ISSUES IN CONTEMPORARY ECONOMICS
Volume 4: Women's Work in the World Economy

ISSUES IN CONTEMPORARY ECONOMICS

Issues in Contemporary Economics

Proceedings of the Ninth World Congress of the
International Economic Association, Athens, Greece

Volume 4
WOMEN'S WORK IN THE WORLD ECONOMY

Edited by
Nancy Folbre
Barbara Bergmann
Bina Agarwal
and
Maria Floro

NEW YORK UNIVERSITY PRESS
Washington Square, New York

First published in the U.S.A. in 1992 by
NEW YORK UNIVERSITY PRESS
Washington Square
New York, N.Y. 10003

Printed in Hong Kong

Library of Congress Cataloging-in-Publication Data
(Revised for vol. 4)
International Economic Association. World Congress.
(9th : 1989 : Athens, Greece)
Issues in contemporary economics.
Contents: v. 1. Markets and welfare / edited by
Kenneth J. Arrow — v. 2. Aspects of macroeconomics
and econometrics / edited by Marc Nerlove —   —
v. 4. Women's work in the world economy / edited by
Nancy Folbre . . . [et al.].
1. Economics—Congresses. 2. Economic policy—
Congresses. 3. Women—Employment—Congresses.
4. Greece—Economic conditions—1974—   —
Congresses. I. Arrow, Kenneth Joseph, 1921–   .
II. Nerlove, Marc, 1933–   .III. Folbre, Nancy.   IV. Title.
HB21.I65   1992   330   90–6649
ISBN 0–8147–0598–7 (v. 1)
ISBN 0–8147–5767–7 (v. 2)
ISBN 0–8147–2606–2 (v. 4)

Contents

v

Preface

Amartya Sen

'Reading maketh a full man', according to Francis Bacon, and 'conference a ready man'. Those who missed the Ninth World Congress of the International Economic Association, held at Athens during August–September 1989, may no longer have the chance of being 'ready' (for whatever), but these proceedings offer them an opportunity of reading the papers presented there, and thus achieving 'fullness' (presumably, a solid, if somewhat obscure, virtue). Less immodestly, we at the International Economic Association are happy to be able to make a selection of the many interesting and productive papers presented at the Ninth World Congress available in book form (in five volumes).

Each of the previous World Congresses of the International Economic Association had one 'unifying' theme (the last one had the theme 'The Balance between Industry and Agriculture in Economic Development'[1]). The Ninth Congress had no such unique theme. Instead papers were invited and contributions sought in a number of different theme areas, covering different parts of the discipline of economics. The purpose of choosing a plurality of themes was to make it possible for economists all over the world to participate in this World Congress despite wide variations in their specialisation. To some extent this had been implicitly permitted in previous conferences too by taking a rather liberal view of the allegedly unifying theme – and by practising what I can only describe as 'diversity in unity'.

The Ninth Congress went a good deal further in making the conference open to economists of different interests and expertise. Since these conferences are three-yearly phenomena, it seems unreasonable to make economists of particular specialisation wait many multiples of three years for their turn to come up. We were rewarded in the Ninth Congress by the attendance of economists of widely different fields and practice. As the variety of papers in these volumes indicate, the range of economic issues covered was quite remarkable.

The programme consisted of twenty-two sections – fifteen sections for presentation of invited and contributed papers and seven sections

ix

for panel discussion. The conference was planned by a Programme Committee, which I was privileged to chair. Each member of the committee took particular responsibility for inviting and selecting papers for one session.

Paper Sections

1. *General microeconomics* (Takashi Negishi)
2. *General macroeconomics* (Jean-Paul Fitoussi)
3. *Welfare and social choice* (Kenneth Arrow)
4. *Econometrics* (Marc Nerlove)
5. *Centrally Planned Economies* (Béla Csikós-Nagy)
6. *Economic History* (Marcello de Cecco)
7. *International Economics* (Elhanan Helpman)
8. *Economic Development* (Victor Urquidi)
9. *Labour Economics* (Richard Layard)
10. *Public Economics* (Lawrence Summers)
11. *Industrial Economics* (Jean Gabszewicz)
12. *Agricultural Economics* (Glenn Johnson)
13. *Food and Nutrition* (Amartya Sen)
14. *Theory of Policy* (Heraklis Polemarchakis)
15. *Economics of Integration* (George Kottis)

Panel Sections

P.1. *Women's and Men's Role in the Economy of the Future* (Barbara Bergmann)
P.2. *The Greek Economy Today* (Thanos Skouros)
P.3. *Game Theory and Economics* (Partha Dasgupta)
P.4. *Rational Expectations after the Event* (Frank Hahn)
P.5. *Neo-Marxian Perspectives on Production Relations and Property Rights* (Stephen Marglin)
P.6. *What Remains of Development Economics?* (Louis Lefeber)
P.7. *Social Justice and Quality of Life* (Zdzislaw Sadowski)

The Programme Committee refereed the papers proposed for presentation, and the final programme was drawn up on that basis. I take this opportunity of thanking the members of the Programme Committee for their immense help in making the Ninth World Congress a success. Not only did they select, severally or jointly, the invited paper writers and assess the contributed papers, but they were also responsible for the selection and appropriate revision of the invited papers for inclusion in these proceedings.

Neither the discussants' comments, nor any reports of the general deliberation in the sessions, are being published. Instead, the paper writers were encouraged to take note of the comments and suggestions made in the sessions, with appropriate acknowledgement.

There were also five invited plenary lectures (in addition to the presidential address), and we were lucky enough to have as plenary speakers: Abel G. Aganbegyan ('Economic Restructuring of the USSR and International Economic Relations'); A. B. Atkinson ('Basic Income Schemes and the Lessons from Public Economics'); Zsuzsa Ferge ('Mechanisms of Social Integration: the Role of the Market'); Frank Hahn ('History and Economic Theory'); and Mahar Mangahas ('Monitoring the Economic and Social Weather in the Philippines').

The proceedings of the congress are being published in five volumes, edited respectively by: Kenneth J. Arrow (vol. 1: *Markets and Welfare*); Marc Nerlove (vol. 2: *Macroeconomics and Econometrics*); Partha Dasgupta (vol. 3: *Policy and Development*); Nancy Folbre, Barbara Bergmann, Bina Agarwal and Maria Floro (vol. 4: *Women's Work in the World Economy*); Thanos S. Skouras (vol. 5: *The Greek Economy: Economic Policy for the 1990s*).

Each editor has his or her own 'Introduction' to the respective volume, and so I need not go into substantive contents of the volumes in this general Preface. I take this chance of thanking the volume editors for their tremendous help in producing these proceedings.

One of the new things in the Ninth Congress was a very active working session – spread over two full days – on 'women's and men's roles in the economy of the future', organised by Barbara Bergmann. This is the first time the International Economic Association has had a special session on gender issues in economics, and the idea met with remarkably active and positive response. There were so many contributions in this field that a special volume is devoted to the papers presented at this session (volume 4).

There was also a full day meeting on the Greek economy. This too had many participants, with presentation of different interpretations and approaches, and the papers from this session are being published also in a separate volume edited by Thanos Skouras.

I should like to put on record our great debt to our Greek hosts.

We are most grateful for the cooperation of the respective Greek governments and the Bank of Greece, and for the superb work done by the Local Organising Committee, under the leadership of Maria Constantopoulos (the others on the committee were Panayotis Korliras, George Kottis and Thanos Skouras). The Local Advisory Board was chaired by George Kottis.

I would also like to thank Patricia Hillebrandt, Rita Maurice and Maureen Hadfield for looking after the editorial arrangements for these proceedings. Without their efficient help, my task as general editor of these volumes would have been impossibly hard. I am also most grateful to Michael Kaser, the Editor, and Jean-Paul Fitoussi, the Secretary General, of the International Economic Association for their constant help in organising the congress and in the publication of these proceedings. I would also like to acknowledge my debt to Kenneth Arrow, the preceding President of the IEA, whose wise counsel I have had to seek on many occasions.

Note

1. The proceedings of that conference were published in five volumes (*The Balance between Industry and Agriculture in Economic Development*, London, Macmillan, 1988), edited respectively by Kenneth J. Arrow (the last President of the IEA), Jeffrey G. Williamson and Vadiraj R. Panchamukhi, Sukhamoy Chakravarty, Irma Adelman and Sylvia Lane, and Nurul Islam.

The International Economic Association

A non-profit organisation with purely scientific aims, the International Economic Association (IEA) was founded in 1950. It is in fact a federation of national economic associations and presently includes fifty-eight such professional organisations from all parts of the world. Its basic purpose is the development of economics as an intellectual discipline. Its approach recognises a diversity of problems, systems and values in the world and also takes note of methodological diversities.

The IEA has, since its creation, tried to fulfil that purpose by promoting mutual understanding of economists from the West and the East, as well as from the North and the South, through the organisation of scientific meetings and common research programmes, and by means of publications on problems of current importance. During its thirty-nine years of existence, it has organised eighty-six round-table conferences for specialists on topics ranging from fundamental theories to methods and tools of analysis and major problems of the present-day world. Nine triennial World Congresses have also been held, which have regularly attracted the participation of a great many economists from all over the world.

The Association is governed by a Council, composed of representatives of all member associations, and by a fifteen-member Executive Committee which is elected by the Council. The present Executive Committee (1989–92) is composed as follows:

President :	Professor Anthony B. Atkinson, UK
Vice-President :	Professor Luo Yuanzheng, China
Treasurer :	Professor Alexandre Lamfalussy, Belgium
Past President :	Professor Amartya Sen, India
Other Members :	Professor Abel Aganbegyan, USSR
	Professor Kenneth J. Arrow, USA
	Professor Edmar Lisboa Bacha, Brazil
	Professor B. R. Brahmananda, India
	Professor Wolfgang Heinrichs, GDR
	Professor Edmond Malinvaud, France
	Professor Takashi Negishi, Japan

The Association has also been fortunate in having secured the following outstanding economists to serve as President:

Gottfried Haberler (1950–53), Howard S. Ellis (1953–56), Erik Lindahl (1956–59), E. A. G. Robinson (1959–62), G. Ugo Papi (1962–65), Paul A. Samuelson (1965–68), Erik Lundberg (1968–71), Fritz Machlup (1971–74), Edmond Malinvaud (1974–77), Shigeto Tsuru (1977–80), Victor L. Urquidi (1980–83), Kenneth J. Arrow (1983–86), Amartya Sen (1986–89).

The activities of the Association are mainly funded from the subscriptions of members and grants from a number of organisations, including continuing support from UNESCO.

Acknowledgements

The hosts for the Ninth World Congress of the International Economic Association were the Hellenic Economic Association and the Athens School of Economics and Business Science. We are grateful to them for the organisation of the Congress, for a stimulating social programme with generous hospitality and for the welcome given to economists from all over the world. The task was daunting but the execution ensured a successful Congress. The International Economic Association wishes to express its thanks on behalf of all participants.

The Congress would not have been possible without the financial help from the Greek Government and the Bank of Greece. The International Economic Association and the Greek host organisations express their appreciation for this support.

The members of the IEA Programme Committee and the Local Organising Committee and Advisory Board are listed overleaf. Our special thanks go to Professor Maria Constantopoulos, the Managing Chairman of the Local Organising Committee, who gave unstintingly of her time and energy to make the Congress a success.

This volume is published by the International Economic Association under the auspices of ISSC and with the financial assistance of UNESCO.

The IEA Programme Committee

Kenneth J. Arrow
Barbara Bergmann
Marcello de Cecco
Béla Csikós-Nagy
Partha Dasgupta
Jean-Paul Fitoussi
J. J. Gabszewicz
Frank Hahn
Elhanan Helpman
Glenn L. Johnson
George Kottis
Richard Layard
Louis Lefeber
Stephen Marglin
Takashi Negishi
Marc Nerlove
Heraklis Polemarchakis
Amartya Sen
Thanos Skouras
Lawrence Summers
Victor L. Urquidi

Local Organising Committee

Panayotis Korliras (Chairman)
Maria Constantopoulos (Managing Chairman)
George Kottis
Thanos Skouras

Local Advisory Board
George Kottis (Chairman)
Angelos Angelopoulos
Dimitris Chalikias
Nickolas Consolas
Constantine Drakatos
George Drakos
Rossetos Fakiolas
Argyris Fatouros
Constantine Kyriazis
Maria Negreponti-Delivanis
George Oekonomou
Stylianos Panagopoulos
Alexandros Yanniotis
Xenophon Zolotas

List of Contributors and Editors

Contributors

Ms Tuovi Allèn, Labour Institute for Economic Research, Helsinki, Finland.

Professor Günseli Berik, Department of Economics, New School for Social Research, New York, USA.

Dr Marga Bruyn-Hundt, Department of Economics and Econometrics, University of Amsterdam, Holland.

Professor Nilüfer Çağatay, Department of Economics, Ramapo College of New Jersey, Mahwah, New Jersey, USA.

Dr Mariam K. Chamberlain, National Council for Research on Women, New York, USA.

Dr Marie-Gabrielle David, Centre d'Étude des Revenus et des Coûts, Paris, France.

Ms Lynn Duggan, University of Massachusetts, Amherst, Massachusetts, USA.

Professor John F. Ermisch, National Institute of Economic and Social Research, London, UK.

Dr Lynne Evans, Department of Economics, University of Durham, UK.

Professor Jean Fletcher, Department of Economics, Gettysburg College, Gettysburg, Pennsylvania, USA.

Professor Maria S. Floro, Department of Economics, American University, Washington DC, USA.

Professor Sandy Gill, Department of Economics, University of Massachusetts, Amherst, Massachusetts, USA.

Dr Jeanne Koopman, Centre d'Étude d'Afrique Noire, University of Bordeaux, France.

Professor Athena Petraki Kottis, Athens University of Economics and Business, Greece.

Professor Yasmeen Mohiuddin, Department of Economics, University of the South, Sewanee, Tennessee, USA.

Professor Aiko Shibata, Economics Department, Tezukayama University, Japan.

Dr Christophe Starzec, Centre d'Étude des Revenus et des Coûts, Paris, France.

Dr Marianne Sundström, Swedish Centre for Working Life, Stockholm, Sweden.
Dr Robert E. Wright, Department of Economics, Birkbeck College, University of London, UK.

Editors

Professor Bina Agarwal, Bunting Institute, Radcliffe, Harvard University, Boston, Massachusetts, USA.
Professor Barbara Bergmann, Department of Economics, American University, Washington DC, USA.
Professor Nancy Folbre, Department of Economics, University of Massachusetts, Amherst, Massachusetts, USA.
Professor Maria S. Floro, Department of Economics, American University, Washington DC, USA.

Abbreviations and Acronyms

BLS	Bureau of Labor Statistics, US Department of Labor, Washington DC
CBI	Confederation of British Industry
CERC	Centre d'Étude des Revenus et des Coûts, Paris, France
CSO	Central Statistical Office, London, UK
DDR	German Democratic Republic
DI	Dissimilarity Index
EC	European Community
FM	Female Marginalisation
FRG	Federal Republic of Germany
GDR	German Democratic Republic
GNP	Gross National Product
HMSO	Her Majesty's Stationery Office, London, UK
IER	Institute for Employment Research, University of Warwick, UK
ILO	International Labour Organisation
IMF	International Monetary Fund
INSEE	Institut Nationale de la Statistique et des Études Economiques, Paris, France
ISI	Import Substituting Industrialisation
LDC	Less-developed country
MNC	Multinational corporation
NIESR	National Institute of Economic and Social Research, London, UK
OECD	Organisation for Economic Cooperation and Development, Paris, France
OLS	Ordinary least squares
PCC	Population Crisis Committee, Washington DC, USA
PSI	Policy Studies Institute, London, UK
SIC	Standard industrial classification
SOEC	Statistical Office of the European Communities, Luxembourg

SZS	Statistisches Zentralverwaltung für Statistik, Ministerrat der Deutschen Demokratischen Republik, Berlin
UN	United Nations
UNCTAD	United Nations Conference on Trade and Development
UNICEF	United Nations International Children's Fund
VFP	Vie Familiale et Vie Professionnelle
WES	Women's Employment Survey
WIDER	World Institute of Development Economics Research

Introduction: The Feminist Sphinx

Nancy Folbre

Our topic was 'Women's and Men's Roles in the Economy of the Future' and our venue was Athens, Greece. Therefore it seemed appropriate to consult the oracle, with the assistance of a feminist poet. Muriel Rukeysar re-tells the myth of Oedipus, and I paraphrase her here, in a special translation, for economists (Rukeysar, 1944).

One day, towards the end of his rather miserable life, the old blind hero of the tragedy sensed the presence of the Sphinx. He asked her why things had turned out so badly for him. 'Well,' the Sphinx explained, 'Your answer to the riddle was only partially correct.' 'Wait a minute,' he said. 'You asked me, "What walks on four legs in the morning, two at noon, and three in the evening?" I answered Man – who crawls as a child, walks upright as an adult, but upon reaching old age must use a cane. That's a perfectly good answer.' 'Well,' said the Sphinx, 'What about Woman?' 'Come on,' said Oedipus, 'When you say Man, of course that implies Woman too. Everyone knows that.' The Sphinx smiled as she replied, 'That's what you think.'

The moral of this story is that feminist theory offers more than some new insights into women's work, more even than insistence that women have the same economic rights as men. Feminist economic theory affects the answers to some of the basic riddles of political economy. Of course, it also poses a riddle of its own. Before exploring that final riddle, let us speculate on what might be prophecies of the feminist sphinx:

In the economics textbooks of the future, introductory chapters might record an important theoretical shift which took place in the late twentieth century, a shift distinct from the Keynesian revolution and counter-revolution that preoccupied most economists at the time. Theorists emerging from both the neoclassical and the Marxian tradition began to consolidate the feminist insights of earlier writers such as Mary Wollstonecraft, William Thompson, Harriet Taylor,

xxiii

John Stuart Mill, Friedrich Engels, Charlotte Gilman, Edith Abbott and Eleanor Rathbone.

Under the aegis of scholars such as those who attended the meetings of the International Economic Association in Athens in 1989, feminist economic theory might come into its own as a distinct paradigm, critical of aspects of both capitalist and socialist economies. It would reject reliance on either market economics or planning and call attention to traditionally unpriced goods – the health, happiness and skills of children, clean air, a stable climate, peace and cooperation – vital to the long-run condition of the species.

In the economics seminars of the future, graduate students might be surprised by the outdated assumptions of pre-feminist economic theories which:

- Failed to acknowledge the importance of non-market production, relying on national accounts that seriously mismeasured economic growth and bore little relationship to actual levels of social welfare.
- Oversimplified the role of both men and women, treating only the former as rational, self-interested people, in search of free choice and efficiency, and the latter as intuitive, altruistic guardians of social obligation.
- Did not take account of the forms of gender-based collective action in which men and women consciously and unconsciously, explicitly and implicitly organised themselves to advance or defend their gender interests with varying degrees of success.

In the social theory of the future, economics might be one aspect of an interdisciplinary social science. Rather than taking tastes, preferences and property endowments as a given, it might explore the cultural and political, as well as economic aspects. Numerous studies might trace the complex evolution of partriarchal capitalism, which gradually provided women with new economic opportunities and increased bargaining power but also increased the economic vulnerability of mothers and children, offering women male privileges only on the condition that they act like men and find someone less well off than they (such as a low-wage worker from a poorer country) to assume responsibility for the basic tasks of cleaning up and taking care.

Whether these prophecies will be fulfilled or not, we do not know. But feminist economists today should consider them, as they seek to answer the riddle of what should be the future of men's and women's economic roles. At least two alternative visions shimmer in the distance, which I will describe as feminist nirvanas numbers 1 and 2.

In the first feminist nirvana, the trend towards a market in the services once provided in the family would continue. The very concept of production for one's own personal use, for the sake of the process and the product itself, would become increasingly obsolete, even in childrearing. Explicit contractual relationships with employers and the state would supercede all forms of personal commitment to family, friends, neighbours and kin. Women's life cycle would closely resemble that now characteristic of men.

We would have reached feminist nirvana number 1 when:

- The full-time labour-force participation rate of women reaches that of men.
- The wage rate is exactly the same for men and women of equal education, experience and productivity.
- Men and women have exactly the same access to education and experience.
- The tax rate on individual men and women is exactly the same and no tax subsidies or family allowances encourage women to engage in non-market activities, such as childrearing, that diminish their market experience.
- Children are cared for by the most efficient means.

Most economists currently writing about gender issues, including many represented in this volume, seem to have this vision implicitly in mind. I believe their answer to the riddle, like that of Oedipus, is only partially correct. A far better, if more remote, vision, lies in the possibility that men and women may choose to retain their personal territory and continue to work for rewards that cannot be priced, sharing the responsibilities of bringing up children and rejecting economic boundaries based on nation, race and ethnicity.

Feminist nirvana number 2 would be reached if and when:

- Men substantially increase their hours of unpaid work, devoting more time to home, children and community. Their formal labour-force participation rate would decline to the level now characteristic of women. Men and women would enjoy the same amount of leisure time.
- The wage rate is exactly the same for all individuals with the same levels of education, experience, and productivity, irrespective of

differences in nation, race, class or gender.
- All men and all women have the same access to education and experience, regardless of differences in nation, race, class or gender.
- Public policies, including tax and social welfare policies, recognise and reward family labour and personal attention to the health, welfare and education of children, adults and the elderly – wherever these responsibilities are shared by men and women.

These two visions of nirvana share complementary intents. They are not, of course, mutually exclusive. But they are somewhat at odds, and the choice between them is shaped by perceptions of the logic of patriarchal capitalism. The first vision is the more expedient, because it does not seek to change the direction of nationalism or of capitalism, but simply to make these gender blind. The second vision is the more impractical, because it seeks to bend the logic of our economy to our will.

Fortunately, feminist economists today do not have to choose one vision or the other. We can continue to explore the territory in between the expedient and the impractical, to zigzag back and forth according to cultural context and historical circumstance. For either vision to materialise we need to know more about how gender works within our economies, and about how the promises of this nascent theoretical paradigm might be fulfilled.

Not all the essays in this volume are feminist in orientation, but they all address feminist issues. The larger theoretical issues of measurement and misperception among economists are aptly summarised by the statement by the working group jointly sponsored by the Mediterranean Women's Studies Institute and the United Nations International Research and Training Institute for the Advancement of Women, which took place immediately before the meetings of the International Economic Association. This statement was presented at the Congress in Athens and is reproduced as an Appendix to this Introduction. Women and men from all over the world produced a concise statement of common concerns about the male bias of conventional economic theory.

The first group of papers concerns issues of women and development. Maria Floro utilises household survey data from the Mindanao region of the Philippines to examine important differences in women's allocation of time between housework, farm work and formal labour-force participation in areas of corn and sugar cultivation. Günseli Berik and Nilüfer Çağatay criticise simplistic generalisations about the impact of economic development on women's share in manufacturing employment. Their detailed analysis of Turkish manufacturing employment shows that the shift in national development strategies in Turkey had no discernable impact on female employment, but that women are most concentrated in export-oriented industries. Yasmeen Mohiuddin questions conventional definitions of female headship, using a sample survey of 100 maid servants in Karachi, Pakistan, to show that many women who do not describe themselves as household heads nonetheless bear primary economic responsibility for the families they live with. Jeanne Koopman discusses the consequences of ignoring the gender aspects of Africa's food crisis and emphasises the contributions of women farmers to household food security and aggregate food supply.

The second part examines the gains and losses women have experienced in the advanced capitalist countries. Tuovi Allèn, taking a global perspective, emphasises that there is no simple relationship between levels of women's welfare and GNP per capita. Women's gains within the labour markets of the advanced capitalist countries, she points out, have been counterbalanced by growth in the number of families maintained by women alone. Marga Bruyn-Hundt explores similar themes within the context of the Netherlands, proposing new criteria for measuring women's economic independence which encompass some consideration of household labour. She also evaluates the level of female economic independence in her country.

The next two papers address factors that affect women's relative bargaining power. Lynne Evans analyses projections of demographic trends in the United Kingdom, and cautiously raises the possibility that women may be able to take advantage of a growing scarcity of labour. Jean Fletcher and Sandra Gill summarise data on the relationship between levels of unionisation and relative wages in Western Europe and the USA, concluding that women have made more progress toward wage equality in countries with strong trade union traditions.

The third part focuses more narrowly on the causes and consequences of part-time market work. Aiko Shibata demonstrates the ways Japanese tax policies penalise working wives and reinforce their traditional role within the household. As Marie-Gabrielle David and Christophe Starzec show in their comparison of part-time employment in Great Britain and France, public policies have a significant impact. Although overall levels of labour-force participation are quite similar in the two countries, part-time employment is far more widespread in Great Britain, where tax and benefit policies make it attractive to employers. A relative shortage of high-quality child care facilities also makes many British mothers unwilling to work full-time.

The economic consequences for women are adverse. As Wright and Ermisch show, using data from the 1980 Women and Employment Survey in Great Britain, the returns in the labour market are substantially lower in part-time work. Still, in certain contexts, part-time work can have a positive impact. Marianne Sundström argues this case for Sweden, pointing out that the growth of part-time employment with pro-rated social benefits has contributed to high levels of female labour-force participation in Sweden, where women often reduce their hours of market work for a portion of their life cycle in order to accommodate the demands of parenthood. Swedish policies have also encouraged men to take advantage of leave for parenthood.

The final part considers issues of education and family policy. Athena Petraka Kottis describes the difficulties that educated women face in trying to re-enter the labour market after a long absence. The training programme she helped to design proved successful, partly because it surveyed carefully the needs and capabilities of the target group. Mariam Chamberlin summarises the findings of a recent benchmark study of women in colleges and universities in the United States. The anti-discrimination laws of the 1970s contributed to a rapid increase in women's entry into junior level positions, but progress at senior levels – particularly within economics – has been limited.

The final paper, Lynn Duggan's assessment of family policy in the German Democratic Republic, takes issue with the common assumption that such policies should be evaluated purely in terms of their effects on the birth rate. Largely unsuccessful efforts to increase fertility in East Germany (as in West Germany) have had negative effects on women's position in the labour market. Duggan insists, in keeping with the feminist sphinx, that effective family policies must seek to reconcile fatherhood, as well as motherhood, with paid employment.

Reference

Rukeysan, M. (1944) *Breaking Open* (New York: Random House).

APPENDIX: ALTERNATIVE ECONOMIC ANALYSIS FOR WOMEN

Elements Proposed by a Workshop Sponsored by the Mediterranean Women's Studies Institute (KEGME) and the United Nations International Research and Training Institute for the Advancement of Women (INSTRAW), August 1990, coordinated by Eleni Stamiris.

To assess the impact of theories and policies on women and development, the following conceptual framework should be considered:

A. Before their application, it is essential to determine whether or not policies/theories favour the integration of women. The existing structures (which are usually detrimental to women) should be re-examined with theories/policies that seek to change these structures.
B. Micro analysis should take into account the impact of the macro level (and *vice versa*) from a gender perspective.
C. Economic analysis and policies should consider the social, cultural and political dimensions from a gender perspective.

Main Elements

1. A strictly economic approach does not capture the complexities of development, a process determined by the interdependence of social, cultural, environmental and political dimensions. Therefore, economic theory and empirical analysis should incorporate these dimensions, on a gender basis.
2. Economic science should extend its scope beyond the market to cover production of 'human welfare' and incorporate that part of the non-monetary economy which includes production within the household, housework, childcare and emotional labour (nurturing children, spouses, personal relations).
3. Short-term economic policies, programmes, and projects often have negative social, environmental and political consequences, particularly for women and children. Therefore, economic research, analysis and planning should have a longer-term framework, specifying long-term and medium-term policy implications and objectives.
4. The household as a unit of analysis does not adequately represent the rights, needs and priorities of women. The unit of analysis for economic research and policy should be individual members of the household. This would facilitate assessment of intra-household relations and the distribution of resources, income and labour, and bring about changes in favour of women.
5. Economists and others need to pay closer attention to the adverse effects of the debt crisis and structural adjustment policies on women in general and women in low-income countries in particular.
6. National income accounts should be revised to include the economic activity of women in the informal sector and in housework.
7. The political use (and abuse) of crude indicators such as GNP and aggregate rates of employment often leads to policies that have a negative impact on women's lives.

8. We need better qualitative and quantitative data on women in employment, their working conditions, pay, and larger contributions to economic welfare in all countries.
9. Existing data and indicators do not fully take into account important aspects of women's employment, unemployment and underemployment.
10. Existing techniques of data collection and analysis should be improved and internationally standardised to capture fully the conditions of work and life for women (such as unpaid family work, employment contracts, temporary and seasonal work, part-time and self-employment).
11. Macro-econometric model builders usually neglect and ignore data and information on gender differences even when available (such as in the employment sector). This leads to inaccurate estimates of the employment impact of public policies.
12. Social, political and cultural dimensions based on gender analysis should be better integrated in economic analysis, research and policy recommendations.
13. It should be recognised that fiscal systems discriminate against women's work and social security rights. They reinforce the dependent status of women. The tax system should be reformed by implementing separate assessment of women's earnings, so as not to penalise women's work.
14. Like women, nature is frequently taken for granted. It is undervalued, exploited and being depleted for future generations. Planning for future development should include a set of indicators emphasising the preservation of natural resources and encouraging policies that contribute to sustainable development.
15. To create conditions of equity for women and sustainable development, it is urgent that the following steps be taken:

    – Identification and analysis of the distinct characteristics of economic processes that have not received sufficient attention: work devoted to the production of human welfare in the household, the cultivation of renewable natural resources, and the extraction and processing of non-renewable resources.
    – Analysis of the interplay and dynamics between these three areas in the totality of the human economy.
    – The development of new methods and measures for taking these crucial components of human economy into consideration in future economic policies.

Part I

Gender and Development

1 Women, Work and Agricultural Commercialisation in the Philippines

Maria Floro[1]

AMERICAN UNIVERSITY, WASHINGTON, DC

1 INTRODUCTION

Several studies on the promotion of 'non-traditional' exports in LDCs have examined the deleterious consequences on the predominantly female workers in export-processing zones.[2] There has been less systematic research, however, on the effects of agricultural-export expansion on women.[3] This is despite the fact that the majority of women in developing countries live in rural areas where the push for export-oriented growth is taking place as well (Quisumbing, 1988; Heyzer, 1986). This paper attempts to fill this gap in the literature by examining how agricultural commercialisation, as a result of export cropping, has affected rural women – both as workers and as family members.

The effect of a development strategy on women can be attributed to a host of factors that leads to their marginalisation in the development process. Some of these factors relate to the persistent gender inequalities in society, at the level of production, and within the household. Others are generated by a pattern of economic change that heightens class differences and economic hierarchies.[4] The second section examines conceptually the interplay of these gender-related and economic status-related factors in determining the impact of agricultural commercialisation on women.

Unfortunately, the paper cannot analyse empirically the complexity of class and gender issues as a whole. While the question of changes in women's time-allocation pattern is related to the changes in men's time-allocation pattern as well, this interesting and important dimension cannot be explored in the present study given the limitations of the data. The study rather will concentrate on the economic status dimension of the issue. As agricultural commercialisation affects the economic position of the household, this has important ramifications on the type of trade-offs done by women with respect to their time use. A brief description of the data used in the empirical investigation of the study as well as pertinent survey method problems are presented in the third section of the paper.

The fourth and fifth sections present the statistical results obtained in the study of 374 rural women in the Mindanao region of the Philippines. The changes brought about by the shift from semi-subsistence cropping to cash (export) cropping on the magnitude and form of women's participation in home production as well as in the farm and labour market are examined using mothers' time-allocation data collected in 1983–84.[5]

2   THE IMPACT OF AGRICULTURAL COMMERCIALISATION ON WOMEN'S WORK

Much of the growth in crop production for Philippine exports has occurred in the past decades in the Mindanao region. Partly because of increased difficulties in penetrating the world market for light manufactures and partly because of the IMF, the World Bank and the Philippine government's preoccupation with foreign debt-burden payment, export cropping continued to expand in the Philippines and has encroached even in remote areas traditionally devoted to food staples such as rice and corn. The reallocation of resources as a result of a crop shift has not only drawn the semi-subsistence households in the affected rural areas to the market.[6] It has also altered the entire production system including landholding, labour-use pattern and production techniques, and has modified the allocation of household labour. The extent to which these affect women's work, however, is in part conditioned by the existing social rules and prevailing gender role concepts.

Within the Philippine household, members have broadly defined duties based in part on their sex and in part on their age. This gender-age role differentiation has been enforced by centuries-old legal, social and political structures. King and Evenson (1983) and Yoto-poulos and Mergos (1986) showed in their respective Laguna and Mindanao household labour-allocation studies that the Filipino women's work domain is traditionally defined to be that of home production while the farm and the market are that of the men's.[7] This household division of labour, moreover, is characterised by inequality in work effort. King and Evenson (1983) demonstrated that women in farm households worked longer hours (66.6 hours per week on average) than men (55.3 hours per week on average). But while women (and children) tend to 'specialise' in home production and men in farming activities and wage employment, Yotopoulos and Mergos (1986) showed that there is a significant amount of labour substitution and complementarity on the part of women in the male-dominated farming activities and wage employment. Men's contribution in the female-dominated home-production activities, on the other hand, was negligible. The male farmer-cultivators in both household studies often required the assistance of other household members especially women in such tasks as weeding, planting, and harvesting.[8] Men, on the other hand, spend little time in childcare and other home production activities. Using the 1975 Laguna survey data, Folbre (1984) examined the time devoted to childcare by men and found that:

'Fathers spent an average of less than an hour a week caring for children. In households with a child under 3 present, fathers devoted slightly more, at 1.19 hours per week, to child care . . . Even those fathers who were unemployed or employed less than 20 hours a week devoted very little time to child care. These results suggest that men not only had no taste for childcare but may have an aversion to it.' (p. 317).

As Folbre (1984) argues, the increased time spent by women on childcare in the presence of young children (under 3 years) has been provided largely by a sacrifice of women's own leisure (p. 322). This may be perceived by women themselves not so much as a sacrifice as it is their 'duty'.

This gender-role perception has yielded unequal positions in the household decision-making as well. Major decisions usually rest upon the male household head. Mothers are relegated the responsibility of overseeing the household budget and are in charge of designating household duties among the family members but *within* the boundaries dictated by social norms, cultural fetters and legal statutes. While respect for elders engenders in Filipino adult women (mothers) authority over children, the former are subordinate to their husbands or the male household head.[9]

This pattern of commitment and authority within the family is carried over to farm activities as well. The organisation of crop production is strongly hierarchical, with women having a subsidiary role (Heyzer, 1986). Women work in agriculture as 'assistants to men' or 'extensions of their husbands' at certain stages in the production cycle.[10] Even as a wage labourer, the household head or 'primary worker' would bring in his own helpers, usually his wife and children, whenever the wage payment is on a piecemeal basis or a share of the harvest.

While there is clear evidence of gender inequality in the distribution of work and in Philippine rural households, little research has been done on how this gender-based inequality may be more or less pronounced among women of different socio-economic positions. While women on average worked longer hours than men, the economic status and demographic composition of the household may provide them with resources to minimise their work load or may increase their work burden relative to men. The complex relationship between economic change and women's time allocation reflects any modification in the sexual division of labour and any shift in the economic status of the household which in turn determine the range of options and choices available to women.

The shift from semi-subsistence to commercial cropping (such as for export) affects, for example, not only the demand for family labour on the farm, but also the wealth position and tenure status of households. This is because commercial crop production is organised in a different way from subsistence production. For instance, the technical requirements of cash cropping change the length of the production cycle and alter the demand for family labour. The more labour is hired, the less the demand for family labour on the farm. This in turn affects the need for women's assistance in crop production. Secondly, its market orientation involves not only an increased dependence of household consumption on the market but also that of inputs acquisition. The less food grown for home consumption, the more monetary income is needed to buy food and other household needs from the market. This may increase the need for women's participation in non-farm activities such as wage labour. Thirdly, there is a shift in farm revenue as output yield and relative prices change. This determines the resources available to women in performing their roles as main food providers and managers of households. It also affects the range of options available to women, their access to education, credit and other resources. In other words, changes in the economic position of the households involves readjustments on women's time allocation and hence, on trade-offs among different activities.

The shift to export crop, in addition, brings about changes in land distribution and production relations. The decision to convert farms to export crop, for example, may lead to increased expansion and consolidation of landholdings by cultivators. This implies that some landholdings increase or diminish over time. The nature of the relations of production are also modified as a result of crop shift. Although this affects the share of the output or farm revenue received by the household in the short run, the long-term consequences are even more important. Tenurial security (or insecurity) largely determines the certainty (or uncertainty) of the future source of livelihood. The smaller the landholding size and the less secure the tenure, the greater the economic compulsion and the more time women must spend in generating supplementary non-farm income. Given the absence of women's effective control over land use, women with little or no access to funds have their own labour time and that of their children (especially daughters) as the only resource over which they have any control (Sen and Grown, 1987). Women's work hours, in attempting to cope with the increased economic pressure, may lengthen considerably.

Economic change brought about by commercialisation of agriculture therefore affects both the length of work and the way women make use of their time. These differences in women's work emanate from differences in the ensuing changes in the tenure status, the earning capacity of the farm, the labour requirements of crop cultivation as well as market integration, all of which affect the choices and constraints faced by women.

Any discussion of the relationship between the development process and women's work needs to take into account the extent of women's reproductive responsibilities and the household composition as determined by the lifecycle stage of the household. Bouls and Kennedy (1989) argued that women decrease the time spent in strenuous activities, or time spent away from home when they are pregnant or breast feeding. The age structure of children within the household also sets the boundaries by which women's time may vary in response to changing economic conditions. Young children place a demand on women's time that competes with their availability to perform tasks in the fields or outside the home. On the other hand, older children, especially daughters, may allow for substitution of women's time in domestic and child care chores, relieving them of some household work.

An econometric model can be drawn out of the above discussion. The time spent by women in household i to home production, H_{ij}, farm cultivation, F_{ij}, and labour market participation, L_{ij}, is jointly determined by their relative bargaining power in the household, B_i, the type of crop adopted, C_{ij}, and a vector of exogenous factors, V_i. That is,

$$H_{ij} = f(B_i, C_{ij}, V_i)$$
$$F_{ij} = g(B_i, C_{ij}, V_i)$$
$$L_{ij} = h(B_i, C_{ij}, V_i) \tag{1.1a}$$

Subject to the following time constraint:

$$Z = H_{ij} + F_{ij} + L_{ij} \tag{1.1b}$$

where Z = Total amount of time available excluding leisure time and personal care.

The term B_i reflects the degree of asymmetrical relations between men and women. The decision of a particular household head to adopt a certain crop, C_{ij}, reflects the household tenure status, T_{ij}, size of landholding, N_{ij}, level of market integration, M_{ij}, and farm profitability, P_{ij}. That is,

$$C_{ij} = t(T_{ij}, N_{ij}, M_{ij}, P_{ij}) \tag{1.2}$$

V_i is a vector of exogenous variables that affect the dependent variable as well, that is the household demographic composition, D_i, women's skill endowment, S_i, and the level of their reproductive responsibilities, R_i.

The set of reduced-form equations for rural women's work is thus given:

$$H_{ij} = f(B_i, T_{ij}, N_{ij}, M_{ij}, P_{ij}, D_i, S_i, R_i)$$
$$F_{ij} = g(B_i, T_{ij}, N_{ij}, M_{ij}, P_{ij}, D_i, S_i, R_i)$$
$$L_{ij} = h(B_i, T_{ij}, N_{ij}, M_{ij}, P_{ij}, D_i, S_i, R_i) \tag{1.3a}$$

subject to the time constraint:

$$Z = H_{ij} + F_{ij} + L_{ij} \tag{1.3b}$$

where Z = Total amount of time available excluding leisure time and personal care.

3 SAMPLING METHOD AND DATA LIMITATIONS

Empirical analysis of the effect of agricultural commercialisation on women's work is based on mothers' time-allocation data collected during 1984 and 1985 in the Mindanao region of the Philippines. The data is part of a nutrition survey conducted among 510 households by the International Food Policy Research Institute and the Research Institute for Mindanao Culture and involved four survey rounds at four-month intervals. For the purpose of this study, the empirical analysis will focus on women in corn and sugar households only, specifically mothers, reducing the sample size to 374 and the number of cases to 1496.[11]

The study area used to be predominantly engaged in smallholder semi-subsistence agriculture. The establishment of a large sugar mill in the area in 1977 eventually led to shifts from corn production to sugar growing by households with access to the necessary funds and within close proximity to the sugar mill.[12] The sample selection involved only rural households with at least one child under the age of five. Pertinent demographic characteristics and the physiological status of mothers in the households are thus identified, so the effect of reproductive responsibilities and the presence of older daughters in the household on women's time allocation can be examined as well.

The absence of men's time allocation data in the same survey unfortunately does not allow for any comparative study of male/female time allocation within the household and hence an analysis regarding any difference in gender distribution of work between sugar and corn households cannot be made. This is admittedly a serious limitation of this study. There is, nonetheless, the need to examine the economic-status related factors that may diminish or reinforce the prevailing gender stratification and the subordinate placement of women in societies. More concretely, it will be examined empirically how women's participation is affected by the shifts in economic hierarchies and redistribution of resources that are created in the process of economic change.

Although effort was made by the survey interviewers to record the activities of women accurately, there is still reason to believe that the time spent on certain activities may be underestimated. One reason is that there is no clear delineation of some activities as 'leisure' or as 'work'. Childcare for instance, may be done in a collective manner by mothers who gather for a chat in the afternoon. The social nature of the activity may be perceived and hence reported by women as 'leisure'. A woman who pays a visit to her uncle to borrow money may also be reported as a 'social visit' even if there is a clear economic purpose for doing so.

Another underestimation problem arises from the prevalence of overlapping tasks. Some mothers may not know whether to call the activity at a particular moment childcare or gardening, for example. The same is true of a woman who rocks the cradle with her foot while she mends clothes. Data collection on time allocation tends, however, to ignore this problem in accounting for activities that can be performed simultaneously. The presence of overlapping activities suggests the importance of differences in work intensity that may compensate or heighten any difference in hours worked between household members. The data obtained in the women's time-allocation surveys thus provide only the quantitative dimension of household activities and allow for analysis of the economic-status factors on women's work alone.

4 ECONOMIC DETERMINANTS OF WOMEN'S TIME USE

4.1 Shift in Crop Effect on Women's Time

Table 1.1 presents the economic characteristics of the rural household sample. As the table suggests, there is considerable difference in the average landholding size as well as land accessibility between households engaged in semi-subsistence (corn) production and those involved primarily in export crop (sugar) growing. These observations are confirmed by the assertion of Bouis and Haddad (1990) that consolidation of certain landholdings in the sugar-growing area has taken place since the introduction of the sugar mill. This is accompanied by a shift in the tenure arrangement from sharecropping to leasehold tenancy, and in some cases to landlessness. In fact, the number of landless (and near landless) households has increased, thus explaining the more skewed tenure pattern and land distribution among sugar households.

Table 1.1 Characteristics of rural households by crop

Characteristics	Corn households	Sugar households	All households
Number of households	227	147	374
Mean household size	7.1	7.9	7.5
Household composition			
Men (per cent)	1.5 (21%)	1.6 (20%)	1.5 (21%)
Women (per cent)	1.2 (17%)	1.3 (16%)	1.2 (16%)
Children (per cent)	4.5 (63%)	5.0 (63%)	4.7 (63%)
Mean landholding available for cultivation (in hectares)	2.9	4.6	3.6
Mean landholding owned (in hectares)	1.8	3.1	2.3
Tenure distribution (per cent)			
Landless	22	35	27
Tenant	39	20	32
Mixed	19	19	19
Owner	20	26	22
Total	100	100	100
Mean household income (in pesos per year)	9 593	15 879	12 068

The data on time allocation of mothers in rural households are classified under three main work categories: home production, farm cultivation and labour market participation.[13] The women in both sugar and corn households spend, on average, more than 60 per cent of their time on home production (see Table 1.2). The data also seems to show that women in sugar households have a shorter work day than women in corn households, a result mainly of their reduced participation in farming. This suggests that agricultural commercialisation may have altered the demand for family labour and specifically the participation of household members. The change in female labour use in crop production is examined in the next section.

The broad crop categories, however, do not take into account the variation of women's experience within each crop. It may be the case that some women have an increased workload, trading off time spent on the farm as unpaid family labour for increased participation in wage employment or in proprietorship. There may also be different

Table 1.2 Time allocation[a] of rural women by crop category
(374 households)

Activities	Corn		Sugar		All households	
	Percentage distribution	Mean minutes per day	Percentage distribution	Mean minutes per day	Percentage distribution	Mean minutes per day
Home	62.9	355	63.8	339	63.3	348
Domestic[b]	51.9	293	52.7	279	52.4	288
Childcare[c]	10.9	62	11.1	60	10.9	60
Farm	27.6	156	24.2	129	26.4	145
Maincrop[d]	17.0	96	14.0	75	16.0	88
Backyard[e]	10.6	60	10.2	54	10.4	57
Labour force	9.4	53	12.0	64	10.5	57
Agriculture[f]	2.8	16	4.1	22	3.4	18
Non-agriculture[g]	6.6	37	7.8	42	7.1	39
Total work time	100.0	564	100.0	532	100.0	550

Notes: a Based on a 24-hour recall of mothers in corn and sugar households. The
following activities exclude time spent on sleeping, personal care, eating and
leisure.
b Time spent on the following domestic chores: cooking, cleaning, fetching
water, gathering wood, laundering, marketing, household repair and shop-
ping for non-food items.
c Time spent on directly taking care of pre-schoolers, for example breastfeeding, feeding/bathing/playing with children.
d Time spent on working in own farm devoted to main crop cultivation.
e Time spent on animal raising, vegetable/fruit cultivation.
f Time spent as paid agricultural worker.
g Time spent on own business, for example general (*sari-sari*) store retailing,
dressmaking, market vending or as an employee in a non-agricultural establishment.

reasons for the reduction in working hours. In some cases, economic
change relieves women from farmwork obligations and hence increases their own leisure time. On the other hand, the reduced
worktime may reflect women's inability to get non-farm jobs. These
differences are significant since economic changes brought about by
agricultural commercialisation are conditioning elements which determine women's available choices and constraints. This requires
further examination and is addressed in sections 4.2 and 4.3 below.

4.2 Female Labour Use in Crop Production

Rural women in the Philippines widely participate in the farm operation as shown in Table 1.3, particularly in backyard production

Table 1.3 Women's participation in selected economic activities by crop
category
(374 households)

Activities	Corn		Sugar	
	Participation rate[a]	Mean hours per day[b]	Participation rate[a]	Mean hours per day[b]
Farm	81.9	3.1	71.8	2.9
Main crop	40.1	3.9	29.2	4.2
Backyard	69.1	1.4	62.1	1.4
Labour force	16.0	5.4	20.6	5.1
Agriculture	5.2	5.0	6.8	5.4
Non-agriculture	10.8	5.5	13.9	4.9

Notes: a The percentage of women in the total sample who participated in
the activity.
b The mean time spent by women who participated in the activity.

which generates roughly one-fifth of the household income. About
two-fifths of women in the corn households performed certain tasks
in the production process. The introduction of export cropping in the
area, however, has reduced the role of women in farm production
sphere so that not only has their farmwork time declined but the
proportion of women who performed any task in sugar production as
household members declined as well. This marked decline in
women's farm role is offset by the increased participation in the
labour market, as agricultural wage workers and as proprietors in
non-agricultural economic activities.

The change in the relative participation of women in crop production is illuminated by the difference in labour use patterns between corn and sugar production. Table 1.4 shows the distribution of
labour for each crop.[14] The results suggest that the substitution of
sugar for corn increases the use of hired labour. This is, in large part,
due to the different way sugar production is organised and the
production technique used in sugar growing. With the subsistence
crop, rural households can decide independently as to the timing of
their production schedule, usually having the rainfall cycle as their
main constraint. The sugar production schedule, on the other hand,
is derived strictly from the schedule of the sugar mill in the area. In
fact, sugar 'production (among the smallholder cultivators) must be
coordinated among producers so that milling capacity is as fully
utilized as possible without overproduction' (Bouis and Haddad,

Table 1.4 Labour use pattern crop category

Labour type	Corn[a]	Sugar[a]	Percentage change
Household labour	.6410	.2724	−57.5
Women	.1135	.0241	−78.8
Men	.3681	.1584	−57.0
Children	.1594	.0899	−43.6
Hired labour	.3590	.7271	102.5
Women	.1010	.0814	−19.5
Men	.2369	.6392	165.7
Children	.0211	.0065	−69.3
All labour	1.0000	1.0000	

Note: a Conditional probabilities of labour type.

1988, p. 80). This intensifies the labour requirement for certain tasks, e.g. harvesting, thereby compelling the sugar farmers to hire labour. The more prevalent use of tractors and sprayers in sugar growing also heightens the tendency of the male farmer-cultivator to use male hired labour since the latter is perceived to be more adept and skilful in handling machines than women workers. Harvesting of sugar cane requires physical strength which increases the preference for male labour.

Among members of the household, women's participation declined most dramatically as a result of the shift to sugar cultivation. This is most prominent in women-intensive tasks such as weeding and planting where they are replaced by hired labour (see Table 1.5). Post-harvest activities predominantly done by women, such as shelling and drying of corn, are now performed by another market agent, the sugar miller (Bouis and Haddad, 1988).

The decline in farm work done by women does not necessarily mean that agricultural commercialisation has improved women's work status, let alone improved gender relations. This question largely depends on whether it has reduced the 'duty component' of their workload and hence increased women's available choices and control of their own time. Men still retain legal ownership (unless stated otherwise) and decision-making powers over resource allocation and output disposal. In certain cases, women's primary 'duty' for the reproduction and maintenance of the household still requires them to make use of their 'freed' labour time to conduct housework and/or to earn supplementary income in order to fulfil

Table 1.5 Change in women's participation in corn and sugar production
by type of labour and by task categories
(286 households, in person days per hectare per production cycle)

Selected tasks	Household labour			Hired labour		
	Corn	Sugar	Change	Corn	Sugar	Change
Land preparation	0.4	0.0	−0.4	–	–	–
Planting	3.3	0.8	−2.5	3.5	2.2	−1.3
Weeding	10.4	2.1	−8.3	0.2	0.8	+0.6
Fertiliser	1.0	0.0	−1.0	–	–	–
Harvest	1.4	0.3	−1.1	3.8	0.0	−3.8
All tasks	16.5	3.2	−13.3	7.5	3.0	−4.5

their roles as providers. The complexity of the issue requires that we
take the reproductive and economic responsibilities of women into
account. The latter requires further examination of the other effect of
a crop shift – the change in the economic security and viability of the
households – since this determines the extent to which women are
'compelled' to seek alternative sources of income.

4.3 The Effect of Women's Reproductive and Economic Position on Their Time

One obvious difference between women and men concerns their
biological roles in reproduction. Indeed, it is sometimes assumed that
this difference sufficiently explains the gender division of labour. A
woman's capacity to perform other productive activities is constrained, to some extent, by her physiological status so that women's
participation in this study is analysed for three categories: a) non-
pregnant, non-lactating women, b) childbearing or pregnant women,
and c) lactating women.

But while childbearing is biologically limited to women, the roles
of childrearing and doing household chores, as mentioned earlier, are
socially determined. Moreover, the extent to which women are
constrained to perform these tasks is an economic question as well.
One factor that may affect women's time use is the household's access
to land.

Since ownership and control over land and tenancy contracts solely
involves the male head in most cases, land tenure *per se* does not
define the degree of women's control over resources. But it determines the proportion of output received by the household as well as

stability of the household income over time. Land tenure affects women's time by determining the extent of economic compulsion of women to look for other sources of income. This economic compulsion may intensify in situations of high household-income instability and lower share of the output. To control for any variation in time-use pattern due to differences in the tenure status of the household, the mean participation of women in productive activities is computed for four tenure subcategories, namely a) landless, b) tenant, c) part-tenant, part-owner or mixed, and d) full owner-cultivator.[15] To detect any difference in the mean time spent in various productive activities by women in landless households and those in other tenure categories, *t*-tests are employed. The results are presented in Tables 1.6–1.8.

Among non-pregnant, non-lactating women, the shift towards more secured land-tenure significantly affects their participation in the labour market as shown in Table 1.6. Tenure security is inversely related to agricultural wage employment and positively correlated with non-agricultural employment especially proprietorship. For women in sugar households, access to land leads both to increased involvement in crop cultivation and to shortening of their workday.

Table 1.7 examines the differences in the participation of childbearing women. Pregnancy in some cultures translates to more 'rest periods' for women, since procreation, that is bringing up the next generation, alongside maintenance of the family, is perceived to be the primary duty of women.[16] Hence, the 'rest is best' policy is strongly recommended for childbearing women in order to secure a higher probability of live birth. In practice, adherence to this 'optimal' childbearing principle appears to depend on the circumstances facing pregnant women.

Empirical results show that in the Philippines, those with more secure tenure-status are able to reduce their participation in women's most time-intensive activity, homework (see Table 1.7). One possible explanation is that those in landowning households can well afford to hire other (female) domestic help to lessen their housework or childcare time. This is especially true for women in sugar households. Pregnancy, however, does not seem to deter their participation in 'men's domain' – main crop cultivation – whenever their assistance is required. This holds true for pregnant women in corn households whose contribution to crop production is considerable (Table 1.7).

Lactating women with better land access have considerably more time for breastfeeding than women in the landless category (see

Table 1.6 Effect of tenure on the time allocation of non-pregnant, non-lactating women, by crop category (231 households, in minutes per day)

Activities	Corn				Sugar			
	Landless (basis)	Tenant (Change from landless)	Mixed	Owner	Landless (basis)	Tenant (Change from landless)	Mixed	Owner
Home	360	−16	−28	−36	331	+12	−38	−68*
Domestic	320	−32*	−33	−37*	287	+24	−21	−42
Childcare	40	+16	−5	+1	45	−12	−17*	−26
Farm	149	+15	−21*	+20	114	+68*	+38*	+44*
Main crop	80	+23	−31*	+21	62	+48*	+40*	+41*
Backyard	69	−8	+10	−1	53	+20*	−2	+3
Labour force	36	+24	+11	+32*	83	−2	−19	−21
Agriculture	28	−20*	−27*	−23*	48	−29	−48*	−54*
Non-agriculture	8	+45*	+38*	+55*	35	+27	+29*	+33*
Net change		+23	−38*	+16		+78*	−19	−45*
Total work time (in minutes)	545	568	507	561	528	606	509	483

* Significance level of 10 per cent or better using t-test.

Table 1.7 Effect of tenure on the time allocation of pregnant women, by crop category (43 households, in minutes per day)

Activities	Corn				Sugar			
	Landless (basis)	Tenant	Mixed (Change from landless)	Owner	Landless (basis)	Tenant	Mixed (Change from landless)	Owner
Home	390	−52	−50	−150*	375	+51	−60	−152*
Domestic	349	−71	−38*	−143*	312	+53	−13	−131*
Childcare	41	+18	−11	−7	63	−2	−46*	−21
Farm	125	−30*	+10	+35	121	+24	−49	+23
Main crop	72	−41*	+26*	+68	30	−32	—	+34
Backyard	53	+11	−17	−32	91	+56	−49	−10
Labour force	23	+32	+9	+70*	28	−27	+55	−25
Agriculture	22	+18*	−22	+26	2	−2	+25*	—
Non-agriculture	–	+14*	+31	+45	25	−25	+30	−25
Net change		−50*	−31*	−45*		+48*	−54*	−154*
Total work time (in minutes)	538	488	507	493	524	572	470	370

* Significance level of 10 per cent or better using *t*-test.

Table 1.8). Among sugar households, these women are able to reduce their time in farm production as well as agricultural wage employment. Breastfeeding women in more secured corn households, on the other hand, spend relatively more time in household chores as well as in corn production than women in the landless category (see Table 1.8). One explanation is that breastfeeding increases the time spent by women on other home-based activities such as cooking and some post-harvest activities, for example shelling or husking of corn.

The increased market integration of sugar households provides, in a sense, more business prospects for women with resources than those in corn households. This may explain why sugar women's time for non-agricultural income generating activities increases as tenure status improves. Such activities may not necessarily take women away from the home. For example, running a 'sari-sari' (convenience or general store) adjacent to the house or managing a dress shop are some of the activities that lactating women can do within the confines of their homes.

The preceding discussion highlights some of the complexity of the causal relationship between economic change and women's time allocation. The interplay of economic forces and other social and demographic factors requires a more comprehensive analysis which is made in the next section.

5 TWO-STEP ECONOMETRIC ANALYSIS OF WOMEN'S PARTICIPATION

The economic consequences of a crop shift on women's participation includes not only a possible change in land tenure but also changes in farm revenue (P_{ij}), level of market integration (M_{ij}) and wealth (landholding size) (N_{ij}). In addition, pertinent household and women attributes such as women's reproductive responsibilities (R_i), the life-cycle stage of the household (D_i), and women's schooling (S_i) need to be taken into account as well since they are conditioning elements of women's time use. These variables represent the two sets of factors identified in the econometric model namely: (a) crop shift or export promotion effect, C_{ij}, and (b) other explanatory factors, V_i. The third variable pertaining to the relative bargaining power of women, B_i, is excluded unfortunately due to data constraints. The set of reduced equations (1–3a) is estimated using the two-step maximum

Table 1.8 Effect of tenure on the time allocation of lactating women, by crop category (100 households, in minutes per day)

	Corn				Sugar			
Activities	*Landless (basis)*	*Tenant (Change from landless)*	*Mixed (Change from landless)*	*Owner (Change from landless)*	*Landless (basis)*	*Tenant (Change from landless)*	*Mixed (Change from landless)*	*Owner (Change from landless)*
Home	331	+47	+71*	+49	388	+57	−22	+6
Domestic	236	+39*	+59*	+65*	291	+1	−59*	+5
Childcare	95	+8	+12	−17	97	+56*	+38*	+1
Farm	117	+1	+9	+73*	120	+37*	−62*	−10
Main crop	55	+22	+31	+98*	75	+37	−51	−7
Backyard	63	−21	−21*	−25	44	−	−10	−3
Labour force	68	−24*	−34	−60*	42	−29*	+30	−2
Agriculture	61	−50*	−50*	−57*	29	−19	−29	−6
Non-agriculture	7	+25*	+16	−3	13	−10	+58*	+4
Net change		+24	+46	+63*		+65*	−54	−6
Total work time (in minutes)	516	540	562	579	550	615	496	544

* Significance level of 10 per cent or better using *t*-test.

likelihood method for each work category. Given the cyclical nature of agriculture, labour demands may vary from season to season. Hence, a dummy variable to control for the seasonality of labour requirements is included in the model as well.

5.1 Methodology

All women in the sample allocate some of their time to home production. Since whether women participate in market production or not is an endogenously determined decision, the estimates of time allocation on home production and farm cultivation may suffer from a sample selection bias. This poses great difficulty in accepting the ordinary least squares estimates as unbiased.[17]

If the unmeasured characteristics influencing sample selection and home time allocation are jointly distributed, then the influence of the selectivity associated with labour force participation can be substantially reduced by using two-step maximum likelihood estimation (Khandker, 1988). The revised estimation procedure requires, first of all, that the likelihood function of a probit model is estimated for corn and sugar household samples where the dependent variable is one or zero, depending on whether women participated in the labour market or not. This provides a consistent estimator such as the inverse-Mills ratio. The second step involves the inclusion of the inverse-Mills ratio estimate associated with the self-selected subsample in the original regression function and the application of ordinary least squares to the resulting equation for the whole corn and sugar household samples. The estimation results for each equation in (1.3a) are presented in Tables 1.9–1.13.[18]

5.2 Women's Participation in Home Production

Although women's time is concentrated in home production activities, there is a wide variation of time actually spent by women in performing these tasks. The adjusted regression estimation presented in Table 1.9 is used to analyse the extent by which this variation is due to the crop shift effect as well as to women's physiological, skills and household attributes.

The effect of tenure status on home production turns out to be positive but negligible for corn and sugar households as shown in Table 1.9.[19] There is however, a stronger, negative wealth effect of landholding size on women's time for domestic chores and childcare.

Table 1.9 Determinants of rural women's time allocation in home production

Explanatory variable	Corn households		Sugar households		All households	
	Coefficient	t-ratio	Coefficient	t-ratio	Coefficient	t-ratio
One	432.792	14.548**	299.936	9.138**	369.620	17.338
Mills[a]	−58.0511	−6.766**	−65.2016	−6.855**	−60.5758	−9.530**
Tenured 1[b]	2.59593	.161	43.1772	2.188**	21.0595	1.774*
Tenured 2[c]	19.6611	.954	25.4948	1.083	24.7584	1.638*
Tenured 3[d]	7.36982	.348	15.6418	.710	12.9311	.867
Physiod 1[e]	−.218596	−.012	23.1769	1.004	4.27682	.304
Physiod 2[f]	14.3537	2.147**	36.2915	4.629**	23.4129	4.591**
Noolddau[g]	−26.7354	−2.609**	−46.2029	−3.551**	−33.4896	−4.182**
Schooling[h]	−.933155	−.414	2.09152	.770	.698620	.405
Profitability[i]	−.006087	−.513	−.015600	−.568	−.028009	−.912
Popden[j]	−.599794	−4.569**	.095767	.599	−.283830	−2.938**
Landsize[k]	−5.74356	−2.510**	−4.66646	−2.861**	−4.77931	−3.710**
Seasonality[l]	32.5932	2.890**	4.26515	.314	21.6289	2.482**
R-squared	.097648		.167661		.111109	
F-ratio	15.4476		9.6688		15.4476	
	(12,894)		(12,576)		(12,1483)	

Notes: a Inverse-Mills ratio estimated from probit model.

b Tenure dummy variable with value = 1 if tenant household;
= 0 if otherwise;

c Tenure dummy variable with value = 1 if mixed household;
= 0 if otherwise;

d Tenure dummy variable with value = 1 if owner household;
= 0 if otherwise;

e Physiological status dummy variable with value = 1 if the woman is pregnant;
= 0 if otherwise;

f Physiological status dummy variable with value = 1 if woman is lactating;
= 0 if otherwise;

g Number of daughters aged 15 and above in the household.

h Years of mother's schooling.

i Net farm revenue per hectare per production cycle.

j Proxy for extent of market integration. This is the population density of the village to which the household belongs.

k Total land area cultivated by the household.

l Seasonality dummy variable with value = 1 if slack period;
= 0 if otherwise.

** Significance level of 5 per cent or better.
* Significance level of 10 per cent or better.

One possible explanation is that, holding tenure status constant, the demand for labour (both family and hired) increases as the household landsize increases. Hence, women's time for home production is lessened. This explanation only holds, however, if there is some degree of substitutability between male and female household labour as in corn production.

In situations where little or no substitutability between types of household labour exists, as in sugar production, a different explanation is required. Since an increase in landsize may be met by hiring more labour and not necessarily by increasing the time demanded of women for assisting in farm cultivation, then the decline in women's home production time cannot be explained by increase in farm participation. The income effect of the increased land size may be significant and this enables women in such households to hire female domestic help.

The physiological status of women is found to affect significantly women's time in home production due to its major component, childrearing (see Table 1.9). Breastfeeding physically constrains women to stay at home so that women's time for domestic chores increases as well.

The significant negative correlation between the number of older daughters in the household and women's home production time confirms the claim made by Yotopoulos and Mergos (1986) that some degree of substitution occurs between women's and children's work, especially in home production. Households with fewer daughters have more work contributed by women. This illustrates in part children's significant contribution in home production.

The regression results presented in Table 1.9 also show the significant effect of seasonality in home production time of women in corn households. The strong positive coefficient of the dummy variable suggests that home production time in corn households increases significantly during the slack season.

5.3 Women's Participation in Farm Cultivation

The relatively low level of women's participation in both corn and sugar farming has been discussed elsewhere in this paper. Having made the necessary statistical adjustment for this selectivity bias, we now examine the significance of agricultural commercialisation and other factors in explaining any variation in women's time that may exist. Table 1.10 indicates that among the various characteristics of cropping systems, it is the level of market integration that significantly affects women's involvement in farm production. Landholding size effect also tends to be significant but only in the case of corn households.

The physiological status and the level of women's schooling seem to affect significantly women's participation in corn production. As women have more reproductive responsibilities, they tend to spend less time in farm production. Since years of schooling affect both their incentive and the probability to get an off-farm job, the more educated women in corn households tend to spend less time in farm production. The negative schooling (push) effect on women's participation is somewhat dampened, however, by the positive landsize (pull) effect.[20]

The generally weak correlation found between these determinants and time spent by sugar women in farm production may be explained by their diminished overall involvement in sugar growing. The presence of older daughters at home proved to be one of the few significant factors and it is positively related with sugar women's farm participation. This is consistent with our *a priori* expectations that (older) children take on some of the maternal duties in the household, thus reducing the demand for women's time in home production.

5.4 Women's Participation in the Labour Market

Women's participation in the labour market has been the focus of several labour studies. Scant attention is paid, however, to the constraints faced by women and to the nature of the labour market activity. Women's labour force participation is affected not only by their physiological status and skills as shown in Table 1.11 but also by the structural changes in the economic environment.

The effect of the cropping system on women's labour force participation yields results that are rather surprising at first glance. Farm profitability is positively correlated with women's time in labour market activities and this is found to be statistically significant in the case of sugar households (see Table 1.11). This seems to contradict the notion that higher (farm) income reduces the incentive as well as the need for household members to work outside the farm.

A further decomposition of the labour force participation of women between agricultural wage employment (Table 1.12) and non-agricultural activities (Table 1.13) sheds light on the effect of export cropping on women's time. The tenure dummy variables are

Table 1.10 Determinants of rural women's time allocation in farm production

Explanatory variable	Corn households		Sugar households		All households	
	Coefficient	t-ratio	Coefficient	t-ratio	Coefficient	t-ratio
One[a]	104.942	3.935**	56.5696	1.790**	101.542	5.152**
Mills[a]	-47.6317	-6.192**	-39.5959	-4.323**	-47.0417	-8.005**
Tenured 1[b]	4.93796	.342	34.6977	1.826*	24.6947	2.250*
Tenured 2[c]	2.02553	.110	6.68261	.295	20.6016	1.475
Tenured 3[d]	3.15753	.166	17.2039	.811	22.3281	1.618
Physiod 1[e]	-40.5832	-2.546**	-6.13587	-.276	-28.2094	-2.170*
Physiod 2[f]	-18.1335	-3.026**	-10.8900	-1.442	-16.5465	-3.509**
Noolddau[g]	15.7970	1.720	25.2980	2.019**	19.6159	2.650**
Schooling[h]	-4.35632	-2.157*	-.690469	-.264	-3.37017	-2.113*
Profitability[i]	.058185	1.087	-.034618	-1.309	-.026102	-1.129
Popden[j]	.377489	3.207**	.340977	2.216**	.028300	3.168**
Landsize[k]	7.71598	3.761**	2.35466	1.499	3.03265	2.546*
Seasonality[l]	.142276	.014	.414987	-.032	-.836085	-.104
R-squared	.110750		.076105		.081359	
F-ratio	9.2784		3.9540		10.9451	
	(12,894)		(12,576)		(12,1483)	

Notes: a Inverse-Mills ratio estimated from probit model.

  b Tenure dummy variable with value = 1 if tenant household;
                                    = 0 if otherwise;

  c Tenure dummy variable with value = 1 if mixed household;
                                    = 0 if otherwise;

  d Tenure dummy variable with value = 1 if owner household;
                                    = 0 if otherwise;

  e Physiological status dummy variable with value = 1 if the woman is pregnant;
                                                            = 0 if otherwise;

  f Physiological status dummy variable with value = 1 if woman is lactating;
                                                            = 0 if otherwise;

  g Number of daughters aged 15 and above in the household.

  h Years of mother's schooling.

  i Net farm revenue per hectare per production cycle.

  j Proxy for extent of market integration. This is the population density of the village to which the household belongs.

  k Total land area cultivated by the household.

  l Seasonality dummy variable with value = 1 if slack period;
                                 = 0 if otherwise.

** Significance level of 5 per cent or better.
* Significance level of 10 per cent or better.

Table 1.11 Determinants of rural women's participation in the labour market

Explanatory variable	Corn households		Sugar households		All households	
	Coefficient	t-ratio	Coefficient	t-ratio	Coefficient	t-ratio
One	52.4456	3.774**	36.6128	1.997**	45.0477	4.210**
Mills[a]	179.681	44.834**	171.309	32.238**	176.373	55.292**
Tenured 1[b]	-8.36159	-1.112	-10.8943	-.988	-5.50547	-.924
Tenured 2[c]	-9.98380	-1.038	-9.93409	-.755	-9.23948	-1.218
Tenured 3[d]	-12.9339	-1.309	-3.26406	-.265	-3.94239	-.526
Physiod 1[e]	-21.3301	-2.568**	-28.7387	-2.228**	-23.0696	-3.269**
Physiod 2[f]	-5.06876	-1.623*	-14.3933	-3.286**	-8.51320	-3.326**
Nooldau[g]	2.31325	.483	9.04843	1.245	5.86870	1.460
Schooling[h]	3.08654	2.934**	.071552	.047	2.12193	2.451**
Profitability[i]	.003165	.114	.053656	3.496**	.042075	3.353**
Popden[j]	-.022821	-.372	.205607	2.303**	.056012	1.155
Landsize[k]	-.309177	.179	-1.14615	-1.658*	-1.05721	-1.635*
Seasonality[l]	2.73160	.519	-3.14368	-1.114	.579987	-.633
R-squared	.696857		.660123		.677572	
F-ratio	171.2586		93.2276		4.4351	
	(12,894)		(12,576)		(12,1483)	

Notes: a Inverse-Mills ratio estimated from probit model.

b Tenure dummy variable with value = 1 if tenant household;
= 0 if otherwise;

c Tenure dummy variable with value = 1 if mixed household;
= 0 if otherwise;

d Tenure dummy variable with value = 1 if owner household;
= 0 if otherwise;

e Physiological status dummy variable with value = 1 if the woman is pregnant;
= 0 if otherwise;

f Physiological status dummy variable with value = 1 if woman is lactating;
= 0 if otherwise;

g Number of daughters aged 15 and above in the household.

h Years of mother's schooling.

i Net farm revenue per hectare per production cycle.

j Proxy for extent of market integration. This is the population density of the village to which the household belongs.

k Total land area cultivated by the household.

l Seasonality dummy variable with value = 1 if slack period;
= 0 if otherwise.

** Significance level of 5 per cent or better.
* Significance level of 10 per cent or better.

Table 1.12 Determinants of rural women's participation in agricultural wage employment.

Explanatory variable	Corn households		Sugar households		All households	
	Coefficient	t-ratio	Coefficient	t-ratio	Coefficient	t-ratio
One	49.2771	4.096**	39.0369	2.393**	43.2281	4.607**
Mills[a]	58.0579	16.732**	60.3391	12.763**	58.9501	21.074**
Tenured 1[b]	-17.9270	-2.753**	-18.8138	-1.918**	-17.4552	-3.341**
Tenured 2[c]	-22.2560	-2.671**	-37.7207	-3.223**	-25.8208	-3.883**
Tenured 3[d]	-18.5098	-2.164*	-32.3426	-2.953**	-22.7102	-3.458**
Physiod 1[e]	11.9060	1.656*	-21.5863	-1.881*	-.768189	-.124
Physiod 2[f]	4.24111	1.569	-5.03130	-1.291	.350439	.156
Noolddau[g]	-6.88216	-1.661*	5.37114	.831	-2.38332	-.676
Schooling[h]	-5.38988	-5.917**	-2.53426	-1.878*	-4.16457	-5.485**
Profitability[i]	.010988	.455	-.009869	-.723	-.008575	-.417
Popden[j]	.120250	2.265**	.151799	1.911*	.143782	3.381**
Landsize[k]	-.461993	-.499	-.320860	-.396	-.553607	-.976
Seasonality[l]	-4.78396	-1.049	-7.87189	-1.651*	-6.29163	-1.941*
R-squared	.292863		.271711		.274879	
F-ratio	30.8544		17.9079		46.8480	
	(12,894)		(12,576)		(12,1483)	

Notes: a Inverse-Mills ratio estimated from probit model.

b Tenure dummy variable with value = 1 if tenant household;
= 0 if otherwise;

c Tenure dummy variable with value = 1 if mixed household;
= 0 if otherwise;

d Tenure dummy variable with value = 1 if owner household;
= 0 if otherwise;

e Physiological status dummy variable with value = 1 if the woman is pregnant;
= 0 if otherwise;

f Physiological status dummy variable with value = 1 if woman is lactating;
= 0 if otherwise;

g Number of daughters aged 15 and above in the household.

h Years of mother's schooling.

i Net farm revenue per hectare per production cycle.

j Proxy for extent of market integration. This is the population density of the village to which the household belongs.

k Total land area cultivated by the household.

l Seasonality dummy variable with value = 1 if slack period;
= 0 if otherwise.

** Significance level of 5 per cent or better.
* Significance level of 10 per cent or better.

Table 1.13 Determinants of rural women's participation in non-agricultural employment

Explanatory variable	Corn households		Sugar households		All households	
	Coefficient	t-ratio	Coefficient	t-ratio	Coefficient	t-ratio
One	-22.8272	-1.293	9.76820	.412	440.854	1.548
Mills[a]	117.448	26.229**	113.031	19.596**	-187.024	-1.072
Tenured 1[b]	23.8839	2.472**	31.8361	2.321**	133.914	3.383**
Tenured 2[c]	28.0473	2.287**	47.4984	2.767**	184.995	3.730**
Tenured 3[d]	34.4736	2.757**	48.5372	3.032**	202.316	4.043**
Physiod 1[e]	-26.6256	-2.379**	-28.7988	-1.736*	15.1004	.233
Physiod 2[f]	-12.1396	-2.961**	-12.6271	-2.195**	-17.1408	-.932
Noolddau[g]	11.4098	1.803*	14.4154	1.582*	15.1785	.632
Schooling[h]	7.92829	5.905**	9.20269	4.995**	4.56045	.761
Profitability[i]	.075892	3.173**	.049382	2.300**	.0430539	.659
Popden[j]	-.070340	-.887	-.317983	-2.937**	-.626369	-2.134**
Landsize[k]	-.462856	-.368	-1.76711	-1.434	-5.26821	-1.406
Seasonality[l]	8.74255	1.257	11.3255	1.160	12.8322	.495
R-squared	.444481		.422764		.213537	
F-ratio	67.6766		44.0046		5.7245	
	(12,894)		(12,576)		(12,1483)	

Notes: a Inverse-Mills ratio estimated from probit model.
   b Tenure dummy variable with value = 1 if tenant household;
     = 0 if otherwise;
   c Tenure dummy variable with value = 1 if mixed household;
     = 0 if otherwise;
   d Tenure dummy variable with value = 1 if owner household;
     = 0 if otherwise;
   e Physiological status dummy variable with value = 1 if the woman is pregnant;
     = 0 if otherwise;
   f Physiological status dummy variable with value = 1 if woman is lactating;
     = 0 if otherwise;
   g Number of daughters aged 15 and above in the household.
   h Years of mother's schooling.
   i Net farm revenue per hectare per production cycle.
   j Proxy for extent of market integration. This is the population density of the village to which the household belongs.
   k Total land area cultivated by the household.
   l Seasonality dummy variable with value = 1 if slack period;
     = 0 if otherwise.

   ** Significance level of 5 per cent or better.
   * Significance level of 10 per cent or better.

found to be a significant factor on women's labour force participation but their effect on women's agricultural wage employment is opposite to their effect on women's non-agricultural employment (see Tables 1.12 and 1.13). As the tenure status of the household deteriorates and the source of income from the farm becomes more unstable, there is greater compulsion for women to work as agricultural wage labourers. In this case, the labour market participation of women is a coping mechanism triggered by income instability.

An improvement in the tenure status of the household, on the other hand, is positively correlated with the involvement of women in non-agricultural activities. This is consistent with the strong positive effect of farm profitability on non-agricultural employment of women. The above results suggest that women in more secured and more wealthy households have more access to funds. Income stability as represented by better tenure status and bigger landholdings open opportunities for this class of women to engage in their own business activity e.g. running a 'sari-sari' (convenience or general store), dressmaking, etc. Such opportunities do not exist, however, for women with inadequate or little access to funds. Women's schooling has an ambiguous effect on labour force participation since it discourages women from engaging in agricultural wage employment but encourages them in non-agricultural activities.

The seasonality dummy variable is found to have negligible effect on women's labour force participation except for agricultural wage employment of women in sugar households. This significant seasonal effect indicates that wage employment opportunities for women are not only difficult to come by in the sugar area but also that these opportunities vary highly from season to season. The seasonality of wage employment only intensifies the search for employment of women in sugar households. For those women whose entry into the labour market is 'economic necessity-driven', the added responsibilities borne by these mothers to move their family out of poverty becomes even harder to fulfil. The relative shortness of their workday is not so much a matter of choice as a result of their inability to find employment.

6 CONCLUSIONS

The preceding discussion examines and measures the impact of agricultural commercialisation on Philippine rural women. Taking the women in Mindanao as an example, this study demonstrated how a crop shift changes women's time allocation pattern. As in many development policy formulations, this dimension is largely ignored in studies of the impact of policy because women's economic contribution is not recognised. Thus, any benefits or costs in terms of women's work (or availability of work) are not taken into account in any evaluation of trade or growth strategies; less so in any formulation of displacement or structural adjustment plans.

The policy of export promotion in the rural sector has transformed women's roles in an uneven and complex manner. The resulting trade-offs made by women on their time use, as this study shows, are anything but uniform. Economic change alters the parameters and boundaries of women's time allocation decisions and thereby reconstitutes women's productive roles. The tendency towards more land concentration, for example, implies that while some women have access to more resources and can acquire domestic help or engage in their own enterprise, others, especially in landless households, must find jobs or new survival strategies. But the general tendency against hiring women workers in sugar production ensures that as cash cropping expands to replace subsistence production, women will find it more difficult to get off-farm work.

The diminished role of women in farm cultivation therefore does not necessarily lead to increased women's control of their time. The results of the study suggests that, in certain cases, only the work domain of women has changed as they adapt various strategies to cope with new situations. The dynamic consequence of agricultural commercialisation has been the replacement of a stagnant semi-subsistence production with a combination of commercial farming and a marginalised landless segment that can neither subsist on land cultivation nor find adequate employment as a substitute. In the process, it has led to increased differentiation among women.

Notes

1. The author would like to thank especially Howarth Bouis for providing the data and Nancy Folbre and Bina Agarwal for their comments and suggestions. This study would not have been possible without the technical support of the International Food Policy Research Institute and the financial assistance of the Center for Excellence Fund of the American University. The computer expertise of Elizabeth Jacinto, Winnie Alvarado and Ellen Payongayong and discussions with Orville Solon, Michael

Alba, Barbara Bergmann, Laurence Haddad, Michael Lipton, Mieke Meurs and Stephanie Seguino are also gratefully acknowledged.

2. A few examples are Dixon (1978), Grossman (1979), Deere and de Leal (1981), Fawcett *et al.* (1984), ILO (1985) and Costello *et al.* (1987).

3. Earlier works on the study of women's time allocation in rural Philippines include King and Evenson (1983) and University of the Philippines at Los Banos *et al.* (1985).

4. See Beneria (1982), Bourque and Warren (1981), Nash *et al.* (1986) and Beneria and Roldan (1987).

5. The lack of data on women as well as the quality of available data are well-acknowledged problems. One area where data on women has been particularly deficient refers to their economic activities (United Nations, 1988). For the purpose of this study, the author makes use of data collected through a time allocation survey. Although there are problems inherent in such data, this is one of the better existing methods for capturing the wide range of work performed by women since it seeks an account of all activities during the specified period.

6. The category of semi-subsistence households is defined by the significant proportion of the farm output that is consumed and of the inputs that is provided by the household. In households that grew corn, Bouis and Haddad (1988) have shown that about a third of the output is for home consumption. The figures are much higher (50–60 per cent) for landless households, or households with less than one hectare of land. Sugar, on the other hand, is grown exclusively for sale to the sugar millers and is destined for the export market.

It should be noted that corn households receive, on average, 50 per cent of their farm income from corn production. Sugar households, on the other hand, continue to produce corn, but this represents only 16 per cent of their farm income. (Bouis and Haddad, 1990, p. 38) The per capita consumption of own-produced corn in sugar households is about 65 per cent of the per capita consumption level of own-produced corn in corn households, even though sugar households produced sufficient corn to have consumption levels equal that of the corn households. (p. 31)

The difference in the degree of market integration is also reflected in the ratio of imputed household-owned inputs to total market-based expenditure outlays. Using the data from Tables 4.7, 6.1 and 6.2 in Bouis and Haddad (1988), the ratio for corn households ranges from 1.2 (mixed and tenant) to 2.5 (landless) while for sugar households it ranges from 0.64 (owners) to 1.8 (landless).

7. The study by King and Evenson (1983) is based on a 1975 survey of 576 households in the Laguna Province of the Philippines. The Yotopoulos and Mergos (1986) study is based on a 1980 survey of 690 households in the Mindanao region of the Philippines.

8. Unlike in some African societies, male and female contributions in Philippine farm cultivation tend to complement each other within the same crop production, rather than engage in separate production of different crops (Bouis and Kennedy, 1989; Joekes, 1987).

9. Sex discrimination is supported by certain provisions of the Philippine

law. Cortes (1975) cites the Civil Code and the Penal Code of the Philippines as two of the many legal statutes which uphold male authority in important positions. The choice of family residence under Philippine law is given to the husband. In case of disagreement concerning parental authority, the husband is given the upper hand. The husband is also the legal administrator of the conjugal as well as the children's property. The husband's consent is needed before the wife can accept expensive gifts, except from close relatives. The wife has the right to purchase things for the house, but not without the consent of the husband in the case of expensive purchases. The husband has the right to object to the wife's profession. If the wife is involved in a legal suit, the husband must be involved; if the husband is involved in a court suit, the wife has no say.

10. For example, in the Philippines, women themselves speak of 'helping with the harvesting' rather than of 'harvesting'.
11. Almost all households grow a variety of crops such as rice, fruits and vegetables in addition to corn and/or sugar. But for purposes of analysis, households are categorised on the basis of the primary crop grown (at least 50 per cent of farm income). Virtually all 'corn' households do not grow any sugar but 'sugar' households produce some corn, a portion of which is for home consumption.
12. The Bukidnon Sugar Company began operations in 1977, established in response to the high world sugar prices in the mid 1970s. The early years of operation were sufficiently profitable for the mill's capacity to be expanded in 1981 (Bouis and Haddad, 1988, p. 18).
13. Home production includes domestic chores performed for family maintenance such as cooking, cleaning, laundering and childrearing. Farm cultivation takes into account both main crop (corn or sugar) production and backyard production such as vegetable gardening, animal raising and growing fruit trees. Participation in the labour market includes not only agricultural wage employment but also non-agricultural activities such as shopkeeping, dressmaking, cottage industry, market vending, etc.
14. The concept of conditional probabilities is discussed in Lindgren (1976) and Mood, Graybill and Boes (1974). This assumes that there exists a probability space, say $(S, A, P[\cdot])$; that is, some random experiment for which a sample space S, collection of events A, and probability function $P[\cdot]$ are defined. The probability $p[\cdot]$ is said to be conditional on the occurrence of the event A defined by the information B. Conditioning with the information that event B has occurred simply introduces a smaller probability space; thus the adjective 'conditional' is used to refer to the reduced model. Hence the conditional probability of event A, given event B, denoted by $P[A/B]$ is defined as:

$$P[A/B] = \frac{P[A,B]}{P[B]} \qquad \text{if } P[B] > 0$$

and is undefined if $P[B] = 0$.

15. For purposes of analysis, households which cultivated less than one

hectare of land are characterised as 'near-landless or landless'. About half of the households in this category have no land at all. Although there is some degree of labour mobility between the two crops, there are skills specific to sugar production that are obtained over time. Certain labour arrangements also tend to develop which restrict labour mobility. Sugar landless households are those whose sugar wage is greater than other agricultural wage incomes; corn landless households are those whose sugar wages were less than half of total agricultural wages. (Bouis and Haddad, 1988).

With respect to tenancy arrangements, land rented typically for sugar production was rented on a fixed rate basis. For corn, the typical rental arrangement was sharecropping, usually on a 50–50 basis.

16. 'The all-round duties of the housewife have as purpose the production of . . . human beings in contrast to the production of things' (Mies *et al.*, 1988, p. 178).

17. A censored sample is one in which some observations on the dependent variable corresponding to known sets of independent variables are not observable (Heckman, 1974; Judge *et al.*, 1985; Maddala, 1983). In a sense, the extent of the labour force participation of rural women is observed only if it is non-negative and otherwise takes the value zero, although the choice of zero is arbitrary. Thus, the labour force participation model can be written as:

$$a_i = B_j X_j + e \qquad \text{if } a_i > 0$$
$$= 0 \qquad \text{if otherwise.}$$

18. The negative inverse-Mills ratio in Tables 1.9 and 1.10 means that time spent in labour force participation reduces the time allocated to home and farm production.

19. The weak positive effect of tenure may reflect the desirability of increased home production time, given the traditional view of women's primary role.

20. As the landholding size of the family increases, there is increased demand for labour, including female household labour.

References

Beneria, L. (1982) *Women and Development: The Sexual Division of Labor in Rural Societies* (New York: Praeger).

Beneria, L. and Roldan, M. (1987) *Crossroads of Class and Gender: Industrial Homework, Subcontracting, and Household Dynamics in Mexico City* (Chicago, Illinois: University of Chicago Press).

Bouis, H. and Haddad, L. (1988) 'A Case Study of the Commercialization of Agriculture in the Southern Philippines: The Income, Consumption and Nutrition Effects of a Switch from Corn to Sugar Production in Bukidnon', unpublished paper, International Food Policy Research Institute, Washington DC.

Bouis, H. and Haddad, L. (1990) *Effects of Agricultural Commercialization on Land Tenure, Household Resource Allocation and Nutrition in the Philippines* (Washington DC: International Food Policy Research Institute).

Bouis, H. and Kennedy, E. (1989) 'Traditional Cash Crop Schemes' Effects on Production, Consumption and Nutrition', Paper presented at the International Food Policy Research Institute and the Institute for Nutrition in Central America and Panama Policy Workshop, Antigua, Guatemala, 9–11 March.

Bourque, S. and Warren, K. (1981) *Patriarchy and Social Change in Rural Peru* (Ann Arbor: University of Michigan Press).

Cortes, I. (1975) 'Status of Women', in *Law and Population in the Philippines: A Country Monograph* (Quezon City: University of the Philippines Law Center).

Costello, M. *et al.* (1987) *Mobility and Employment in Urban Southeast Asia – Examples from Indonesia and the Philippines* (Boulder, Colorado: Westview Press).

Deere, C. D. and de Leal, L. (1981) *Women in Andean Agriculture* (Geneva: International Labour Office).

Dixon, R. B. (1978) *Rural Women at Work: Strategies for Development in South Asia* (Baltimore: John Hopkins University Press).

Fawcett, J. *et al.* (1984) *Women in the Cities of Asia – Migration and Urban Adaptation* (Boulder: Westview Press).

Folbre, Nancy (1984) 'Household Production in the Philippines: A Non-neoclassical Approach', *Economic Development and Cultural Change*, vol. 32, no. 2, pp. 303–29.

Grossman, R. (1979) 'Women's Place in the Integrated Circuit', *Southeast Asia Chronicle*, no. 66, January–February.

Heckman, J. (1974) 'Sample Bias as a Specification Error', *Econometrica*, vol. 42, no. 1, pp. 153–62.

Heyzer, N. (1986) *Working Women in Southeast Asia: Development, Subordination and Emancipation* (Milton Keynes: Open University Press).

International Labour Office (ILO) (1985) *Women Workers in Multinational Enterprises in Developing Countries* (Geneva: International Labour Office).

Judge, G., Griffiths, W. F. *et al.* (1985) *The Theory and Practice of Econometrics* (New York: Wiley).

Joekes, S. (1987) *Women in the World Economy* (Oxford: Oxford University Press).

Khandker, S. (1988) 'Determinants of Women's Time Allocation in Rural Bangladesh', *Economic Development and Cultural Change*, vol. 37, no. 1, October.

King, E. and Evenson, R. (1983) 'Time Allocation Study and Home Production in the Philippine Rural Household', in Buvinic, M. *et al.* (eds) *Women and Poverty in the Third World* (Baltimore, Maryland: Johns Hopkins University Press), pp. 35–61.

Lindgren, G. (1976) *Statistical Theory* (New York: Macmillan).

Maddala, G. S. (1983) *Limited Dependent and Qualitative Variables in Econometrics* (London: Cambridge University Press).

Mies, M. *et al.* (1988) *Women: the Last Colony* (London: Zed).

Mood, A., Graybill, F. and Boes, D. (1974) *Introduction to the Theory of Statistics* (New York: McGraw-Hill).

Nash, J., Safa, H. *et al.* (1986) *Women and Change in Latin America* (South Hadley, Massachusetts: Bergin and Garvey).

Quisumbing, A. (1988) 'Women and Agrarian Transformation in the Philippines: Food Crops, Cash Crops and Technical Change', Paper presented at the 1988 Tokyo Symposium on Women, Tokyo Women's Christian University, 25–8 August.

Sen, G. and Grown, C. (1987) *Development, Crises and Alternative Visions* (New York: Monthly Review Press).

United Nations (UN) (1988) *Improving Statistics and Indices on Women Using Household Surveys*, Department of International Economic and Social Affairs, Studies in Methods, Series, F, no. 48 (New York: United Nations).

University of the Philippines at Los Banos, *et al.* (1985) *Filipino Women in Rice Farming Systems* (Los Banos, Philippines: International Rice Research Institute).

Yotopoulos, P. A. and Mergos, G. (1986) 'Labor Allocation in the Agricultural Household', *Food Research Institute Studies*, vol. 20, no. 1, pp. 87–104.

2 Industrialisation Strategies and Gender Composition of Manufacturing Employment in Turkey

Günseli Berik[1]
NEW SCHOOL FOR SOCIAL RESEARCH, NEW YORK, USA

and

Nilüfer Çağatay[1]
RAMAPO COLLEGE OF NEW JERSEY, USA

1 INTRODUCTION

During the past decade, the literature on women and development as well as the literature on the new international division of labour have frequently emphasised the growing share of female employment in manufacturing under export-led industrialisation. Many authors have documented the often repressive conditions of women's employment (Elson and Pearson, 1981; Nash and Fernandez-Kelly, 1983), some characterising this industrialisation strategy as 'female-led industrialisation' (Joekes, 1982), others as a process of 'bloody taylorization' (Lipietz, 1987, pp. 75–6). Beyond an appreciation of the repressive working conditions, these conceptualisations include widely accepted characterisations of women's location in manufacturing employment. It is held as a near-axiomatic truth that in the current phase of the international division of labour, Third World countries specialise in labour intensive production of commodities with low skill content, and women constitute a high proportion of the labour force in these sectors. Such characterisations of women's employment raise the question of whether these characteristics are peculiar to export-led

41

industrialisation or are more general features of women's employment in the industrialisation process.

Despite the rapid growth of the literature on women and development in the last two decades, there are relatively few studies on patterns of industrial employment by sex in the Third World, and even fewer attempts to establish the relationships between industrial characteristics and gender composition of manufacturing employment. This blindspot in research is primarily due to the relative paucity of detailed data on occupational and industrial distributions of employment by gender, which precludes the examination of the processes of incorporation, exclusion and substitution by gender in manufacturing industry. Much of the literature on women and development, therefore, pursues detailed case studies focusing on gender at the household, enterprise or industry subsector levels.

Using Turkey as a case study, this paper attempts to investigate econometrically the characteristics of manufacturing industries in which women tend to be concentrated. Turkey constitutes an interesting case study because Turkish industrialisation since 1960 is characterised by two distinct sub-periods of rapid economic growth and structural change interrupted by a period of economic crisis. The first period between 1963 and 1977 is characterised by import-substituting industrialisation, and the post-1980 period by export-oriented growth. Using cross-sectional data from annual manufacturing surveys corresponding to 1966 and 1982, we assess the separate effects of micro level industry characteristics, such as capital intensity or export orientation of a sector, as well as the effect of the change in industrialisation strategy, which are often found to co-determine patterns of employment by sex in manufacturing in the Third World. Thus, our method is complementary to the existing studies of gender in the course of industrialisation, in that we seek to identify econometrically where women are located in manufacturing industry subsectors.

2   INDUSTRIALISATION STRATEGIES AND GENDER COMPOSITION OF EMPLOYMENT IN THE THIRD WORLD

The literature on changes in women's relative position during the industrialisation process can be divided into two phases since the seminal study by Boserup (1970). While the earlier studies emphasise women's marginalisation from modern manufacturing employment, the more recent studies focus on the integration of women into manufacturing employment in the course of capitalist development. Boserup noted that women's economic roles in home industries eroded as the latter were displaced by modern manufacturing without providing employment for the displaced women. According to Boserup, employers discriminated against women in hiring, and women, because of their reproductive responsibilities, did not prefer modern industrial employment. The literature of the 1970s provided further documentation of the slow growth of women's manufacturing employment accompanying the post-World War II industrialisation process, particularly in Latin America. This outcome was widely attributed to the specific strategy of industrialisation, that is, capital-intensive, import-substituting industrialisation with a high degree of involvement of multinational corporations (Chinchilla, 1977; Schmink, 1977; Saffioti, 1978; de Miranda, 1977), and to the functionality of women's unpaid labour in the household for employers (Saffioti, 1977). This 'marginalisation' literature largely relies on *aggregate* employment statistics for the economy and manufacturing industry of the countries under investigation.

Studies of the last decade have produced evidence which qualifies somewhat the bleak picture drawn by the first generation of studies. These studies focus on the post-1960s industrial growth in selected economies of the Third World, which has been fuelled both by growth of export markets and by the expansion of domestic demand and has partly been accompanied by the relocation of manufacturing industry from developed to developing economies. These studies provide empirical evidence which supports the association of growth in exports of manufactured goods and growth in female industrial employment.[2] The industries in which women constitute the majority of employment, such as apparel and textiles, happen to be the ones which account for the largest proportion of Third World exports to the developed countries (Joekes, 1986). This later vintage of studies, therefore, emphasises not so much the marginalisation of women by *exclusion* from capitalist development and industrialisation, but rather women's marginalisation by *inclusion* and *segregation* into labour-intensive sectors with 'low wages' and 'low skills'.

This literature identifies lower wage rates associated with female employment as key to the high and growing proportion of women in export-oriented as well as labour-intensive sectors of manufacturing industry. Many case studies show that employers value the reliability, stability and flexibility of women workers relative to men workers

(Humphrey, 1985; Joekes, 1985; ILO, 1985; Hein, 1984), which translate into lower unit labour costs with female workers than with male workers (Anker and Hein, 1986; Elson and Pearson, 1981; Safa, 1981; Nash, 1983; Lim, 1983).[3]

For the purposes of this discussion, we identify these two approaches to the study of the impact of industrialisation on women's employment as the 'Female Marginalisation 1' (FM1) and 'Female Marginalisation 2' (FM2) theses.[4] Even though FM1 and FM2 literatures contain different conclusions with respect to changes in employment patterns of men and women during the course of industrialisation (particularly in manufacturing industry), they posit similar hypotheses about the determinants of women's location in manufacturing industry *at any point in time.*

The proponents of the FM1 thesis, which emerges from the Latin American experience of import-substituting industrialisation (ISI), argue that *over time* women's share of employment in manufacturing falls. The FM2 discussions, on the other hand, which mostly emerge from a later period of Latin American as well as the South East Asian experiences with export-led industrialisation, emphasise an increase of women's share of employment. Neither literature examines the effect of the shift in industrialisation strategy on the gender composition of manufacturing employment, but focuses on trends within each strategy. Given that in recent decades export-led industrialisation is commonly adopted following ISI, however, the implication of the FM2 literature is an increase in the share of women's employment with the shift to export-led industrialisation.

The FM1 literature characterises import-substituting industrialisation as 'capital-intensive' with the consequence that industrial employment can only absorb a small proportion of the labour force. It is also argued that the character of the technology adopted by the multinational firms in this type of industrialisation increases the availability of skilled jobs. As the large number of unskilled jobs are replaced by a small number of skilled positions, men are favoured over women in filling these jobs. For example, Chaney and Schmink (1976, pp. 168) state that, unlike the countries that embarked on industrialisation in the nineteenth century, those undergoing the industrialisation process in the second half of twentieth century skip the relatively labour-intensive stages of industrialisation, and in these late industrialisers 'the demand for skilled labour to manage complicated machines is explicitly a "male-favoured" demand'.

By contrast, the FM2 literature is based on the argument that the relocation of manufacturing processes in the Third World is the outcome of technological progress, which has fragmented and standardised production processes and resulted in deskilling. It is argued that the 'success' of the export-oriented industrialisation strategy is premised on labour-intensive manufacturing under the auspices of multinational corporations (MNCs) using unskilled labour. Despite the assumption that technological advancement on a world scale brings about deskilling and therefore increasing reliance on unskilled labour, the implicit connection between type of technology and skill requirements of the labour force in this literature is identical to the one posited by the proponents of FM1: capital-intensive production processes require skilled labour and labour-intensive ones use unskilled labour. Furthermore, the association between the skill requirement of the technology and the gender composition of the labour force is also identical: women constitute the unskilled and men the skilled labour force.[5] In addition, country studies informed by both approaches imply that women will be concentrated in the exporting as well as the relatively unskilled sectors of manufacturing industry. Similarly, both sets of literature assign a privileged status to the role of MNCs in determining patterns of employment by sex.

There are studies contradicting these somewhat stylised arguments about women's employment in the Third World. The association of female employment with export-oriented industrialisation is not universal. Pyle (1986), for example, shows that the ideological imperative to give priority to male employment may outweigh the favourable cost conditions of female employment. Humphrey (1987), who examines the changes in gender composition of employment in Brazilian manufacturing industry, observes that the dramatic growth of women's share of employment in the 1970s is neither limited to export-oriented industries and firms nor to assembly production processes. Moreover, while export-oriented multinationals account for the majority of women's employment in multinational firms in industry in the Third World, the majority of women's manufacturing employment in the Third World is in national and import-substituting firms (ILO, 1985).[6] At the same time, a few studies suggest that the growing proportion of women's employment in manufacturing may be associated with the upswing of the cycle and may not represent a trend, suggesting reversibility of the growth of women's employment in manufacturing (Joekes, 1986) under export-led industrialisation.

3   INDUSTRIALISATION AND GENDER COMPOSITION OF MANUFACTURING INDUSTRY IN TURKEY

Like many Third World economies, Turkey embarked on its industrialisation process under the import-substituting industrialisation (ISI) strategy, but has recently shifted to an export-oriented growth regime. The Turkish industrialisation process, which began in the 1930s with a high degree of public sector involvement in manufacturing industry, gained momentum in the 1960s. Between 1963 and 1977 the industrial sector exhibited consistently high growth rates, with manufacturing as the most dynamic sector of the economy. Over this period the composition of output changed towards industrial goods and services, but both the labour force and exports remained predominantly agricultural.[7] The largest manufactured export product group was textiles and clothing, which increased as a share of both total exports and manufactured exports during this period.

The characteristic features of manufacturing industry during the 1963–77 period were continued public sector involvement in manufacturing, orientation of production to the domestic market, an insignificant level of foreign direct investment, and differentiation between public and private sectors. In contrast to the private sector, the public sector consists of larger firms, has a higher degree of capital intensity and greater representation in intermediate and capital goods industries, and is less exposed to international competition.

The import-substitution industrialisation strategy was abandoned in favour of an export-oriented regime following the balance of payments crisis in the late 1970s. Key features of the structural adjustment programme implemented from 1980 onwards were export promotion and liberalisation of capital flows and imports. Recently there have also been efforts to diminish the significance of the public sector in manufacturing production by privatising public sector firms. The trade policies adopted in this period have resulted in:

(a) an increase in the volume of exports;
(b) an increase in the share of manufactured goods in exports; and
(c) a diversification in the composition of exports and manufactured output.

From 1980 onwards, Turkish exports grew significantly faster than the world demand and the sectoral composition of Turkish exports changed sharply in favour of industrial goods, especially manufactured goods, which accounted for three-quarters of exports in 1985. Textiles and clothing remained as the largest manufactured export category, increasing its share in total exports, albeit with a decline of its share of manufactured exports between 1980 and 1985 (OECD, 1987). In the same period, the composition of gross domestic product continued to change in favour of industry, with manufacturing industry's share reaching 25 per cent in 1985. By 1985 the share of industrial employment had risen to nearly 20 per cent of total civilian employment (OECD, 1987). However, the post-1980 period is also marked by increasing unemployment and a worsening income distribution. In this period the rate of unemployment remained around 15 per cent. Wages in large-scale manufacturing suffered a setback. Overall, under the export-led regime the labour market conditions deteriorated.[8]

Despite the macro picture of shifts in output, employment and exports, women's share in manufacturing employment remained constant both throughout the ISI period as well as in the early 1980s. Between 1960 and 1985, this figure declined slightly from 16.3 per cent to 15.2 per cent, according to population census data. According to manufacturing survey data, between 1966 and 1982 (the last year for which data on the gender breakdown of manufacturing employment is available) women's share in manufacturing employment declined from 20.3 to 18.2 per cent.[9]

The relative constancy of the female share at the aggregate levels, however, conceals both the changes in gender composition of employment at disaggregated levels and the growth of female employment outside the large manufacturing enterprises (that is, those establishments that employ 10 or more workers). There is some evidence that in this period homeworking increased, particularly in the clothing industry, where women constitute the homeworking labour force. While it is difficult to estimate the extent of homeworking, preliminary evidence indicates that it became widespread in major cities and women were 'pushed' into homeworking as wage levels in manufacturing jobs declined. In Turkey, as elsewhere, women in homeworking do not enjoy any legal protection and the wage rates are lower than even the minimum wage (Cinar, 1987).

The aggregate female share of employment in large scale manufacturing also conceals differences between public and private sector firms: public sector manufacturing employs a lower proportion of women than private manufacturing.[10] During the 1964–82 period, the female employment share in the private sector was consistently around 20 per cent, while in the public sector this share remained around 14 per cent.[11] Between 1966 and 1982 the dissimilarity index (DI) value for manufacturing industry (at the 3-digit SIC level)[12] declined from 43.3 to 42.7.[13] However, the public and private sectors registered change in opposite directions: for the private establishments the DI increased over this period from 32.69 to 38.44. For the public sector, there was a decrease from 59.28 to 55.92. This means that even though the degree of segregation in the public sector decreased, it still remains higher than in the private sector.

In manufacturing industry, in both 1966 and 1982 the first five most female-intensive industries included tobacco, apparel and textile industries. Moreover, the rankings according to female intensity of employment were similar in both public and private firms for both years (see Tables 2.1 and 2.2). These industries were also significant export sectors of Turkey during import-substituting industrialisation and the importance of these sectors (textile and apparel) continued in the 1980s. In 1966 food, textiles, apparel and tobacco accounted for 81 per cent of female employment, while in 1982 this figure fell to 71 per cent. We should note that this decline reflects the greater degree of diversification of employment in Turkish manufacturing as a whole rather than a fall in the degree of segregation since the comparable figures for male workers also fell from 47 per cent to 35 per cent. This indicates that even though female employment became more diversified by 1982, their employment remained much more concentrated in certain industries than male workers.

4 REGRESSION ANALYSIS

In this section, employing regression analysis, we explore the relationship between characteristics of manufacturing industry subsectors and the degree of 'feminisation' of each sector, measured by the share of female employment in a manufacturing subsector. Using annual surveys of manufacturing for Turkey, we pooled 3-digit SIC level data provided separately for the public and private manufacturing establishments for the two years 1966 and 1982.[14] During 1966, as discussed above, the industrialisation strategy was of the ISI type, while in 1982 export-led industrialisation was in place. Using dummy variables, we also tested the impact of the shift in the overall strategy as well as the effect of the type of ownership of establishment to determine whether or not there were any behavioural differences between private and public enterprises that affected the gender pattern of employment as distinct from industry characteristics.

The following specification was adopted to test the various hypotheses that emerge from the literature discussed in section 2 above as well as hypotheses informed by the peculiar characteristics of Turkish industrialisation.

$$PERC_i = a_0 + a_1 SKILL_i + a_2 HP_i + a_3 EXP_i + a_4 SIZE_i +$$
$$a_5 DPR_i + a_6 D82_i + a_7 EXPD82_i$$

where i = manufacturing industry subsector at 3-digit SIC-level of disaggregation.

$PERC$ = the share of women wage workers.

$SKILL$ = the ratio of skilled to non-skilled production workers.

HP = total power of equipment installed per worker.

EXP = the ratio of exports to output.

$SIZE$ = average establishment size in terms of employment.

DPR = dummy variable for type of ownership; 1 = private establishment component of subsector i, 0 = public establishment component of subsector i.

$D82$ = dummy variable for year; 1 = 1982, 0 = 1966.

$EXPD82 = EXP \times D82$.

The first three variables, $SKILL$, HP and EXP, are used to test the three hypotheses suggested by both sets of 'female marginalisation' literature about women's location in manufacturing employment, namely that women are concentrated in sectors of low skill intensity, high labour intensity, and export orientation. The variable $SIZE$ is used to examine whether establishment size affects demand for labour by sex in an industry, since in Turkey the comparison of data obtained from censuses of the population with that from manufacturing industry surveys suggests that in 'large' establishments (that is, those with 10 or more workers) the female share of employment is, on average, higher than in 'small' workplaces (that is, those with fewer than 10 workers). We test to see whether a similar pattern holds among large enterprises.

The dummy variable DPR distinguishes private establishments from public ones. As pointed out in section 3, public establishments have consistently had a lower share of female employment than

Table 2.1 Employment by sex for manufacturing industry subsectors, 1966 (3-digit SIC; ranked by female share of total employment in subsector)

SIC code	Sector	Public Employment (number)	Public Female (percent)	Private Employment (number)	Private Female (percent)	Total Employment (number)	Total Female (percent)
314	Tobacco	32 229	65.62	2 926	40.74	35 155	63.55
322	Wearing apparel (except footwear)	241	34.85	614	44.63	855	41.87
321	Textiles	32 509	20.36	84 022	34.22	116 531	30.36
352	Other chemical products	1 382	13.17	13 497	31.51	14 879	29.81
361	Pottery, china and earthenware	688	23.26	3 292	29.80	3 980	28.67
383	Electrical machinery	187	0.00	8 443	19.15	8 630	18.74
341	Paper products	7 840	17.87	1 030	19.13	8 870	18.02
385	Professional, scientific measuring and controlling equipment (not elsewhere classified)	–		2 534	17.05	2 534	17.05
390	Other manufacturing industry	–		2 535	17.04	2 535	17.04
356	Plastic products (not elsewhere classified)	–		5 731	16.68	5 731	16.68
312	Food products (not elsewhere classified)	4 851	5.90	13 830	20.20	18 681	16.48
311	Food	27 122	3.41	24 170	22.88	51 292	12.58
313	Beverages	4 262	14.34	1 312	6.33	5 574	12.45

Code	Industry						
324	Footwear	2 273	11.17	612	3.27	2 885	9.50
362	Glass products	–		4 726	8.23	4 726	8.23
342	Printing, publishing and allied industry	1 538	5.01	4 658	6.72	6 196	6.29
369	Other non-metallic products	5 880	1.92	11 899	6.33	17 779	4.87
355	Rubber products	–		2 366	4.65	2 366	4.65
353	Petroleum refinery	1 124	4.63	–		1 124	4.63
381	Fabricated metal products	11 265	3.87	17 604	4.74	28 869	4.40
331	Wood and cork products (except furniture)	4 066	1.13	3 442	6.74	7 508	3.70
323	Leather products (except footwear and wearing apparel)	–		1 755	2.34	1 755	2.34
382	Machinery (except electrical)	1 940	1.55	8 168	2.49	10 108	2.31
371	Basic iron and steel	10 901	2.35	3 132	0.70	14 033	1.98
351	Basic industrial chemicals	4 209	1.81	1 438	2.02	5 647	1.86
372	Basic non-ferrous metals	6 166	1.30	1 198	0.42	7 364	1.15
384	Transportation equipment	17 592	0.68	5 017	1.49	22 609	0.86
354	Petroleum and coal derivatives	1 236	0.73	–		1 236	0.73
332	Furniture and fixtures (except primarily of metal)	–		1 338	0.52	1 338	0.52
	Total (average)	179 501	18.37	231 289	21.85	410 790	20.33

Source: State Institute of Statistics, *Annual Survey of Manufacturing*, 1966.

Table 2.2 Employment by sex for manufacturing industry subsectors, 1982
(3-digit SIC; ranked by female share of total employment in subsector)

SIC Code	Sector	Public		Private		Total	
		Employment (number)	Female (percent)	Employment (number)	Female (percent)	Employment (number)	Female (percent)
322	Wearing apparel (except footwear)	221	31.22	17 696	53.45	17 917	53.17
314	Tobacco	38 380	48.66	1 316	25.00	39 696	47.87
390	Other manufacturing industry	–		4 715	36.97	4 715	34.97
321	Textiles	33 019	20.71	146 122	37.42	179 141	34.34
385	Professional, scientific measuring and controlling equipment (not elsewhere classified)	395	15.44	1 983	37.82	2 378	34.10
352	Other chemical products	2 339	9.45	20 518	28.93	22 857	26.93
361	Pottery, china and earthenware	2 188	19.20	5 965	27.11	8 153	24.98
312	Food products (not elsewhere classified)	8 961	4.27	10 703	39.79	19 664	23.61
383	Electrical machinery	3 120	24.81	36 034	20.85	39 154	21.17
356	Plastic products (not elsewhere classified)	53	7.55	14 600	15.79	14 653	15.76
323	Leather products (except footwear and wearing apparel)	–		5 662	13.46	5 662	13.46

Code	Industry					
342	Printing, publishing and allied industry	2 460	13.78	9 076	13.38	11 536	13.46
311	Food	35 417	5.29	64 151	17.04	99 568	12.86
324	Footwear	1 962	8.26	3 501	14.00	5 463	11.93
381	Fabricated metal products	2 340	7.56	38 476	9.87	40 816	9.73
341	Paper products	12 117	7.55	6 803	10.67	18 920	8.67
332	Furniture and fixtures (except primarily of metal)	664	1.96	4 006	9.46	4 670	8.39
313	Beverages	4 965	7.96	6 314	8.63	11 279	8.33
362	Glass products	–		12 510	6.64	12 510	6.64
355	Rubber products	–		10 743	5.95	10 743	5.95
354	Petroleum and coal derivatives	662	3.78	2 733	6.26	3 395	5.77
369	Other non-metallic products	8 826	3.09	29 691	6.54	38 517	5.75
331	Wood and cork products (except furniture)	5 980	3.29	7 555	7.64	13 535	5.72
351	Basic industrial chemicals	12 185	2.49	12 800	7.49	24 985	5.05
384	Transportation equipment	17 193	1.97	32 869	6.33	50 062	4.83
382	Machinery (except electrical)	13 386	2.05	38 851	4.95	52 237	4.21
371	Basic iron and steel	35 934	3.32	19 591	3.11	55 525	3.24
372	Basic non-ferrous metals	12 050	2.14	9 477	4.26	21 527	3.08
353	Petroleum refinery	6 975	2.82	–		6 975	2.82
	Total (average)	261 792	13.13	574 461	20.47	836 253	18.17

Source: State Institute of Statistics, *Annual Survey of Manufacturing*, 1982.

private ones. However, this difference may be due to the differences in industrial characteristics of public manufacturing as opposed to private manufacturing, rather than differences with regard to employment policy between the two sectors. Indeed, public firms tend to utilise more capital-intensive techniques and are more oriented toward production for the domestic rather than the export market. At the same time, jobs in the public sector are said to be allocated through patron–client relationships, which tend to be more advantageous to men than women. Assessing the public sector's role with respect to the gender composition of employment is especially important in the context of the present move toward privatisation in the Turkish economy.

The dummy variable $D82$ is used to capture the effect of the switch in industrialisation strategy to export-led industrialisation and the changes in the macro economy, and the interaction variable $EXPD82$ is used to test whether or not the export orientation of an industry has an even greater impact under the export-led regime than under the regime of import-substituting industrialisation.

The results of the OLS regression and the correlation matrix are presented in Tables 2.3 and 2.4 respectively. By and large, estimation results (first column of Table 2.3) are consistent with the hypotheses common to the FM1 and FM2 literatures. While the variables $SKILL$ and HP each have a statistically significant negative effect on women's representation in an industry, EXP has a statistically significant positive effect. On the other hand, none of the other variables has any statistically significant effect on the degree of women's representation in an industry.

Because of the high degree of collinearity between EXP and $EXPD82$ (correlation coefficient $= 0.79$), we also estimated the model by leaving out the interaction term. These results, reported in the second column of Table 2.3, indicate that collinearity does not affect the first set of results. The latter set of results indicate that EXP has an even stronger effect in explaining women's location in manufacturing industry compared to the model that includes the interaction term.

This analysis has several implications:

1. While women indeed have greater representation in low-skill and labour-intensive industries, the degree of export-orientation *per se* also leads to a higher female share in an industry. This may be due either to the greater disciplining effect of international competition

Table 2.3 Determinants of share of women in manufacturing industry subsectors (dependent variable: *PERC*)

	Including interaction term	Excluding interaction term
Intercept	16.454	16.227
	(3.543)***	(3.527)***
SKILL	−16.309	−16.342
	(−1.845)*	(−1.856)*
HP	−0.411	−0.420
	(−2.440)**	(−2.526)**
EXP	−0.365	−0.427
	(−2.149)**	(−3.951)***
SIZE	−0.0005	−0.0005
	(−0.357)	(−0.352)
DPR	3.310	−3.353
	(1.169)	(1.189)
D82	−1.553	−0.823
	(−0.433)	(−0.255)
EXPD82	0.103	
	(0.476)	
	$R^2 = 0.31$	$R^2 = 0.30$
	Adjusted $R^2 = 0.25$	Adjusted $R^2 = 0.26$
	$N = 102$	$N = 102$

Notes: *t*-statistics are given in brackets.
*** Significant at the 1 per cent level
** Significant at the 5 per cent level
* Significant at the 10 per cent level

Table 2.4 Correlation matrix

	SKILL	HP	EXP	SIZE	DPR	D82	EXPD82
SKILL	1.000	−0.118	−0.290	0.024	−0.314	−0.520	−0.386
HP		1.000	−0.014	0.072	0.064	0.464	0.081
EXP			1.000	0.122	−0.017	0.284	0.790
SIZE				1.000	−0.437	0.064	0.099
DPR					1.000	−0.022	−0.005
D82						1.000	0.516
							1.000

on wage rates and profitability in the export-oriented industries or to the greater need to employ a flexible and controllable labour force.[15]

2. In the case of Turkey, the relatively low degree of female share of employment in the public sector does not seem to be due to the form of ownership *per se* but solely due to the differences of public sector firms from private ones in terms of industrial characteristics.

3. Insofar as the year dummy (*D82*) and the interactive dummy (*EXPD82*) are not statistically significant this implies that the industrialisation strategy *per se* does not have a significant effect on gender composition of employment. In both periods, women's concentration in subsectors of manufacturing industry was determined by industry characteristics and these determinants have not been affected by the outward orientation of the economy.

This result contrasts with the implication of the FM2 literature, which associates export-led industrialisation with women's prominence in manufacturing industry. Thus, study of the Turkish case suggests that the widely-accepted characteristics of women's manufacturing employment under export-led industrialisation are not peculiar to this strategy but are more general features of women's employment in the industrialisation process. It is important to note, however, that by 1982 the export-led growth strategy in Turkey was in effect for only two years. Therefore, this result may reflect only the short-run effects of the implementation of this strategy. It is also likely that employment growth associated with export-led industrialisation may be occurring outside of large enterprises, particularly in homes under homeworking arrangements, in which case it is not captured by the manufacturing industry statistics.

Notes

1. We would like to thank Mehmet Köymen for his skilful research assistance on this project, Bina Agarwal for helpful comments on this paper and members of the New York City Women in Development group for discussions in the early stages of this research.
2. Joekes (1986) and ILO (1985). Country case studies, such as those by Cho and Koo (1983) and Hein (1984) in Korea and Mauritius, respectively, document the changes in the pattern of employment by sex in the course of export-led industrialisation, without engaging in a discussion of the characteristics of this industrialisation strategy.
3. Women's concentration in labour-intensive industries is widely noted and documented in the literature for the Western capitalist economies.

Through econometric techniques Bridges (1980) establishes that in the USA, among various indicators of industrial structure, capital-intensity of a subsector explains the underrepresentation of women in that sector. Dean (1988) finds evidence for the hypothesis that because women are historically lower paid workers they tend to be concentrated in highly labour-intensive occupations and industries in the USA.

4. Our purpose is not to engage in a critique of these marginalisation theses but rather to draw some of the implicit and explicit similarities in the two literatures. For a timely critique of the analytical issues in substantiating 'marginalisation' see Scott (1986).

5. Needless to say, many countries, which have successfully implemented export-oriented industrialisation (for example, South Korea), have moved up the skill ladder towards production and export of commodities with high skill content.

6. Most employment in export-oriented manufacturing in the Third World is in national and not MNCs, more MNCs are engaged in import-substituting than export-oriented manufacturing, and MNCs directly employ a very small proportion of the total labour force in the Third World (ILO, 1985, pp. 8, 27).

7. In 1963, agriculture, industry and services constituted 29.3, 19.1 and 51.6 per cent of the output, respectively. By 1977 the shares had changed to 22.0, 24.1 and 52.9 per cent, respectively. However, in 1977 agriculture still accounted for 58 per cent of the labour force (Kopenok, 1904, pp. 408-9).

8. For a more detailed analysis of labour market conditions and labour standards in Turkey from the early 1960s to the present see Çağatay (1990).

9. Figures from the State Institute of Statistics, Annual Surveys of Manufacturing for 1966 and 1982 and Censuses of population for 1960 and 1985. The discrepancy between population census and manufacturing survey figures is due to the fact that annual manufacturing surveys provide information only on establishments with 10 or more employees (25 or more employees after 1982). The higher shares of female employment in manufacturing obtained from the manufacturing surveys could be a reflection of proportionally greater employment of women in establishments employing 10 or more workers compared to smaller workplaces.

10. This is an interesting contrast with evidence reported by Anker and Hein (1985) p 77, according to whom because of stronger profitability pressures there is a lower representation of women in the private than in the public sector. The underlying reason is the higher cost of women workers, mainly arising from maternity leave benefits.

11. Figures from the State Institute of Statistics, Annual Surveys of Manufacturing for 1964, 1966 and 1982. For a more comprehensive discussion of the gender composition of Turkish manufacturing and analysis of segregation indices see Çağatay and Berik (forthcoming).

12. The Standard Industrial Classification (SIC) at the 3-digit level includes 29 manufacturing industries. For a breakdown of industries at the 3-digit level and their ranking by female share of total employment see Tables 2.1 and 2.2.

13. The dissimilarity index is defined as

$$DI = 1/2 \sum_{i=1}^{k} \mid N_{fi}/N_f - N_{mi}/N_m \mid \times 100,$$

where N_{fi} = number of females in industry i,
 N_f = total female employment in industry
 N_{mi} = number of males in industry i
 N_m = total male employment in industry.

The value of DI ranges from 0 to 100, 0 corresponding to a state of no sex segregation when the distribution of women across industrial sectors is identical to that of men, and 100 corresponding to total segregation by sex.

14. We first ran separate regressions for the two years and the Chow test indicated the stability of the regression coefficients. We are therefore reporting the results of the pooled regression here. For discussion of the Chow test see Maddala (1977) pp. 198–9.

15. See Çağatay (1986) for an analysis of the relationship between international competition on the one hand and wage rates and profitability on the other hand in Turkish manufacturing.

References

Anker, R. and Hein, C. (1985) 'Why Third World Urban Employers Usually Prefer Men', *International Labour Review*, vol. 24, no. 1.
Anker, R. and Hein, C. (1986) 'Introduction and Overview' and 'Sex Inequalities in Third World Employment: Statistical Evidence', in Anker R. and Hein, C. (eds) *Sex Inequalities in Urban Employment in the Third World* (New York: St Martin's).
Boserup, E. (1970) *Woman's Role in Economic Development* (New York: St Martin's).
Bridges, W. (1980) 'Industry Marginality and Female Employment: A New Appraisal', *American Sociological Review*, vol. 45, no. 1.
Çağatay, N. (1986) 'The Interindustry Structure of Wages and Markups in Turkish Manufacturing', unpublished PhD thesis, Stanford University, USA.
Çağatay, N. (1990) 'Economic Development Policies and Workers' Rights: The Case of Turkey', in Herzenberg, S. and Perez-Lopez, J. (eds) *Labor Standards and Development in the Global Economy* (Washington DC: Bureau of International Labor Affairs, US Department of Labor).
Çağatay, N. and Berik, G. (forthcoming) 'Transition to Export-led Growth in Turkey: Is there a feminisation of Employment?', *Capital and Class/ Review of Radical Political Economics*, joint special issue.
Chaney, E. and Schmink, M. (1976) 'Women and Modernization: Access to Tools', in Nash, J. and Safa, H. (eds) *Sex and Class in Latin America* (New York: Praeger).

Chinchilla, N. (1977) 'Industrialisation, Monopoly Capitalism and Women's Work in Guatemala', in Wellesley Editorial Committee (eds) *Women and National Development: The Complexities of Change* (Chicago, Illinois: University of Chicago Press).

Cho, U. and Koo, H. (1983) 'Economic Development and Women's Work in a Newly Industrializing Country: The Case of Korea', *Development and Change*, vol. 14, no. 4.

Cinar, Mine E. (1987) 'Sub-Contracting at Home: Disguised Female Employment in Urban Turkey', paper presented at the Middle East Studies Association meetings, Maryland, November.

Dean, J. (1988) 'Sex Segregation, Relative Wages and the Technical Conditions of Production: A Theoretical and Empirical Analysis', unpublished PhD thesis, New School for Social Research, USA.

de Miranda, G. V. (1977) 'Women's Labor Force Participation in a Developing Country', in Wellesley Editorial Committee (eds) *Women and National Development: The Complexities of Change* (Chicago, Illinois: University of Chicago Press).

Elson, D. and Pearson, R. (1981) 'The Subordination of Women and the Internationalization of Factory Production', in Young, K., Wolkowitz, C. and McCullagh, R. (eds) *Of Marriage and the Market* (London: Conference of Socialist Economists).

Hein, C. (1984) 'Jobs for the Girls: Export Manufacturing in Mauritius', *International Labour Review*, vol. 123, no. 2.

Humphrey, J. (1985) 'Gender, Pay and Skill: Manual Workers in Brazilian Industry', in Afshar, H. (ed.) *Women, Work and Ideology in the Third World* (London: Tavistock).

Humphrey, J. (1987) *Gender and Work in the Third World: Sexual Divisions in Brazilian Industry* (London and New York: Tavistock).

ILO (1985) *Women Workers in Multinational Enterprises in Developing Countries* (Geneva: ILO).

Joekes, S. (1982) 'Female-led Industrialisation, Women's Jobs in Third World Export Manufacturing: The Case of Moroccan Clothing Industry', Research Report no. 15, Institute of Development Studies Brighton, Sussex.

Joekes, S. (1985) 'Working for a Lipstick? Male and Female Labour in the Clothing Industry in Morocco', in Afshar, H. (ed.) *Women, Work and Ideology in the Third World* (London: Tavistock).

Joekes, S. (1986) *Industrialisation, Trade and Female Employment: Experiences of the 1970s and After* (Dominican Republic: International Research and Training Institute for the Advancement of Women, United Nations).

Kepenek, Y. (1984) *Gelisimi ve Uretim Yapisi ve Sorunlariyla Turkiye Ekonomisi* (Ankara: Savas).

Lim, L. (1983) 'Capitalism, Imperialism, and Patriarchy: The Dilemma of Third World Women Workers in Multinational Factories', in Nash, J. and Fernandez-Kelly, M. P. (eds) (1983).

Lipietz, A. (1987) *Mirages and Miracles: The Crisis of Global Fordism* (London: Verso).

Maddala, G. S. (1977) *Econometrics* (New York: McGraw Hill).

Nash, J. (1983) 'The Impact of Changing International Division of Labor on

Different Sectors of the Labor Force', in Nash, J. and Fernandez-Kelly, M. P. (1983)

Nash, J. and Fernandez-Kelly, M. P. (1983) (eds) *Women, Men and the International Division of Labor* (Albany: State University of New York).

OECD. (1987) *Turkey*, OECD Economic Surveys, Paris.

Pyle, J. (1986) 'Export-led Development and the Underemployment of Women: The Impact of Discriminatory Development Policy in the Republic of Ireland, unpublished paper, Smith College, Northampton, Mass.

Safa, H. (1981) 'Runaway Shops and Female Employment: The Search for Cheap Labor', *Signs*, vol. 7, no. 2.

Saffioti, H. (1977) 'Women, Mode of Production and Social Formations', *Latin American Perspectives*, nos. 1 and 2.

Saffioti, H. (1978) *Women in a Class Society* (New York: Monthly Review).

Schmink, M. (1977) 'Dependency, Development and Division of Labor by Sex: Venezuela', *Latin American Perspectives*, Winter–Spring.

Scott, A. (1986) 'Women and Industrialisation: Examining the "Female Marginalisation" Thesis', *Journal of Development Studies*, vol. 22, no. 4.

3 Female-Headed Households and Urban Poverty in Pakistan

Yasmeen Mohiuddin
UNIVERSITY OF THE SOUTH, SEWANEE,
TENNESSEE, USA

1 INTRODUCTION

There is growing evidence not only of a substantial increase in woman-headed households all over the world but also of the severely disadvantaged economic condition of these households. These women are amongst the poorest of the poor – belonging to what may be termed a 'Fifth World'. In the urban areas, they are concentrated in the informal sector which serves as a catchment area and source of identification of such household heads as well as other poor women desperate for some income to eke out a living in urban areas. The main characteristics of woman-headed households are reported to be extreme poverty, large-sized families, the need for all family members to work, and low levels of education and skills.

A household may be designated as woman-headed, *de facto* or *de jure* or both, if the male spouse or partner is absent (widows, divorcees, unmarried mothers, abandoned women), or is present but contributes marginally to the economic maintenance of the household. Thus, even those women workers who are not sole providers (for example, married women with their spouse present) often qualify as primary breadwinners due to the irregularity and uncertainty of their spouse's income (due to old age, sickness or the nature of his job, for example self-employed), their lack of control over such income, or gender specific differences in the disposition of income. In certain extreme cases, women assume economic responsibilities for their families' survival due to male drug addiction, loafing about and social acceptance of male idleness within that particular community (see Mohiuddin, 1985).

These woman-headed households are especially vulnerable to poverty because of the marital status of most of the household heads (widowed, separated, divorced, single motherhood), their lack of access to productive resources and income (land, credit, farming and technical assistance, wage labour and employment, regular income), the decline of the traditional familial support system, lack of access to services (health care and education), size and composition of household (higher dependency burdens, fewer male secondary workers), etc. They are also more vulnerable because they face the challenge of making market-oriented activities compatible with domestic responsibilities. With the education and training at their disposal and their dual role as mothers and workers, the type of jobs available to them are the informal sector jobs. Within the informal sector there are very few options for poor women, since in the religious/cultural setting of Pakistan females are confined to jobs where sex seclusion can be assured. One of the most likely options is to work as a domestic servant (in people's homes at a time when the master of the house is away at work and have dealings only with the mistress). It is the purpose of this paper to investigate the economic role and status of households headed by female domestics in Karachi, Pakistan. It analyses the socio-economic characteristics of these women in female-headed households as well as the nature and extent of poverty of these women, and compares them with male-headed households.

The data used for this study are derived from a sample survey of female domestics in East, West, and South Karachi. A total of nine study sites was selected: three middle-income neighbourhoods from each of the three zones (East, West and South). The sample size was 100 and each neighbourhood was given a weight equal to its share of the total population. Within each neighbourhood, homes were randomly selected, and the domestic servant working in the house was the respondent to the survey. Thus the survey was conducted at the point of demand for these workers. A total of 100 such respondents were chosen.

This paper is organised into five sections. Section 2 presents the description of labour market conditions faced by the women domestics in Karachi, Pakistan. Section 3 presents the issues involved in research on breadwinning women and applies economic criteria to the definition of a household head. Section 4 deals with an analysis of the economic role of women and the extent of poverty in female-headed households. Section 5 presents the policy implications of the study.

2 THE LABOUR MARKET FOR WOMEN DOMESTICS

Karachi's urban labour market, like that of other large cities, is segmented into a modern formal sector geared toward capital intensive, large scale production, and a traditional informal sector geared toward labour intensive small scale production. The informal sector is also characterised by poorer earning opportunities, limited bargaining power and job protection, lack of minimum wage regulation and high labour turnover. The usually self-employed workers in this sector are engaged in activities ranging from hawking, street vending, market selling, letter writing, knife sharpening, shoe shining and junk collecting, to selling fireworks. Others find jobs as mechanics, carpenters, small artisans, handicraft workers, potters, barbers and personal servants.

Moreover, Karachi's labour market is also sexually segmented like many Muslim cities in regions of Arab influence and unlike most other cities of Asia, Latin America and Africa. Thus the street vendors, market sellers, carpenters, mechanics, barbers are almost exclusively males, whereas females are confined to home-based production (which can be done within the confines of the home) or those production and service activities where sex seclusion can be assured, and male contact minimised. Examples are handicraft workers, seamstresses, and domestics (maids, washerwomen, sweepers, etc.). This is because Karachi is very much like what Boserup (1970, p. 86) calls male towns where most outdoor activities are taken care of by men, while women live in some seclusion within the family dwelling. With women mostly confined to the homes, the streets, market places, shops, factories, offices, restaurants and cinemas become mostly a male world with a surplus of men over women. Even non-secluded women are greatly affected in their decision making, especially in the choice of occupation, by the general attitude in favour of seclusion. Thus women account for only 1 to 8 per cent of the total labour force in 'Trade and Commerce' (where women cannot avoid male contact) in Muslim countries of Africa and Asia (and 2 per cent in Pakistan) compared with 9 to 65 per cent in Latin America, 6 to 56 per cent in South and East Asia, and 8 to 80 per cent in Africa South of the Sahara (Boserup, 1970 pp. 88–9). Moreover, the association of respectability with seclusion possibilities cuts across economic classes so that it is a binding constraint, overtly or covertly, on women of all classes. Thus most of the high-skilled and middle-class women become teachers (skills for which in Pakistan can be acquired and often used in a segregated environment) and most of the low-skilled and poor women become domestic servants (who work in people's homes at a time when the master of the house is away at work and have dealings only with the mistress) (Mohiuddin, 1980). Domestic service has recently emerged as the single largest source of employment for poor women in the urban informal sector in Karachi. It shares with self-employment the freedom to choose the time, duration and location of work, but unlike self-employment, it does not yield any profit. It shares with wage employment the feature of payment at a contracted rate for work done, but unlike wage employment, there is greater flexibility in hours and a more personalised patron–client type of relationship with the employer. The female domestics, popularly known as 'Masees' (meaning aunts), typically work in three or four houses part-time on a regular basis at one or more of the following chores: washing dishes, washing clothes, cleaning and sweeping, and cooking. They charge Rs 60–100 per activity per month (which is about one-sixth of the salary of a full-time male domestic servant) which has made it possible for most middle-income households to afford them, at least for the most arduous tasks.[1] The poorer women prefer to work as domestics since it represents an extension of the household role not requiring specialised skills, it does not interfere with their household responsibilities, it requires little or no investment, and it guarantees seclusion and therefore respectability. On the other hand, middle-class households prefer to hire only female (rather than male) domestics partly because they are more affordable and partly because the rules of seclusion are more strict in middle-class families (where it is not appropriate to expose women in the family to the constant presence of a male domestic). In fact, the recent surge in demand for female domestic servants has been brought about in part by increasing home remittances of middle-class Pakistanis working in the Gulf States and in part by a rise in the labour force participation and college enrolment rates for middle-class females in Karachi. At the same time, there has also been a significant increase in the number of masees as a result of migration of thousands of poor families from Bangladesh in the 1970s and rural to urban migration from within the country. As a matter of fact, the masee market resembles a perfect market with a large number of buyers and sellers, a 'homogeneous' service (house chores) and perfect knowledge (by masees and hiring households) about charges per activity in different locations. Consequently we find that wages of those women are highly competitive and uniform in a neighbourhood.

3 THE ISSUES INVOLVED IN RESEARCH

One of the most important issues in any research on female-headed households is the question of definition of such households. The problem is that the definition of the head of a household evolved from studying male labour may not remain valid when the problem of women workers is considered. While economic responsibility, decision-making and headship status go together for male heads of households, this is not so for females. A woman might be the only earner in the family but still may neither have decision-making power nor be considered the head of the household by the family or even herself. This is due to cultural pressures on the women, their declared secondary status and their dependency relationship with men. Thus the United Nations (1973) recommended definition that the person reported as the family head be 'either (a) that person who is acknowledged as such by the other members of the census family or of the family nucleus . . . or (b) the member of the family or of the family nucleus who meets specified requirements – identified on the basis of such characteristics as sex, age and marital status' might give an underestimate of the incidence of female-headed households. The United Nations suggests, however, that the more desirable definition is the one that further specifies the role of the household head, by designating the head of the household as 'the person who bears the chief responsibility for the economic maintenance of the household, [although] it is not recommended that this definition be applied because of the difficulty of collecting the information needed to determine economic responsibility'. Thus of the 36 countries reviewed by the United Nations in 1973, 23 censuses defined the head as one who reports himself as such or is so reported by another member of the household or family, seven defined the head as one who controls maintenance of the household – that is, exercises the authority to run the household, and six (Denmark, Finland, Hungary, Norway, Barbados and Grenada) defined the head as the main supporter (chief earner) of the household. Of the 69 developing countries reviewed by the United States Census Bureau,[2] 12 used the first definition, two the second and only one (Israel) the third. The

Asian countries of India, Nepal, Sri Lanka, Malaysia and Pakistan do not even report the incidence of female-headed households in their censuses, not to speak of the definitional issue (Youssef and Hetler, 1983, pp. 227–9). A household head is a male by assumption, since the mere presence of an adult male in the household (husband, son, father, brother, father-in-law, or any other member of the extended family like uncles, cousins, nephews, brothers-in-law, etc.) is enough to confer headship status on him. However even chief or all economic responsibility on a woman is not enough to confer the same status on her. Even in micro level surveys, it is difficult to detect the incidence of female-headed households unless the researcher is extremely careful and there is no male bias in data collection.[3] Thus in our sample of 100 women, most married women (with their spouse present) who had the chief or entire economic responsibility for their family considered their husband to be the head in response to a direct question in the survey. This points to a divergence between the cultural and the economic definition of the head of household. A head of the household, by the cultural definition, is one whose authority is accepted by the family. It is more likely that he would be a male for all the historical, cultural reasons outlined earlier. An economic head of household is one, on the other hand, who accepts the economic responsibility for the family.

In this paper we have defined head of household in economic, rather than cultural, terms. That is, a person is considered the head of household if he/she has the chief economic responsibility for the family. This is different from the first UN definition, the use of which will give the erroneous result that there are no female heads of households among married women. It is in accordance with the more desirable third UN definition which specifies the economic role of the household head. Using this definition, we have identified female-headed households at the processing stage on the basis of such characteristics as income, contribution to family income and disposition of income. More specifically, we have distinguished between five types/degrees of economic responsibility, fulfilling any of which qualifies a woman as head of the household. These types are:

Type 1: Only Earner In this type, the respondent or any other female is the only earner in the family, and therefore has the full economic responsibility for the family. This is likely when the husband/male guardian is dead, sick, old, unemployed or unwilling to work (for example, he loafs about). It may be pointed out that this is a *de facto*, and not *de jure* female-headed household since these women might have other adult non-earning male members (of the extended family) living with them, who would qualify technically as household heads, as outlined earlier.

Type 2: Only Female Earners In this type, only the women in the family are breadwinners, that is there is no male income. It differs from the first in that more than one woman bears the economic responsibility of the household.

Type 3: Female Major Earner In this type, the respondent or another female is the major earner in her family. This means that her earnings are more than that of any other person, male or female, in the family. In our sample, the earnings of these women were more than the combined earnings of everyone else in the family. This is likely in cases where the husband/male guardian is self-employed, or has a low-paying occupation so that his contribution is marginal. Examples are wage labourers, fruit vendors, and other self-employed men.

Type 4: Female Group Major Earner This type of household is different from the other two, in that the combined earnings of all females in the family exceed the combined earnings of all males in the family. This is likely when males get employment only part-time. Thus in our sample, many men have very irregular jobs for irregular intervals.

Type 5: Equal Earner We have included this type in a female-headed household because of gender specific differences in the disposition of income. Thus even if women contribute equally to family income, they spend a much larger proportion of it on the household than do men.

Table 3.1 shows that out of 65 heads of household in our sample, 31 women (48 per cent) are the only earners in their families, 8 are joint earners with other women (12 per cent) and 14 (?? per cent) are major earners. However, not all of these women consider themselves to be heads of the households. Thus 30 of them consider their male guardians to be heads of the families. These male relatives may be either members of the immediate or the extended family.

Table 3.1 Distribution of households by type of economic responsibility

Type of economic responsibility	Number of women	As percentage of female-headed households	As percentage of all households
1 Respondent only earner	31	48	31
2 Only female earners	8	12	8
3 Female major earner	14	22	14
4 Female group major earner	11	17	11
5 Respondent equal earner	1	2	1
All female-headed households	65	100	65
Male-headed households	35	–	35
All households	100	–	100

4 THE ECONOMIC ROLE OF WOMEN AND THE EXTENT OF POVERTY IN FEMALE-HEADED HOUSEHOLDS

This section is concerned with a description and analysis of certain socio-economic characteristics of the sampled women, (marital status, occupation of husband and family income), and comparison of these in female- and male-headed households; an estimate of the extent of poverty in each and an analysis of the earnings differential between the two.

Marital Status

Data regarding marital status (Table 3.2) indicates that in our sample of 100 maid servants, 55 per cent are married, 12 per cent are single, 22 per cent are widowed and 11 per cent are either divorced or separated. A comparison of female- and male-headed households shows that widowed, divorced/separated and single women are over represented in the former and married in the latter. This is under-standable since those women are likely to have economic responsibility for their families whose husband is not present (either due to death or separation or no marriage).

There are several inferences that can be drawn from this informa-

Table 3.2   Distribution of households by marital status and by type of economic responsibility

Type of economic responsibility	Marital status				
	Single	Married	Widowed	Divorced/ separated	All households
1 Respondent only earner	3(10)	12(39)	10(32)	6(19)	31(100)
2 Only female earners	2(25)	2(25)	2(25)	2(25)	8(100)
3 Female major earner	0(0)	8(57)	4(29)	2(14)	14(100)
4 Female group major earner	4(36)	6(55)	1(9)	0(0)	11(100)
5 Respondent equal earner	0(0)	1(100)	0(0)	0(0)	1(100)
All female-headed households	9(14)	29(45)	17(26)	10(15)	65(100)
Male-headed households	3(9)	26(74)	5(14)	1(3)	35(100)
All households	12(12)	55(55)	22(22)	11(11)	100(100)

Note: Figures in brackets are percentages.

tion. First, widows and divorced/separated women have to fend for themselves, mostly without the aid of anyone else, including the extended family. Thus 17 out of the 22 widows in our overall sample (77 per cent) are household heads, with 10 of these 17 (59 per cent) being the 'only earners' (Type 1). Similarly 10 of the 11 separated/divorced women in our sample (91 per cent) are household heads, with 6 of the 10 (60 per cent) being the sole supporters of their families. Looking at it from another angle, we can say that 51 per cent of women in the 'only earner' category are widows or divorced/separated women, the percentage dropping to 42 for all female-headed households taken together and to 17 for male-headed households. It seems that the extended family system does not serve as a safety net for women in divorce or separation, although married and single women do get some support from it. This can be ascribed to the differential age structure of the two groups of women. On the average, widowed and divorced/separated women are older than married or single women and are thus less likely to have living fathers/elder brothers who can support them.

Secondly, married women are the largest single group among the female-headed (as well as male-headed) households. Thus 29 of the 65 women household heads are married. In exploring the reasons as to why married women, rather than their husbands, have economic responsibility for their families, we found that such women have husbands who are either too old to work, or unemployed or sick. Some women even described their husbands as 'loafers', that is they were able but unwilling to work thus implicitly forcing their wives to work in order to sustain the family, especially children. Others complained that their husbands were drug addicts who made their wives finance their addiction. However, it should be noted that 12 of the 29 married household heads (41 per cent) are 'only earners', which means that the rest get at least some support from their husbands and the extended family.

Lastly, 14 per cent of the female-headed households are maintained by single women. While the reason for the existence of such households in the West may be childbearing outside marriage, in Pakistan it is the practice or social norm whereby unmarried women (of any age) live with their parents or brothers in the absence of parents. For example, there were many young single women who could not or did not want to get married since they were the bread winners for their families (parents and/or siblings) due to death of father, or absence of elder brother, or low income of male family members.

Occupation of Husband

Since the economic condition of poor households depends to a greater extent on the earnings of the husband/guardian rather than the respondent, the former's earning capacity is a key variable in the economic status of these households. Table 3.3 shows that in 48 out of the 65 female-headed households (74 per cent), the husband has no income-earning occupation (either due to absence through death or desertion, or to unemployment or being out of the labour force) while this is true for only 6 out of the 35 male-headed households (17 per cent). Moreover, 29 of the 31 'only earners' (94 per cent) and all 8 of the Type 2 households are confronted with this problem of absence of husband's economic support in maintenance of the household. Table 3.3 also shows that husbands of 2 per cent women in female-headed households (1 out of 65) have a regular or permanent job, whereas the corresponding percentage is 31 (11 out of 35) for male-headed ones. Thus husbands of women in female-headed households, have an average income of Rs 94 per month compared to Rs 619 for husbands in male-headed households.

Table 3.3 Distribution of households by occupation of husband/guardian
and by type of economic responsibility

Type of economic responsibility	Occupation of husband/guardian				
	Regular job	Daily wage labour	Self-employed	No job	All households
1 Respondent only earner	0(0)	1(3)	1(3)	29(94)	31(100)
2 Only female earners	0(0)	0(0)	0(0)	8(100)	8(100)
3 Female major earner	1(7)	6(43)	0(0)	7(50)	14(100)
4 Female group major earner	0(0)	7(64)	0(0)	4(36)	11(100)
5 Respondent equal earner	0(0)	1(100)	0(0)	0(0)	1(100)
All female-headed households	1(2)	15(23)	1(2)	48(74)	65(100)
Male-headed households	11(31)	17(49)	1(3)	6(17)	35(100)
All households	12(12)	32(32)	2(2)	54(54)	100(100)

Note: Figures in brackets are percentages.

Family Income

Table 3.4 presents the data on family income for different types of
female-headed households. We have considered the household as the
accounting unit for estimating poverty, and family income is therefore an important variable to consider in comparing different types of
households. The table shows that about 26 per cent of women in
male-headed households (9 out of 35) have a family income of less
than Rs 1000 per month, whereas this percentage is exceeded by all
types of female-headed households, being 100 per cent for Type 1
and Type 5, and 75 per cent (49 out of 65) for all female-headed
households taken together. On the other hand, 23 per cent of
male-headed but only 3 out of 65 (5 per cent) of female-headed
households have a family income of more than Rs 2000 per month.
The average family income in female-headed households is Rs 869
per month compared to Rs 1830 in male-headed ones, implying that
the former are more likely to be poor.

Gender and Development

Table 3.4 Distribution of households by family income and by type of economic responsibility

Type of economic responsibility	Family income (Rupees)						
	Up to 500	501– 1000	1001– 2000	2001– 3000	3001– 5000	Above 5000	All households
1 Respondent only earner	21(68)	10(32)	0(0)	0(0)	0(0)	0(0)	31(100)
2 Only female earners	1(12)	4(50)	3(38)	0(0)	0(0)	0(0)	8(100)
3 Female major earner	2(14)	6(43)	5(36)	1(7)	0(0)	0(0)	14(100)
4 Female group major earner	0(0)	4(36)	5(45)	1(9)	1(9)	0(0)	11(100)
5 Respondent equal earner	0(0)	1(100)	0(0)	0(0)	0(0)	0(0)	1(100)
All female-headed households	24(37)	25(38)	13(20)	2(3)	1(2)	0(0)	65(100)
Male-headed households	1(3)	8(23)	18(51)	3(9)	4(11)	1(3)	35(100)
All households	25(25)	33(33)	31(31)	5(5)	5(5)	1(1)	100(100)

Note: Figures in brackets are percentages.

Extent of Poverty

In order to estimate the extent of poverty in female- relative to male-headed households, we need to determine the poverty line. This is defined as the line dividing the poor and the non-poor. In line with other studies, we have drawn this line at the so-called basic needs income level, which is the income level required to satisfy basic needs of a household, or at the income level required for achieving a socially acceptable minimum standard of living. All the households whose income falls below the level are considered poor and the rest non-poor. Based on studies of poverty in Pakistan (de Kruijk and van Leeuwen, 1985; Cheema, 1985), we have taken account of differences in household size in computing the poverty line and the basic needs income is fixed at a level of Rs 250 per person per month in urban areas. Accordingly, we have separate poverty lines for different types of female- and male-headed households depending on their household size.

Table 3.5 shows that 83 per cent households which are female-headed fall below the poverty line compared to 43 per cent of those which are male-headed. Moreover in each type of female-headed household the percentage below the poverty line is greater than that

Table 3.5 Distribution of households along the poverty line by type of economic responsibility

Type of economic responsibility	Family income (Rupees)		
	Households below poverty line	Households above poverty line	All households
1 Respondent only earner	29(94)	2(6)	31(100)
2 Only female earners	7(88)	1(12)	8(100)
3 Female major earner	9(64)	5(36)	14(100)
4 Female group major earner	8(73)	3(27)	11(100)
5 Respondent equal earner	1(100)	0(0)	1(100)
All female-headed households	54(83)	11(17)	65(100)
Male-headed households	15(43)	20(57)	35(100)
All households	69(69)	31(31)	100(100)

Note: Figures in brackets are percentages.

in male-headed households. More specifically, 43 per cent of male households are below the poverty line, compared to 94 per cent of Type 1, 88 per cent of Type 2, 64 per cent of Type 3, 73 per cent of Type 4 and 100 per cent of Type 5 female-headed households. Thus the poorest women are those where there is no male earner so that women are the sole earners (either the respondent alone or together with other females), that is Type 1 and Type 2.

Table 3.6 presents a distribution of all households by headship and marital status, and by the level of household income per person. Three household income classes are distinguished: the poor, whose income per person averaged less than Rs 250 per month (in 1985, equivalent to about US $15 – at the time, a kilogram of rice cost about 15 cents and an inexpensive pair of shoes about $3), representing 69 per cent of all households; low-income families, with income per person between Rs 250 and Rs 400, representing 19 per cent of all households; and middle-income classes with income per person of Rs

Table 3.6 Distribution of households by headship, marital status and
household income class

Headship and income class	Marital status				
	Single	Married	Widowed	Divorced/ separated	Total
Female-headed households					
Poor	6(67)	27(93)	13(76)	8(80)	54(83)
Low	2(22)	2(7)	2(12)	2(20)	8(12)
Middle/high	1(11)	0(0)	2(12)	0(0)	3(5)
Total	9(100)	29(100)	17(100)	10(100)	65(100)
Male-headed households					
Poor	0(0)	12(46)	3(60)	0(0)	15(43)
Low	1(33)	8(31)	2(40)	0(0)	11(31)
Middle/high	2(67)	6(23)	0(0)	1(100)	9(26)
Total	3(100)	26(100)	5(100)	1(100)	35(100)

Note: Figures in brackets are percentages.

400 or more, representing 12 per cent of households. The 'poverty' cut-off was the same as used earlier, i.e. Rs 250 per person per month.

As the breakdown by marital status shows, the proportion of poor, woman-headed households is the lowest for households headed by single women, 67 per cent. Of the 56 households headed by married, separated and widowed women, the poverty group accounts for 85 per cent; 76 per cent of women in the widow group and 93 per cent in the married group live at a poverty level. It might at first appear strange that the incidence of poverty is highest among married women who might get some support from their husbands. However, married women are also more likely to have more children, thus requiring a higher family income to maintain a bigger household.

Husband's occupation is another important aspect of the poverty observed among households headed by females. A substantial proportion of the female heads of poor households (41 out of 54 or 76 per cent) have a non-earning husband. The corresponding figure is 33 per cent (5 out of 15) for male heads of poor households (see Table 3.7).

Table 3.7 Distribution of households by headship, occupation of husband/guardian and household income class

	Occupation of husband/guardian				
Headship and income class	Regular job	Daily wage labour	Self-employed	No job	Total
Female-headed households					
Poor	1(100)	11(73)	1(100)	41(85)	54(83)
Low	0(0)	3(20)	0(0)	5(10)	8(12)
Middle/high	0(1)	1(7)	0(0)	2(4)	3(5)
Total	1(100)	15(100)	1(100)	48(100)	65(100)
Male-headed households					
Poor	5(45)	4(24)	1(100)	5(83)	15(43)
Low	3(27)	8(47)	0(0)	0(0)	11(31)
Middle/high	3(27)	5(29)	0(0)	1(17)	9(26)
Total	11(100)	17(100)	1(100)	6(100)	35(100)

Note: Figures in brackets are percentages.

Table 3.8 Distribution of households by headship, dependency ratio and household income class

	Dependency ratio				
Headship and income class	Less than 2.0	2.0– 3.9	4.0– 5.9	6 or more	Total
Female-headed households					
Poor	24 (44)	25(46)	3(6)	2(4)	54(100)
Low	7 (88)	1(12)	0(0)	0(0)	8(100)
Middle/high	2 (67)	1(33)	0(0)	0(0)	3(100)
Total	33	27	3	2	65
Male-headed households					
Poor	10 (67)	3(20)	1(7)	1(7)	15(100)
Low	11(100)	0 (0)	0(0)	0(0)	11(100)
Middle/high	9(100)	0 (0)	0(0)	0(0)	9(100)
Total	30	3	1	1	35

Note: Figures in brackets are percentages.

Another reason for the increased incidence of poverty among households headed by women could be a higher dependency burden – that is, a higher ratio of non-workers to workers than in male-headed households. Table 3.8 shows that this is so. Dependency in poor households is, in fact, slightly higher in households headed by females. Thus, the dependency ratio is 2 or greater in 30 out of 54 (56 per cent) poor female-headed households but only in 5 out of 15 (33 per cent) poor male-headed households. Moreover, when we compare poor households with households in the higher income groups, especially the adjacent low-income group, we find that the differences are striking. Additional workers make a large difference in the comparative economic situation of the poor and low-income groups. Thus low-income households, relative to poor households, and male- relative to female-headed households are able to break through the poverty threshold because of the added earnings of a secondary worker.

Table 3.9 summarises the characteristics of the female- and male-headed households.

Econometric Analysis of Household Income

Table 3.10 reports the results of a regression analysis which estimates the effects of human capital and household composition variables on family income. Separate regression results for the logs of family income are shown for female-headed, male-headed and all households. The independent variables in the regression are:

X_1 age of the household head (in years)
X_2 education of household head (= 1 if literate, = 0 otherwise)
X_3 education of household head (= 1 if primary or above, = 0 otherwise)
X_4 number of children less than 10 years of age
X_5 number of secondary earners, other than household head and spouse
X_6 occupation of husband (= 1 if any occupation, = 0 otherwise)
X_7 headship status (= 1 if female headed, = 0 otherwise)

The results show that the coefficient of multiple determination, R^2, exceeds 0.44 in each regression and all parameter estimates have the expected signs.[4] In each case, education (X_3), secondary earners (X_5) and husband's occupation (X_6) have statistically significant co-

Table 3.9 Characteristics of households by headship

	Female-headed households	Male-headed households	All households
Income or respondent (RS p.m.)	497	453	481
Income of husband/ guardian (RS p.m.)	94	619	278
Income of secondary[1] earners (RS p.m.)	278	759	446
Family income (RS p.m.)	869	1830	1205
Number of secondary earners	0.62	1.11	0.79
Number of earners[2]	1.9	2.94	2.25
Number of household members	5.4	6.2	5.7
Dependency ratio (non-earners/earners)	2.400	1.426	2.032
Children less than 10 years old	1.3	1.5	1.4
All children	2.9	2.8	2.89
Income per person per month	174	318	224
Poverty line (per month per person)	250	250	250
Households below poverty line	54 (83)	15 (43)	69 (69)
Households above poverty line	11 (17)	20 (57)	31 (31)
Poverty index	0.831	0.429	0.69

Notes: Figures in brackets are percentages.
1. Secondary includes other males except husband and other females except the respondent.
2. Includes secondary earners, husband and the respondent.

efficients with expected signs. Thus family income is higher in a household where the head completes primary education or above than in one where he or she is illiterate (reference group), suggesting that human capital variables are important determinants of family income. Similarly the effect of number of secondary earners (siblings, older children, extended family members) on family income is positive, as is the effect of presence of an earning husband. On the other hand, age of the head and presence of small children in the household, who might restrict the activities of female heads, do not appear to have a statistically significant effect. Moreover, in the equation for

Table 3.10 Regression analysis of determinants of household income
from survey data

Independent variables	Female-headed households	Male-headed households	All households
Constant	6.08	7.06	5.97
Age of household head (X_1)	0.003	0.004	0.002
Education of household head: literate (X_2)	0.025	−0.363*	0.518*
Education of household head: completed primary or above (X_3)	0.965***	1.595**	0.736***
Children less than 10 years of age (X_4)	−0.008	−0.062	−0.017
Secondary earners (X_5)	0.339***	0.228***	0.273***
Husband's occupation (X_6)	0.498***	0.377***	0.517***
Headship status (X_7)	–	–	−0.317*
R^2	0.448	0.702	0.619
Adjusted R^2	0.391	0.631	0.589
F	7.8	9.8	20.7
Number of households	65	35	100

*** Significant at 1 per cent level
** Significant at 5 per cent level
* Significant at 10 per cent level

all households, the dummy for headship status has a negative estimated coefficient which is statistically significant at the 10 per cent
level, meaning the female household heads have a lower family
income than male heads. Also education (X_2) has a significant positive effect in the regression for all households taken together.

A comparative analysis of the family income of male- and female-
headed households shows that although human capital variables
(education) are important determinants of the general level of income, household occupational composition explains most of the
differential in income between male and female heads. The male and
female heads differ markedly in their education, number of secondary earners in their households and in occupation of the male (himself household head or husband of household head). Thus 94 per cent
of female heads are illiterate compared to only 71 per cent of male
heads. And husbands of 74 per cent female heads do not earn any
income (either due to absence, temporary or permanent, or unemployment or being out of the labour force) whereas husbands of only
17 per cent of women in male-headed households are in this category.

Similarly, the average number of secondary earners in female-headed households is 0.62 compared to 1.11 in male-headed households. Thus a major part of the disadvantaged economic position of female heads of households derives from fewer earners in such households relative to male-headed ones. The differential in income between the two types of households is also evident from the value of the constant: it is 6.08 in the case of female-headed and 7.06 in the case of male-headed households, indicating that income is higher in the latter.

5 POLICY IMPLICATIONS

One of the objectives of this paper has been to identify and enumerate the female-headed households on the basis of survey data. This has been done by removing the conceptual and methodological bias in the conventional definition of head of household. Our results show that female-headed households exist in substantial numbers and their incidence is surprisingly high in urban slums.

The second objective of this study has been to show the differences in socio-economic and demographic characteristics both between female- and male-headed households and within the female-headed ones. Our results show that there are significant inter-household and intra-household differences in the characteristics which affect the economic condition of the household.

The third objective of the paper has been to show the extent of poverty in female- relative to male-headed households and in different types of the former. Our results show that the incidence of poverty is higher in each single type of female-headed households than in male-headed households.

The incidence of female-headed households and the extent of poverty points to the need to target these women as a special category for development activities. Efforts need to be made to redesign development programmes to focus on their critical as well as long-term needs. However, it needs to be emphasised that the issues of female-headed households should be seen in a broader perspective of the social process. There is great danger in viewing this issue and other women's issues as an isolated category. A better understanding of needs of female-headed households can come only when their roles are viewed in relation to other women's and men's and in the broader social perspective. It should not be forgotten that these women and other women too play an instrumental role in the development process. No development effort is likely to succeed if it bypasses half the population. The mere recording of the secondary status of women and the poverty of female-headed households as has been done until now in most of the women's studies is not enough. They can be retrieved from their submerged status of poverty and virtual invisibility only if a genuine search is made for understanding their roles, in responding to their needs, and in a genuine commitment to bringing about improvement in their status. As a first step in this direction, planners and administrators need to be made aware of the issue. Moreover, the existing inadequate methods of data collection and survey should be improved and attempts should be made at the national and international levels to make women household heads identifiable in official statistics. For example, questions on sex of household head need to be incorporated into data collection procedures and headship needs to be defined in terms of economic responsibility as well.

Notes

1. The upper-income households generally have full-time male domestic servants but are now shifting to 'masees' for the greater protection of their females.
2. Unpublished data from The Women in Development Data Base, Inter Demographic Data Center, Tables 12 and 13; as quoted in Youssef and Hetler (1983).
3. In an earlier study of rural women in Pakistan, male surveyors were satisfied with the first UN definition (as to who is considered head of household) and thereby failed to recognise that many women had reported their dead husbands as household heads (see Mohiuddin, 1985).
4. The only exception to this is the sign of X_2 (education) in the equation for male-headed households, where family income is lower if the head is literate (can read and write) than if he is illiterate. This can be explained by the fact that the literate male head might be earning less than the illiterate because the former's 'literacy' might be inhibiting him from working at a 'blue-collar' though better paid job.

References

Boserup, E. (1970) *Women's Role in Economic Development* (New York: St. Martin's Press).
Buvinic, M., Lycette, M. A. and McGreevey, P. (eds) (1983) *Women and*

Poverty in the Third World (Baltimore: Johns Hopkins University Press).

Cheema, A. A. (1985) 'Poverty in Pakistan: Some New Dimensions,' *Pakistan Development Review*, May.

de Kruijk, H. and van Leeuwen, M. (1985) 'Changes in Poverty and Income Inequality in Pakistan During the 1970's,' *Pakistan Development Review*, May.

Mohiuddin, Y. (1980) 'Women in Urban Labor Market,' *Pakistan Economist*, 5 April.

Mohiuddin, Y. (1985) 'Women's Employment in Handicrafts. A Case of Occupational Dependency,' unpublished discussion paper, Applied Economics Research Centre, Karachi, Pakistan.

United Nations, (1973) *Manuals on Methods of Estimating Population. Manual VII: Methods of Projecting Households and Families*, Population Studies no. 54, Department of Economic and Social Affairs (New York: United Nations).

Youssef, N. H., and Hetler, C. B. (1983) 'Establishing the Economic Condition of Women-Headed Households in the Third World: A New Approach' in Buvinic, M., Lycette, M. A. and McGreevey, P. (eds) (1983).

4 The Hidden Roots of the African Food Problem: Looking Within the Rural Household

Jeanne Koopman
UNIVERSITY OF BORDEAUX

1 INTRODUCTION

As fundamental problems in Africa's food sector intensify under the strains of structural adjustment policies, African governments and international donors have become increasingly concerned about the political and economic implications of declining household food security and rising malnutrition (UNICEF, 1985; World Bank, 1988). As a result, we have witnessed a shift in the analysis of food problems from a focus on aggregate production and macroeconomic price policy (analyses which tend to advocate policies of primary benefit to large farmers and capitalist agro-enterprises) to a focus on the production and marketing problems of resource-poor smallholders, the overwhelming majority of Africa's rural population. Pinstrup-Andersen, for example, argues that policies which improve the access of small farmers to land, modern technology, fertilisers, credit and markets can both raise aggregate food supplies and minimise scarcity pressure on food prices (Pinstrup-Andersen, 1989).

While the argument that the production and marketing problems of the great majority of peasants must be addressed if food output is to be increased in an equitable and cost-effective manner is undoubtedly correct – the second section of this paper makes a similar point – it nonetheless fails to get to the heart of the household food security problem. What Pinstrup Andersen's analysis fails to appreciate is that access to productive resources varies not only by the income level of the household, but also by the gender of the farmer. This is a critical oversight in Africa where the great majority of food farmers are women.

This paper discusses the consequences of ignoring the gender aspects of Africa's food crisis: its goal is to emphasise the contributions of women farmers to household food security and aggregate food supply, to stress the importance of an analysis of gender-specific constraints on food production, and to explore the implications of gender-sensitive analysis for policy. It argues that a progressive and effective approach to Africa's food problems must not only direct resources to the great majority of resource-poor farmers, it must also be based on an adequate understanding of the intra-household separation and interrelation of men's and women's enterprises and incomes. Because most women farmers produce food both to provision their families and to earn a personal income from food sales, women's food output is critical to both rural and urban food supplies. To ignore the tightening constraints on women's food production is to ignore trends that are threatening the health and well-being of large segments of the population.

The second section of the paper attributes the deterioration of Africa's traditional agricultural sector – specifically its declining soil fertility, its loss of male labour, and the increasing overwork and exhaustion of female farmers – to two longstanding practices of African governments: the extraction of significant financial surpluses from the smallholder sector, and the practice of directing improved inputs, credit and other resources toward better-off male peasants and capitalist farmers while neglecting the resource needs of women food farmers.

The third section outlines the basic characteristics of most African smallholder economies and demonstrates how the separation of men's and women's agricultural enterprises and incomes affects the food sector. The fourth section argues that the structure and functioning of African rural households is fundamentally misspecified in standard agricultural household models and in project appraisal methods. Projects and policies based on models that assume that household members pool their labour and incomes in the pursuit of shared objectives tend to direct improved resources at 'households'. This practice has the effect of strengthening male-controlled enterprises, but it rarely meets the specific resource needs of women's food or other enterprises.

The last section demonstrates that despite serious constraints on their economic activities, African women are highly motivated to increase food production. The section describes two cases in which women significantly increased food output after obtaining access to new resources. These cases support the paper's major argument that the general failure to accord women farmers effective access to improved inputs has been a fundamental factor in the decline in African food production.

2 STORMS VERSUS SEA CHANGES: POLICY FAILURES AND THE DECLINE OF TRADITIONAL AGRICULTURE

Africa's recurring food crises and the successive waves of research and policy initiatives regularly following in their wake can be compared to a series of tropical storms which, in capturing our immediate attention during their fury, tend to divert our analyses from the basic 'sea changes' in the resource base and social organisation of traditional peasant agriculture.

The most important 'sea changes' in Africa's smallholder sector over the past several decades have been:

(1) declining soil fertility due to the reduction of fallowing (Hirschmann and Vaughn, 1984; Schoepf and Schoepf, 1988);
(2) continuing male withdrawal from agriculture and out-migration (Brown, 1980; Stichter, 1985); and
(3) increasing exhaustion of overworked women farmers (Bukh, 1979; Cloud and Knowles, 1988; Goheen, 1988; Koopman Henn, 1988).[1]

These fundamental trends are mutually reinforcing. Out-migration of husbands and sons deprives women food farmers of help in clearing new fields thereby limiting their ability to cultivate more fertile land or to employ labour intensive methods of soil regeneration. Declining fertility and smaller harvests reduce food farmers' ability to invest in fertility-restoring and labour-saving technology.

2.1 State Policy toward Smallholders: Export Crop Price Controls

Certain state policies have speeded up the adverse 'sea changes' weakening traditional agriculture and have increased the probability of continuing crises ('storms') in the food sector. State control of producer prices for export crops is a notable example. Export crop marketing boards were ostensibly created to shield producers from the destabilising effects of fluctuations in the international terms of trade, but it is well known that since the late 1960s most African governments have consistently maintained producer prices far below world prices, a practice that has permitted the state to accumulate significant surpluses from the smallholder sector. The bulk of these surpluses have been invested in non-agricultural enterprises and institutions.[2] Marketing boards rarely maintained sufficient reserves to compensate producers for long-term declines in world prices like those experienced in the 1980s.

Since the mid 1980s, the structural adjustment policies of the World Bank and International Monetary Fund have forced most African governments to reduce sharply both implicit and explicit taxation of export crop producers. But since nearly all Third World governments have been under the same international pressure to increase exports, world markets for tropical crops are flooded, and world prices continue to decline. With the exhaustion of marketing board reserves, African smallholders have recently suffered large cuts in producer prices. Since export crop production is a male enterprise, this situation poses an acute problem of sustaining rural men's incomes.

While we can expect to see some transfer of male labour to the food crop sector, state policies to encourage this process by subsidising men's food crop production run the risk of exacerbating both foreign exchange and household food security problems. First, despite their unprecedentedly low prices on world markets, export crops will be a critical source of foreign exchange for most African economies for some time to come. Second, state-subsidised male competition in the more lucrative food markets may threaten the major source of women farmers' personal incomes – food sales. Since most African women are expected to purchase the food products they do not cultivate, a reduction in women's incomes can threaten household food security. (The importance of separate budgets within households and the correlation between women's incomes and children's nutrition will be discussed in section 4.)

2.2 The Limits of a 'Progressive Farmers' Approach to Food Policy

A major problem with many food policies has been their implicit focus on the aspect of the food problem often considered politically most critical – feeding the cities. Since the urban population in most African countries represents only 15–40 per cent of the population

(World Bank, 1989), some analysts and policy makers have argued that the stimulation of larger food surpluses from better-off farmers, from modern farms operated by the urban elite, or from agro-industrial enterprises can most effectively achieve national food self-sufficiency (Cohen, 1988). The basic problem with this approach is its inherent tendency to undermine the food security and food-related incomes of the *majority* of the rural population.

Policies that subsidise larger farmers and agro-industrial estates encourage the wealthier segments of the population to expand their control over rural resources, a process that tends to reduce the access of the poor to land and other critical resources. As a result, poorer men and women may be forced to seek seasonal employment on larger farms, even though this means neglecting their own farms at critical periods. Alternatively, men may be compelled to leave the villages altogether, even in periods of high rural unemployment. Policies that implicitly favour larger farmers and capitalist agro-industries rarely take their potential negative effects on resource-poor farmers into account. Evidence from several African countries that chronic malnutrition is becoming a serious problem for large segments of the rural population highlights the importance of a re-analysis of the effects of this type of policy on the rural majority (Pinstrup-Andersen, 1989; UNICEF, 1985).

Malawi's acute problems with household food security highlight the dangers of neglecting the resource needs of resource-poor farmers. A 1980–81 national survey of Malawi's agricultural sector, the sector that still supports over 85 per cent of the population, found that 56 per cent of rural children had signs of chronic malnutrition (UNICEF and Government of Malawi, 1987). Such high rates of rural malnutrition are particularly striking in a country where the government has long given priority to the agricultural sector and has invested heavily in agricultural extension and smallholder credit programmes. A closer examination of Malawi's agricultural services reveals, however, that production advice and agricultural credit actually reach only about a fifth to a quarter of the better-off small-holders. Within this privileged group, state resources are over-whelmingly directed towards men. Despite the fact that by 1977, 70 per cent of Malawi's full time farmers were women, in 1988 less than a third of the farmers who received credit were women (Christiansen and Kydd, 1987; Evans, 1989).

A recent government-sponsored 'Symposium on Agricultural Policies' in Malawi emphasised the correlation between rising rural malnutrition and declining land availability (Quinn, Chiligo, and Gittinger, 1988). As a result of rapid population growth and massive land alienation for estate production of export crops, about three-quarters of the rural population no longer has access to enough land to produce its own food needs, and 30 per cent cannot earn a sufficient income to purchase adequate food supplies (Carr, 1988). Land scarcity has forced food farmers to abandon fallowing. The use of fertiliser could improve yields, but during the single annual planting season most farmers must allocate their meagre earnings from non-agricultural enterprises and casual labour to immediate survival needs. Land-short farmers desperately need seasonal credit to purchase fertiliser, but the smallholder credit system does not reach them.

Even though the 25–30 per cent of smallholders with access to credit and modern agricultural inputs have increased their output, their rising contribution to aggregate food supplies is rarely adequate to offset the declining production of the majority. The ultimate effect has been increasing rates of malnutrition in rural as well as urban households. In order to achieve *household* food security, the government of Malawi must find a way to deliver improved agricultural inputs to the majority of its food farmers, and in Malawi, as elsewhere in Africa, most food farmers are women.

3 BASIC CHARACTERISTICS OF AFRICAN AGRICULTURAL HOUSEHOLDS

Malawi is by no means unique as a case in which the majority of food farmers are women. Food production is, in fact, the major enterprise of nearly all rural African women. In some cases men also participate heavily, in others minimally or not at all. This section presents an outline of basic characteristics of African smallholder farming systems in which men and women pursue a significant number of separate agricultural and non-agricultural enterprises with each economically active adult managing the investment, labour, output, and income from his or her enterprises on an individual basis.

Most African household production systems have the following characteristics.

i. *In the production and processing of food crops, women's responsibilities and labour inputs normally exceed men's.* There are three basic variants of household food production systems: in the first, women are responsible for the production of all or most staple foods and for all other food crops; in the second, men and women jointly cultivate staple food crops in fields controlled by male household or compound heads, while women grow other essential food products in separate gardens; in the third (encountered far less frequently than the others), men are responsible for most food production, and women specialise in food processing and trade.

In the first variant, household food plots are usually considered women's fields. Men help with the clearing of large trees, but with little else. Women control the distribution of the harvest and derive their personal incomes from the sale of output which exceeds family consumption needs (Bukh, 1979; Funk, 1988; Goheen, 1988; Koopman Henn, 1988; Schoepf and Schoepf, 1988).

In the second variant, staple food crops are grown in household or compound fields, and although both women and dependent males help with planting, weeding and harvesting, the male household or compound head controls the output. Women, however, are still responsible for non-staple food production. Women's incomes are derived primarily from the processing and sale of crops from their individual fields (Cloud, 1986; Hemmings-Gapihan, 1982; Davison, 1988). In both variants, there is normally a clear demarcation between men's and women's crops, a distinction which determines who can claim the income from any marketed output (Guyer, 1984a; Roberts, 1988).

Even in the third variant, usually encountered where Islamic practices of female seclusion prevent most women from engaging in field work, young girls and older women may help on male fields, and married women may cultivate small gardens within compounds. Women are usually heavily engaged in food processing (Hill, 1972); non-Islamic women also specialise in the food trade (Guyer, 1984a).

ii. *In an overwhelming majority of cases, men have ultimate control over the household's most basic productive resource – land* (Davison, 1988, presents ten case studies). In patrilineal inheritance systems, women gain access to land through their husbands. Daughters do not inherit land, divorced women farmers nearly always lose access to their ex-husband's land, and widows often lose a major portion of their deceased husband's land to his patrikin (Goody and Buckley, 1973; Hay, 1982; Wilson, 1982). In matrilineal systems (numerically less significant but still encountered in central and southern Africa), both men and women inherit land from their matrikin. Married women are usually pressured to cede effective land control to their husbands (Hirschmann and Vaughn, 1984), but they are often better able to retain access to land if divorced or widowed (Hill, 1975). In either system, women may be subject to arbitrary withdrawal of certain land rights, particularly with respect to land they allocate to market oriented enterprises from which their husbands receive little or no monetary return (Hay, 1982; Hirschmann and Vaughn, 1984; Rose, 1988). In sum, male control of land significantly increases the uncertainty and risk in women's food production activities.

iii. *With the obvious exception of food produced for family consumption, most 'household income' is not pooled.* Husbands and wives keep separate budgets, make separate investments in their individual enterprises, and have gender-specific as well as joint responsibilities for different categories of family expenditures (Staudt, 1987; Guyer, 1988). In general, men are responsible for housing the family and women for feeding it. Men and women are individually responsible for their personal needs and for investment in their own productive enterprises (Bukh, 1979; Hemmings-Gapihan, 1982; Koopman Henn, 1978). Children's education and medical costs are usually joint expenditure items. It is here that the level of total 'family income' has its primary effect on 'family welfare' (Guyer, 1988).

iv. *In nearly all African farming systems men alone control export crop production and the resulting income.* If export crops are not grown, men normally control the production of the most lucrative food crops grown for market sale. Men's social seniority in household and lineage hierarchies and their ultimate control over land permit male household heads to mobilise considerable amounts of women's and male dependents' labour for the cultivation and processing of 'male crops'. Men nonetheless retain ultimate control over the monetary proceeds, deciding how much to spend on dependents' school fees, gifts to wives, other household needs, and personal expenditures. This is an arena for bargaining, to be sure, but the real returns to wives and other dependents are inevitably far below the returns a man realises for his own work (Carney, 1988; Crehan, 1984; Jones, 1986).

v. *Male farmers also derive income from a wide range of non-agricultural enterprises and from casual or part-time wage labour.* Rural women's opportunities to engage in wage labour and non-agricultural enterprises are far more limited: most, like food processing, beer brewing, and small-scale trade, are directly related to the food sector. Women's non-agricultural enterprises are sometimes explicitly organised to take advantage of seasonal increases in male incomes from export crops or other earnings. Wives' access to their husbands' incomes is more often realised through explicit or implicit market relations than through simple intra-household transfers (Guyer, 1988). Their economic opportunities are nonetheless highly conditioned by the state of the male economy.

vi. *Women's incomes are lower than men's in large part because women are socially required to spend some 40 to 50 hours a week on domestic labour and subsistence food production before they can engage in income earning enterprises.* Men's unpaid family labour obligations are far fewer. Furthermore, a wife is rarely able to mobilise her husband's 'unpaid' labour for her own enterprises in the manner that men mobilise women's labour for male controlled enterprises (Roberts, 1988; Guyer, 1984b). Consequently, women's total labour hours are much higher than men's, while their monetary incomes are much lower (Crehan, 1984; Engberg *et al.*, 1988; Koopman Henn, 1988). This essentially universal outcome seriously constrains women's investment capabilities, but it does not dampen their efforts to maintain individual enterprises and personal incomes.

4   PROBLEMATIC AGRICULTURAL HOUSEHOLD MODELS, PROJECTS AND POLICY

The preceding section's characterisation of African household production systems as a set of gender-specific individual as well as joint enterprises suggests a structure of intra-household economic relations at considerable variance with the basic assumptions of standard agricultural household models. This section elaborates the paper's critique of conventional household models, project appraisal methods, and smallholder sector policies.

4.1   Agricultural Household Models

Most smallholder food projects are based on an implicit model of the household which assumes that all economically active members operate as a single production and consumption unit. The objective of the household production unit is posited as the maximisation of its utility (a concept encompassing preferences for various types of consumption and for leisure), subject to the cash income and time constraints of the household as a whole (Singh, Squire and Strauss, 1986). In simpler versions of the model, the household objective is specified as the maximisation of its total income. All versions assume that household income is pooled and that all members of the household share the same preferences for consumption and leisure.

While the model of the unitary agricultural household has been useful in making predictions about consumption and investment behaviour in economies where its basic assumptions of income pooling and shared preferences reflect actual household behaviour, its relevance for the analysis of African households characterised by the separation of men's and women's budgets (non-pooling of monetary incomes) and by gender differences in spending patterns (differing preferences) is extremely problematic (McKee, 1986).[3]

Most African rural households are not characterised by joint enterprises but by a series of individual enterprises in which the enterprise 'owner' manages the production process and controls the ultimate output. While jointly farmed household or compound fields do exist in many household production systems (those of the Sahel region, for example), their output is normally controlled by male household or compound heads. Furthermore, they are inevitably accompanied by individual fields or non-agricultural enterprises that sustain separate budgets (Cloud, 1986; Carney, 1988; Guyer, 1984a).

The prevalence of separate budgets rather than income pooling between spouses indicates that preferences as to what to produce, sell and consume differ. Guyer's conclusion that 'men and women have different spending preferences, not necessarily because they hold different values, but because they are in structurally different situations' (Guyer, 1988, p. 160) very aptly sums up the importance of recognising the structural differences between men's and women's economies within African households and of incorporating them into the formal models used to analyse policies and projects.

Differences between men's and women's enterprises and spending patterns are linked to food security issues. As the previous section demonstrated, women's enterprises and incomes are more explicitly oriented toward the maintenance of household food security than are men's. While this fact does not, in itself, contradict the implicit assumption of standard models that total household income and family welfare are positively correlated, evidence on the relationship between children's nutrition and gender-specific incomes demonstrates that it is incorrect to assume that total household income is directly associated with nutritional welfare. Recent research has revealed a positive correlation between women's monetary incomes and children's nutrition. It has not been able to establish a similar correlation between increases in men's incomes and improvements in children's nutrition (Blumberg, 1988, surveys the evidence).

4.2 Project Appraisal Methods

Most project appraisal methods retain the same problematic assumptions of shared preferences and pooled incomes that characterise household models. Conventional cost-benefit analysis, for example, assumes that because 'households' seek to maximise total income, both men's and women's labour will be reallocated to project activities when the return to labour on those activities exceeds the return to labour on alternative enterprises available to household members. This assumption not only ignores the existence of separate budgets within households, it grossly underestimates that fundamental importance African women farmers attach to the maintenance of their individual enterprises and incomes.

Because most project appraisal methods assume a single household budget, income resulting from the participation of 'family labour' in project activities tends to be directed at the heads of households – essentially at men (Dey, 1981; Carney, 1988; Hemmings-Gapihan, 1982; Lewis, 1981; Staudt, 1985). When this happens, women often have little incentive to participate, no matter how great the difference between the formally calculated opportunity cost of their labour time and the benefits attributed to their participation in the project. Most African women do not expect to receive the full value of the actual returns to their labour when they work on an enterprise controlled by their husbands or other male family members (Jones, 1986). Since women must protect their personal incomes in order to fulfil their responsibilities in maintaining family food security, projects that threaten to reduce women's personal incomes by transferring their labour to male controlled enterprises will inevitably have problems in attracting female participation (Staudt, 1987).

Women resist pressure to participate in projects that limit their access to land or time to produce family food supplies, even when the project in question has been designed to increase national food supplies (Jones, 1986; Newbury and Schoepf, 1989). Women are often similarly disinclined to reallocate their labour to a project that seeks to increase the production of a male controlled crop because they doubt that the resulting income will be spent in a manner consonant with their own preferences or their children's welfare (Pankhurst and Jacobs, 1988). If male household heads, local political leaders, and/or national authorities force women to participate, there are likely to be serious losses to women's personal incomes and/or to family food security (Conti, 1979; Blumberg, 1988).

Given the basic assumption of project planners that households pool their incomes in the pursuit of jointly held consumption and investment preferences, women's reluctance or refusal to participate in projects that have a clear potential to improve overall household income cannot be explained. The problem, however, is not with women farmers' failure to understand the potential benefit of the project for the 'household', but with the project analyst's failure to understand and evaluate the different effects of the project on women's and men's enterprises and incomes.

African women farmers are neither the simple 'family labourers' that all too many projects still assume them to be, nor are they the free economic agents assumed in neoclassical economic theory. The reality is not only much more complex, it is of critical importance in determining the actual effects of policy and project interventions on food production and household food security. To understand this reality better, we must develop methodologies that focus on the basic differences between men's and women's enterprises, the extent of their interdependencies, and the prevailing patterns of gender responsibilities for household provisioning. This demands a considerably more elaborate analysis of intra-household processes of production, resource control and socially conditioned rights to mobilise labour within households and lineages than has heretofore been characteristic of project analysis (Guyer, 1986). Only by attempting to understand systematic differences in the social, ideological, political and economic constraints on men's and women's enterprises can we hope to understand the probable effects of project interventions on the economic activities and welfare of the different categories of producers and consumers in agricultural households.

4.3 Policy Constraints on Women Farmers

African policy makers and administrators tend to accept the model of the economically unitary household, perhaps because it supports their male constituents' desire to reinforce male control over household resources, in general, and women's labour, in particular. Patriarchal dominance over women's economic opportunities is so deep-rooted historically that it is widely regarded (particularly among men) as either 'natural' or as fully sanctioned by 'custom'. Even today it is not uncommon for men in positions of political or administrative power to suggest that a married woman should not have access to land, credit, or other resources on her own account because it would undermine her husband's position as head of the family.

The constraints on women's access to resources are not limited to constraints emanating from patriarchal relations within households. They have regional, national, and international political and economic determinants as well. At the national level, examples of institutional reinforcement of patriarchal dominance are manifold. State land registration systems and state-sponsored resettlement schemes, for example, rarely allow married women to obtain individual titles to land (Carney, 1988; Feldman, 1984; Goheen, 1988; Tadesse, 1982). While widows or divorced women are sometimes allowed to participate in settlement schemes or in state-sponsored irrigation projects as individuals, most women participate only as wives of a male household head. Married women often lose access to their traditional sources of independent income when they join a resettlement project (Bernal, 1988; Conti, 1979). They also face a significant risk of eviction in the event of divorce or widowhood (Brain, 1976; Jacobs, 1989).

Credit associations and export crop marketing cum credit cooperatives often restrict their membership to household heads, thereby excluding all married and a majority of unmarried women (Goheen, 1988). State sponsored projects to develop and diffuse modern technology have been heavily concentrated on men's export crops, but even innovations in food production technology, such as improved seeds, tools and fertilisers, have in fact been targeted at men because it is men who receive the inputs as heads of households (Crehan, 1984; Lewis, 1981).

At the international level, donor conceived and funded projects have taken essentially the same ideological view of women as subject to male 'leadership' that informs African state policy. Most donor provided resources are directed at households with minimal attention to the nature of intra-household resource use and control. The failure of international agencies to recognise the separation of male and female enterprises has had the effect of drastically limiting women's access to productive resources for their own food production and non-agricultural activities (Staudt, 1985 and 1987).

Colonial governments and international donors have compounded the problems of African women farmers by promoting the Western notion that the most appropriate role for women is that of a dependent housewife (Mies, 1986). Even though the Western view of women as housewives is in direct contradiction to the African assumption that women are responsible for producing most food for home consumption, Western attitudes have had a regressive impact on post-colonial agricultural extension and educational services for rural women which remain heavily oriented toward home economics skills rather than toward training in improved agricultural techniques (Staudt, 1982; Lewis, 1981).

African women farmers still cultivate their fields with the same back-breaking labour, the same hoes, and the same range of inputs they used in the pre-colonial period.[4] As land fertility has declined and men have reduced their contributions to the traditional food sector, neither African states nor international donors have made notable progress in helping women farmers overcome the gender-specific constraints which have prevented them from gaining effective access to the resources and technology they need to raise their productivity and output. Thus, even though women are Africa's most experienced and committed food farmers, women and children have been the primary victims of Africa's continuing food crises.

5 WOMEN WITH RESOURCES: IMPLICATIONS FOR THE FOOD SECTOR

The preceding discussion has emphasised the importance and urgency of making improved production, processing and marketing resources available to women farmers. This orientation need not and should not exclude men. All farmers need secure access to land, credit and technology if the food crisis is to be resolved in a manner that will improve household food security. There is, nonetheless, a critical need to target women, not only because women are more involved in food production than men, but because they face gender-specific intra-household constraints that seriously impede their access to resources targeted at households.

Since the approach advocated here has been tried so rarely, and since women farmers face such daunting social and economic constraints, sceptics may ask: Can it work? Do women have the motivation, the energy and the time to increase both food production and marketing even if they do obtain access to new resources? This section presents two case studies which demonstrate women farmers' ability to respond positively to new economic opportunities.

5.1 Women's Response to Credit for Subsistence Food Production

In the early 1980s, a small 'pilot' project in southern Malawi offered poor women and men credit for fertiliser.[5] Farmers who accepted the credit, primarily women, purchased fertiliser for their subsistence maize plots. Maize is the basic staple food of the region and is cultivated in a single season. Before joining the project, the average participant could only produce enough maize to feed her family for four to five months. With the application of fertiliser, maize yields rose by 100 per cent thereby covering the average family's consumption requirement for nine months (Evans, 1989).

Many observers assumed that since project credit had been used to increase subsistence rather than marketed output, repayment rates would not be adequate to make the credit scheme viable in the long term. These expectations were disproved. Fertiliser loans were repaid primarily with earnings from non-agricultural income generating activities and casual labour from larger farmers. Repayment rates equalled or exceeded the average 95 per cent repayment rates of male farmers in the government's major smallholder seasonal credit programme. Participants in the pilot credit project reported that it was much less costly to repay their loans than to purchase maize for an additional four to five months.

Unfortunately, but perhaps not surprisingly, the obvious 'lesson' of this pilot project – that resource-poor women farmers can repay agricultural credit used to improve subsistence production – has been ignored by Malawi's official smallholder credit fund. The national and international managers of the state credit fund continue to insist that poor farmers are bad credit risks (personal communication, Lilongwe, Malawi, June 1989). The latest national smallholder credit programme has been designed to reach only 30 per cent of farm households. Men still represent 70 per cent of all farmers with effective access to seasonal credit (Evans, 1989).

5.2 Women's Response to Improved Market Access

A case study from southern Cameroon compared the production and marketing of food from two villages with significant differences in access to urban food markets. Market access for farmers in the first village was drastically improved in the early 1980s with the opening of a new highway. In the second village it was necessary, if one wanted to sell food, to headload it to a road situated 1.5 hours walk away and then to wait, possibly for several hours, for public transport. Since the production and marketing situation in the second village was very similar to that of the first before the construction of the highway, data on output, sales and incomes from the second village have been used to approximate the situation of farmers in the first village prior to the improvement in their access to food markets.[6]

With the availability of more efficient and less costly forms of market access, women farmers increased the time they allocated to the production and processing of marketed food by nearly 80 per cent (from 8.5 to 15.2 hours a week), thereby increasing their earnings from food sales by 136 per cent (Koopman Henn, 1989). Women also continued to work about 16 hours a week producing food for family consumption and about 30 hours a week on domestic labour. Even though women's total labour time had been over 61 hours a week prior to the opening of the highway, they responded to the new marketing opportunities by increasing their weekly labour by about seven hours.

Women farmers' impressive response to improved market access contrasts strikingly with the response of men. Even though men's total labour time averaged less than 32 hours per week, only half the men in the village with improved market access increased their output of food products. (Men in this area gain the bulk of their incomes from cocoa production which, in 1985, the year of the survey, still paid a better return to male labour than most food production activities.) Among the men who did increase food production, none produced the variety of food products that women farmers cultivated and sold. Men only increased sales of the two traditionally 'male food crops' in southern Cameroon – plantain and bananas – crops with relatively low labour requirements and high returns to labour. There was no difference in men's total labour times between the two villages: the men who sold more food mobilised unpaid family labour to help increase their output and/or decreased the time they spent on alternative activities, particularly time spent clearing women's food fields (Koopman Henn, 1989).

The significant differences between men's and women's responses to improved food marketing incentives revealed by this case study have several implications for policy. First, the data show that despite their heavy subsistence and domestic labour responsibilities, women farmers are able to increase food production when they have access to new resources. Second, men's failure to allocate additional labour to the food sector in response to the same incentives available to women indicates that even though men have more leisure time than women, they may well require significantly greater monetary incentives if they are to be motivated to increase food production. Men in rural Africa have a much wider range of income earning opportunities than women and generally depend far less heavily on the food sector to generate monetary incomes. In the southern Cameroon case, for example, male farmers with excellent access to food markets obtained only 12 per cent of their total monetary income by selling food, while food sales generated 45 per cent of women's incomes even when they had very poor market access. Thus, women's primary involvement in the food sector and their strong motivation to increase production and sales should figure prominently in project design and policy analysis.

6 CONCLUSION

Until very recently women's food production and marketing problems have received little attention from governments or donors. This paper has argued that agricultural household models and project appraisal methods which assume that household resources are pooled and allocated to consumption and investment on the basis of shared preferences have contributed to the general failure to accord women access to improved productive resources. Models of this type have contributed to a serious misunderstanding of African rural household economies in which men and women conduct separate agricultural and non-agricultural enterprises and maintain separate budgets. When state and donor resources are targeted at households rather than at particular categories of farmers, they become subject to male control and rarely enable women to gain access to the inputs they require to improve the productivity of their food farms.

This paper has attempted to demonstrate that women are highly motivated to increase food production both to improve household food security and to improve their personal incomes. Declining soil fertility and the loss of men's and children's help in the food sector have, however, compounded the negative effects of the gender-specific constraints on women's farming. The failure of African and international authorities to help women overcome these constraints has contributed in a fundamental way to the general decline in Africa's per capita food production.

If women farmers are to increase their food output and sales, they must gain access to improved inputs, technology, and credit. Whether or not this will happen remains an open question. Women's own attempts to improve their access to basic resources often meet fierce resistance at national, local and household levels.[7] The power of the social, ideological, political and economic forces that have impeded women farmers' access to improved resources should not be underestimated. On the other hand, the persistent decline in food production and household food security experienced in many countries may finally force a new, gender-sensitive approach to food policy. There is also the distinct possibility that repeated food crises will provoke an intensified political response from women farmers themselves. African women are unlikely to allow their families to suffer increasing food insecurity without protest, especially if they continue to see state resources being allocated to agro-industrial enterprises or to the large-scale farms of the elite while their own food farms are deprived of desperately needed inputs.

Notes

1. Malawi's 1977 census found that although 88 per cent of the population lived in rural areas, only 50 per cent of economically active men worked full-time (nine months or more per year) on their own farms, down from 76 per cent in 1966. In constrast, 90 per cent of all women were full-time farmers (Hirschmann and Vaughn, 1984).
2. One estimate of the extent of state accumulation from the control of cocoa prices can be found in Koopman Henn (1978). See also an important analysis of the influence of the 'educated elite' in the formulation of agricultural policy in Cameroon by Ntangsi (1987) and a seminal analysis of the elite and the state in Africa by Bayart (1989).
3. The 'new home economics' household model discussed here has also been used to analyse the economic behaviour of urban households. Eleanor Fapohunda's illuminating critique challenges its relevance for the analysis of urban households in Lagos, Nigeria (Fapohunda, 1988).
4. This observation should not be taken to suggest that women have not been capable of making innovations in the range of farming techniques they practice nor in the varieties and types of crops they cultivate. The point being emphasised is women's virtual exclusion from access to state and donor provided inputs for the food production enterprises they manage as individuals.
5. All data in this example are from a paper by Janis Evans (1989) who

participated in the project from its inception. Ms Lucy Liuma, Women's Program Officer in the Blantyre Agricultural Development District, also participated in the project and generously shared both the Evans paper and her own reflections on the project.
6. The data are from field surveys conducted by the author in 1985 with the aid of a grant from the Social Science Research Council. See also Koopman Henn (1988) and (1989).
7. Carney (1988) provides an exceptionally instructive example.

References

Bay, E. G. (ed.) (1982) *Women and Work in Africa*, (Boulder, Colorado: Westview Press)

Bayart, J. F. (1989) *L'Etat en Afrique* (Paris: Fayard).

Bernal, V. (1988) 'Losing Ground – Women and Agriculture on Sudan's Irrigated Schemes: Lessons from a Blue Nile Village', in Davison, J. (ed.) (1988).

Blumberg, R. L. (1988) 'Income Under Female vs. Male Control: Differential Spending Patterns and the Consequences When Women Lose Control of Returns to Labor', World Bank Population and Human Resources Series, Washington DC.

Brain, J. L. (1976) 'Less Than Second-Class: Women in Rural Settlement Schemes in Tanzania', in Hafkin, N.J. and Bay, E. G. (eds) *Women in Africa* (Stanford, California: Stanford University Press).

Brown, B. B. (1980) 'Women, Migrant Labor and Social Change in Botswana', Working paper no. 41, African Studies Centre, Boston University, Massachusetts.

Bukh, J. (1979) *The Village Woman in Ghana* (Uppsala: Scandinavian Institute of African Studies).

Carney, J. A. (1988) 'Struggles Over Land and Crops in an Irrigated Rice Scheme: The Gambia', in Davison, J. (ed.) (1988).

Carr, S. (1988) 'Malawi National Rural Development Program: Technical Issues Review', Paper presented at the Symposium on Agricultural Policies for Growth and Development, Mangochi, Malawi.

Christiansen, R. E. and Kydd, J. G. (1987) 'Malawi's Agricultural Export Strategy and Implications for Income Distribution', Staff Report No. AGES870224, International Economics Division, Economic Research Service, US Department of Agriculture.

Cloud, K. (1986) 'Sex Roles in Food Production and Distribution Systems in the Sahel', in Creevey, L. E. (ed.) *Women Farmers in Africa*, (Syracuse: Syracuse University Press).

Cloud, K. and Knowles, J. B. (1988) 'Where Can We Go from Here? Recommendations for Action', in Davison, J. (ed.) (1988).

Cohen, R. (ed.) (1988) *Satisfying Africa's Food Needs: Food Production and Commercialisation in African Africulture* (Boulder, Colorado: Lynne Rienner).

Conti, A. (1979) 'Capitalist Organisation of Production through non-

Capitalist Relations: Women's Role in a Pilot Resettlement in Upper Volta' *Review of African Political Economy*, no 15–16.

Crehan, K. (1984) 'Women and Development in North Western Zambia: From Producer to Housewife', *Review of African Political Economy*, no. 27–8.

Davison, J. (ed.) (1988) *Agriculture, Women, and Land: The African Experience* (Boulder, Colorado: Westview Press).

Dey, J. (1981) 'Gambian Women: Unequal Partners in Rice Development Projects?', in Nelson, N. (ed.) *African Women in the Development Process* (London: Frank Cass).

Dwyer, D. and Bruce, J. (eds) (1988) *A Home Divided: Women and Income in The Third World*, (Stanford, California: Stanford University Press).

Engberg, L. E., Sabry, J. H., and Beckerson, S. A. (1988) 'A Comparison of Rural Women's Time Use and Nutritional Consequences in Two Villages in Malawi', in Poats, S. V., Schmink, M. and Spring, A. (eds) *Gender Issues in Farming Systems Research and Extension* (Boulder, Colorado: Westview Press).

Evans, J. (1989) 'The Phalombe Rural Development Project', Overseas Development Administration, Lilongwe, Malawi.

Fapohunda, E. R. (1988) 'The Nonpooling Household: A Challenge to Theory', in Dwyer, D. and Bruce, J. (eds) (1988).

Feldman, R. (1984) 'Women's Groups and Women's Subordination: An Analysis of Policies Towards Rural Women in Kenya', *Review of African Political Economy*, no. 27–8.

Funk, U. (1988) 'Land Tenure, Agriculture and Gender in Guinea-Bissau', in Davison, J. (ed.) (1988).

Goheen, M. (1988) 'Land and the Household Economy: Women Farmers of the Grassfields Today', in Davison, J. (ed.) (1988).

Goody, J. and Buckley, J. (1973) 'Inheritance and Women's Labour in Africa', *Africa*, vol. 43, no. 2.

Guyer, J. I. (1984a) 'Women in the Rural Economy: Contemporary Variations', in Hay, M. J. and Stichter, S. (eds) *African Women South of the Sahara* (London: Longman).

Guyer, J. I. (1984b) 'Naturalism in Models of African Production', *Man*, vol. 19, no. 3, pp. 371–88.

Guyer, J. I. (1986) 'Intra-Household Processes and Farming Systems Research: Perspectives from Anthropology', in Moock, J. L. (ed.) *Understanding Africa's Rural Household and Farming Systems* (Boulder, Colorado: Westview Press).

Guyer, J. I. (1988) 'Dynamic Approaches to Domestic Budgeting: Cases and Methods from Africa', Dwyer, D. and Bruce, J. (eds) (1988).

Hay, M. J. (1982) 'Women as Owners, Occupants, and Managers of Property in Colonial Western Kenya', in Hay, M. J. and Wright, M. (eds) (1982).

Hay, M. J. and Wright, M. (eds) (1982) *African Women and the Law: Historical Perspectives* (Boston, Massachusetts: Boston University).

Hemmings-Gapihan, G. S. (1982) 'International Development and the Evolution of Women's Economic Roles: A Case Study from Northern Gulma, Upper Volta', in Bay, E. G. (ed.) (1982).

Hill, P. (1972) *Rural Hausa: A Village and a Setting* (Cambridge, Massachusetts: Cambridge University Press).

Hill, P. (1975) 'The West African Farming Household', in Goody, J. (ed.) *Changing Social Structure in Ghana: Essays in the Comparative Sociology of a New State and an Old Tradition* (London: International African Institute).

Hirschmann, D. and Vaughn (1984) *Women Farmers of Malawi: Food Production in the Zomba District* (Berkeley, California: Institute of International Studies, University of California).

Jacobs, S. (1989) 'Zimbabwe: State, Class, and Gendered Models of Land Resettlement', in Parpart, J. L. and Staudt, K. A. (eds) *Women and the State in Africa* (Boulder, Colorado: Lynne Rienner).

Jones, C. W. (1986) 'Intra-Household Bargaining in Response to the Introduction of New Crops: A Case Study from Northern Cameroon', in Moock, J. L. (ed.) *Understanding Africa's Rural Household and Farming Systems* (Boulder, Colorado: Westview Press).

Koopman Henn, J. (1978) 'Peasants, Workers, and Capital: The Political Economy of Labor and Incomes in Cameroon', unpublished PhD dissertation, Harvard University, Massachusetts.

Koopman Henn (1988) 'Intra-Household Dynamics and State Policies as Constraints on Food Production: Results of a 1985 Agroeconomic Survey in Cameroon', in Poats, S. V., Schmink, M. and Spring, A. (eds) *Gender Issues in Farming Systems Research and Extension* (Boulder, Colorado: Westview Press).

Koopman Henn (1989) 'Food Policy, Food Production, and the Family Farm in Cameroon', in Geschiere, P. and Konings, P. (eds) 'Proceedings: Conference on the Political Economy of Cameroon – Historical Perspectives', Part II, Research Reports No. 35, African Studies Centre, Leiden, The Netherlands.

Lewis, B. (1981) 'Invisible Farmers: Women and the Crisis in Agriculture, AID Office of Women in Development', Washington DC.

Mckee, K. (1986) 'Household Analysis as an Aid to Farming Systems Research: Methodological Issues', in Moock, J. L. (ed.) *Understanding Africa's Rural Household and Farming Systems* (Boulder, Colorado: Westview Press).

Mies, M. (1986) *Patriarchy and Accumulation on a World Scale* (London: Zed).

Newbury, C. and Schoepf, B. G. (1989) 'State, Peasantry, and Agrarian Crisis in Zaire: Does Gender Make a Difference?', in Parpart, J. L. and Staudt, K. A. (eds) *Women and the State in Africa* (Boulder, Colorado: Lynne Rienner).

Ntangsi, J. (1987) 'Political and Economic Dimensions of Agricultural Policy in Cameroon', Managing Agricultural Development in Africa Series, World Bank, Washington DC.

Pankhurst, D. and Jacobs, S. (1988) 'Land Tenure, Gender Relations, and Agricultural Production: The Case of Zimbabwe's Peasantry', in Davison, J. (ed.) (1988).

Pinstrup-Andersen, P. (1989) 'Assuring a Household Food Security and Nutrition Bias in African Government Policies', Paper presented at the Ninth

World Congress of the International Economic Association, Athens, Greece, 28 August – 1 September.

Quinn, V., Chiligo, M. and Gittinger, P. (1988) 'Household Food and Nutritional Security in Malawi', Paper presented at the Symposium on Agricultural Policies for Growth and Development, Mangochi, Malawi.

Roberts, P. A. (1988) 'Rural Women's Access to Labor in West Africa', in Stichter, S. B. and Parpart, J. L. (eds) *Patriarchy and Class: African Women in the Home and the Workforce* (Boulder, Colorado: Westview Press).

Rose, L. (1988) '"A Woman Is Like a Field": Women's Strategies for Land Access in Swaziland', in Davison, J. (ed.) (1988).

Schoepf, B. G. and Schoepf, C. (1988) 'Land, Gender, and Food Security in Eastern Kivu, Zaire', in Davison, J. (ed.) (1988).

Singh, I., Squire, L. and Strauss, J. (eds) (1986) *Agricultural Household Models* (Baltimore, Maryland: Johns Hopkins University Press).

Staudt, K. (1982) 'Women Farmers and Inequities in Agricultural Services', in Bay, E. G. (ed.) (1982).

Staudt, K. (1985) *Women, Foreign Assistance and Advocacy Administration* (New York: Praeger).

Staudt, K. (1987) 'Uncaptured or Unmotivated? Women and the Food Crisis in Africa', *Rural Sociology*, vol. 15, no. 1.

Stichter, S. (1985) *Migrant Labourers* (Cambridge: Cambridge University Press).

Tadesse, Z. (1982) 'The Impact of Land Reform on Women: The Case of Ethiopia', in Beneria, L. (ed.) *Women and Development: The Sexual Division of Labor in Rural Societies* (New York: Praeger).

UNICEF (1985) *Within Human Reach, A Future for Africa's Children* (New York: UNICEF).

UNICEF and Government of Malawi (1987) *The Situation of Children and Women in Malawi* (Lilongwe: UNICEF).

Wilson, F. R. (1982) 'Reinventing the Past and Circumscribing the Future: *Authenticité* and the Negative Image of Women's Work in Zaire', in Bay, E. G. (ed.) (1982).

World Bank (1988) *The Challenge of Hunger In Africa* (Washington DC: World Bank).

World Bank (1989) *World Development Report 1989* (New York: Oxford University Press).

Part II

Developed Countries: Gains and Losses

5 Economic Development and the Feminisation of Poverty

Tuovi Allèn[1]

LABOUR INSTITUTE FOR ECONOMIC RESEARCH, HELSINKI

1 INTRODUCTION

Feminisation of poverty has become a catch phrase of political discussion in many countries. That is to say, there is a gender bias in poverty and a tendency towards the impoverishment of women. The term itself – feminisation of poverty – was first coined by sociologist Diane Pearce (1978), since when many studies have described the factors which make women particularly prone to economic victimisation.

'Feminisation of poverty' has often been used as a catch-all label for a wide variety of problems and some studies have oversimplified reality, making no clearcut distinction between two phenomena: the feminisation of poverty and the impoverishment of women. The former can be defined as an increase in the number or share of women among the poor. The latter refers to the worsening of women's living standards, i.e. women in general and poor women in particular are getting even poorer.

Although the level of economic development is the primary determinant of poverty in general, economic growth is no panacea for female poverty either in developing or in industrialised countries. Despite rapid economic growth and high standards of social security, there is still a growing tendency towards the impoverishment of women and the feminisation of poverty in many industrialised countries.

2   SOME EVIDENCE FROM INDUSTRIALISED AND DEVELOPING COUNTRIES

International comparisons of female poverty and the feminisation of poverty are still rare, and the existing data are not usually comparable. No thorough analysis of the subject exists. But on the basis of official statistics some 'stylised facts' can be developed on key relationships between economic development and the economic status of women.

The Population Crisis Committee (PCC) published a report entitled 'Poor, Powerless and Pregnant' (1988), which was based on aggregate statistics and previous research, including information on social, economic and political inequalities between men and women. If we combine the results of the PCC with some indicators of economic development – derived from World Development Report (World Bank, 1988) – we can roughly say that the lower the GNP per capita of a country, the poorer the women and the greater the inequality between men and women. General inequality has been measured by variables concerning educational attainment, condition of health, labour force participation rate, etc., by gender. A comprehensive rank order 'indicator' is formed on the basis of these variables. This kind of an indicator is of a purely qualitative and rank order nature.

Among the 12 countries with the lowest living standards of women and the greatest inequalities between men and women, there are five of the world's poorest countries. The 'positive correlation' between the level of GNP and gender inequalities in economic, social and political variables seems to be evident. Cultural and religious values, traditions and the underlying economic inequalities in the distribution of income and wealth also explain the poor economic status of women and gender inequalities in the economy.

As an example of cultural impact, the PCC's report revealed that among the 12 countries with the greatest gender bias, three were high income oil producers and seven were Islamic arab countries. Among the industrialised countries, the lowest scores – still well above the average – fell to Ireland and Japan. The former is culturally governed by a strong Roman Catholic church, the latter by extremely patriarchal traditions. The highest score for female status and gender equality fell to the Scandinavian welfare states, Sweden and Finland. These countries were also highly ranked in terms of GNP per capita (World Development Report, World Bank, 1988).

But everything does not count in GNP, especially if we study poverty as the value of living standard. The main importance lies then in the quality of life, and not in income and other resources, or the possession of material assets. This kind of approach emphasises the importance of those features of the economy that relate to the fulfilment of what have been seen as the 'basic needs' of people (Sen, 1987b, pp. 24–5).

The importance of cultural differences becomes apparent when we study the gender bias in poverty on a regional basis. The impact of cultural values on gender bias in poverty has recently been discussed in many studies (Sen, 1987a, pp. 30–1; Sen, 1987b, pp. 36–7; Sen, 1987c, p. 4). In these studies the gender bias in poverty was studied by means of statistics on nutritional levels and population structure.

To go beyond the aggregate nature of living standards when studying female poverty, information at the micro level or at least disaggregated data by gender is needed. Indicators of poverty usually vary from the level and distribution of individual income to life expectancy and mortality rates. In the least developed countries, demographic data are usually the only available source of information that can be used to study economic deprivation and poverty.

The greatest differences between male and female infant mortality rates generally exist in low-income countries. If we accept the gender-specific population structure of the industrialised countries as a standard – 96 female per 100 male children under the age of four years – among the poorest 42 countries, there are at least six countries where the ratio of young females to males is even lower (World Development Report, World Bank, 1988, p. 286). These countries comprise countries of southern Asia: Bangladesh, Bhutan, China, India, Nepal and Pakistan. According to Svedberg (1988, pp. 16–24), Nigeria and Senegal in Africa can also be added to this list. This kind of evidence has often been interpreted to refer to gender bias in infant mortality.

Frequently used explanations for gender bias in infant mortality are cultural preferences in favour of male children, which manifest themselves in inequalities in the division of food between male and female babies. But the empirical evidence is not unambiguous and there seems to be great variation between and within regions (Sen and Sengupta, 1983; Harriss, 1986; Sen, 1987a, p. 27). There is greater agreement on the existence of a gender bias in the division of health care. According to various studies, girls receive less health care and medical attention especially in many countries of Southern

Asia (Kynch and Sen, 1983; Taylor and Faruque, 1983).

Another variable that can be used as a rough proxy for gender bias in living standards and poverty is the life expectancy at birth. In the least developed 42 countries the life expectancy for males and females is rather short – from 32 to 56 years – and the gender difference is very slightly in favour of females. Among these low income countries there were six exceptions in 1986. In the countries of southern Asia mentioned above the life expectancy at birth for females was considerably lower than for males (World Bank, 1988, p. 287). However, this is not a good measure of living standards because it is strongly related to fertility. In countries with high fertility, mortality at childbirth is also high.

This kind of demographic evidence refers to the importance of cultural and other not basically economic factors when explaining the causes of gender bias in poverty. Higher rates of infant mortality and the lower life expectancy of females in some countries have led to exceptionally low female-to-male gender ratios in the population structure (Sen, 1987a, pp. 23–6). However, we have to remember that many demographic and social explanations are related to basic economic factors.

This kind of evidence also leads us to believe that inequality of opportunity may prevail in other spheres of human life as well. When females are deprived of basic economic opportunities and rights from the very beginning of their lives, the existence of a gender bias in living standards and poverty is only to be expected.

3 ECONOMIC ACTIVITY OF WOMEN AND WOMAN-HEADED HOUSEHOLDS

Sen has pointed out an interesting relationship between the gender bias in poverty and the economic activity of women (Sen, 1987a, pp. 35–7). If we consider Asian and African countries by regional blocks, it seems that the female-to-male economic activity ratio coincides exactly with the female-to-male life expectancy. This makes it possible to argue that higher economic activity of women – participation in productive activities in the formal sector – goes with social and economic structures that are more favourable to the overall position of women in the society and act against gender bias.

The only questions left open by Sen's analysis are:

1) which one came first, survival and freedom from poverty or productive activity?
2) what could be the logical regional boundaries of social and cultural influences considered?
3) what determines the economic activity of women?

We consider here only the latter problem.

In many studies the productive activity of women refers to women in paid employment in the formal sector of the economy. This kind of view is very approximate since unpaid work – both in the formal and the informal sector – is also productive. A large number of women in the least developed countries work in the informal sector, the extent of which varies from country to country (Joekes, 1987). Work in the informal sector is most often agricultural household work and in some places also service or manufacturing work.

The original Boserup (1970) hypothesis, that a lower relative involvement of women in formal productive activities may bring about a greater gender bias and *vice versa*, is to some extent confirmed by Sen's comparison of Asian and African low-income countries. The hypothesis also works fairly well in the case of high-income welfare states, especially in the case of Scandinavia.

The relative economic activity and earning power of women *vis-à-vis* men are important when considering both the family welfare of the adult members, and the relative treatment of boys and girls in the family. Women's lives are, from the very beginning, relegated to the private sphere within which the principles of economic equality and independence have no place.

While women's economic activity and participation in wage labour has become more general all over the world, the share of woman-headed households in the total population has been simultaneously growing (Clark, 1986, pp. 103–19). In some industrialised countries (for example, Sweden and Denmark) the share of woman-headed households, with no adult male in the family, has grown to as high as 20 or 40 per cent. The common factors behind these changes in family structure are: more divorce and teenage mothers in developed countries, as well as increasing male unemployment and immigration of husbands to urban manufacturing areas in developing countries.

In industrialised countries, the change in family structure has become one of the most important factors in the feminisation of poverty during the 1970s and 1980s. More and more women are supporting minor children on their own. Many studies have stressed the importance of marital status as a secondary factor of women's poverty (Corcoran, Duncan and Hill, 1986).

One of the most remarkable social changes in most industrialised countries has been the rapid growth in the relative share of woman-headed households since the early 1950s. The usual explanation for this is the increase in the number of divorces and unmarried teenage mothers (Peterson, 1987; Pressman, 1989). For example, nowadays more than one in five American families are supported by a woman on her own (Lefkowitz and Withorn, 1986; Peterson, 1989), and the figure is even greater among ethnic minorities (Sawhill, 1988, p. 1084). The proportion of woman-headed households is still higher in Sweden and other Nordic welfare states (Kamerman, 1986, p. 49).

According to recent research, in most North American and European countries the poverty risk is greatest among woman-headed households and particularly among aged and coloured population subgroups (Kamerman, 1986; Sawhill, 1988; Messinger *et al.*, 1988). The increase in female headship can be regarded as a tendency counter to the trend towards the improvement in women's status with economic development.

4 IMPOVERISHMENT OF WOMEN IN INDUSTRIALISED COUNTRIES

The increase in the number and relative share of women and woman-headed households among the poor in many countries shows that the feminisation of poverty is a real phenomenon irrespective of the level and growth of GNP. It can be argued that the mechanism behind the process is the sexual division of the economy that works through all levels of productive activities. The segmentation of labour markets, occupational segregation and the sharp division of working hours by gender are still reducing the positive impact of increasing economic activity of women (for example, OECD, 1988).

Although the labour market status of women has improved during the 1970s and 1980s in many industrialised countries, the occupational segregation of the labour market and wage differentials by gender still exist. Traditionally, women have worked in the sectors and occupations 'less productive' than those dominated by men.

Many 'women-appropriate' jobs are an extension of women's domestic tasks in the household. Similarly, when the public sector

Table 5.1 The female labour force participation rate and the proportion of employed women in part-time work in OECD countries 1986–87 (percentages)

	Labour force participation rate[1]	Proportion in part-time work
Sweden	78.3	45.1
Denmark	76.5	41.9
Finland	73.5	11.4
Norway	71.0	43.0
USA	64.9	26.1
Canada	63.5	25.3
Great Britain	61.6	45.0
Japan	57.4	30.5
Portugal	56.2	6.6
France	55.3	23.2
Belgium	51.3	22.6
Italy	42.3	9.5
Greece	41.7	10.4
Netherlands	41.1	55.2
Ireland	37.3	14.2

Source: OECD (1988), *Employment Outlook*.
Note: 1. Defined as the total female labour force divided by the female population of working age (aged 15–64) at mid-year.

began to share the woman's burden of mothering, large numbers of women found employment in these publicly provided 'reproductive' tasks, especially in the welfare states. Women's twin role of producer and reproducer and the double burden of domestic and market activities have also resulted in the sharp division of working hours by gender in many – but not all – countries.

Proportionately more women than men are employed in part-time jobs: from 6.6 per cent of Portuguese women to over 50 per cent of women in Denmark and Netherlands in 1987 (see Table 5.1; Meulders and Plassman, 1989). The proportion of employed women in part time work is more than one third in the OECD area, while the labour force participation rate is about 70 per cent. In developing countries most of the work done by women remains unrecorded because of the extensive informal sector.

The differential of hourly earnings by gender in manufacturing is 60 to 70 per cent on average in industrialised countries, from about 50 per cent in Japan to 60 per cent in the United States and 90 per cent in Sweden in 1986 (see Table 5.2). In many countries the reduction of

Table 5.2   Women's hourly earnings as a proportion of men's hourly
earnings in manufacturing, 1975 and 1986
(percentages)

	1975	1986
Sweden	85	90
Norway	78	85
Denmark	84	85
Netherlands	79	78
Finland	73	77
Greece	69	77
FRG	72	73
Ireland	61	69
Great Britain	66	68
Switzerland	66	67
USA	n.a.	60
Japan	51	49

Source: OECD (1988), *Employment Outlook*.
n.a. = not available.

wage differentials has been slowing down or even ceased during the
1980s. For example, in the United States the income inequality
between families headed by males and females has been increasing
from the mid 1970s until the late 1980s mainly because of low levels
of public assistance to families. In the United States, women's wages
have increased relative to men's wages (Peterson, 1989). The wage
and income differentials by gender are even greater in the developing
countries (Joekes, 1987, p. 14).

Many studies have considered the primary causes of the feminisation of poverty, and there is some agreement that the wages paid to
women are so low that not even a considerable increase in female
working hours in the formal sector, for example more frequent
full-time work, would solve the whole problem. But if women were
paid equal wages for equal work, it has been estimated that, for
example in the United States, the number of poor families would
decrease by about 50 per cent (Corcoran *et al.*, 1986; Feldberg,
1986). The relation between women's low pay and the impoverishment of women is even more evident in the developing countries,
since women are often forced to take a job in the informal sector in
addition to full-time work in the formal sector (Joekes, 1987).

In most developed economies there is a comprehensive system of
social security designed for families with children in general and for
single parent families in particular. The nominal level of social

Table 5.3 Annual income[1] of woman-headed households (mother and two children) as a proportion of the annual net earnings of an average production worker in some industrialised countries, 1979 (net earning of an average production worker = 100)

	Mother is not working outside home	Mother is working outside home	Mother is working plus welfare
Sweden	93.8	123.1	123.1
Germany	67.3	70.9	76.3
USA (New York)	55.9	100.8	100.8
USA (Pennsylvania)	44.0	69.2	75.3
France	78.6	79.1	103.4
Canada	52.5	75.9	75.5
Australia	50.0	78.8	82.1
Great Britain	51.7	83.0	91.6
Israel	50.0	71.5	80.1

Source: Kamerman (1986, p. 51).
Note: 1. Labour income, public assistance and private transfers.

assistance to families varies a lot among industrialised countries, as can be seen from Table 5.3. The income for woman-headed households is highest in Sweden – 94 per cent of the annual earnings of an average production worker – and lowest in some parts of the United States, in the case of a mother with no paid job (Kamerman, 1986, p. 51). These figures include both wages, private transfers and public assistance – and in the case of no paid job, only public assistance and private transfers. The last item includes estimated transfers from fathers as well.

Although the labour force participation rate of women is higher than elsewhere, and transfers to woman-headed households are relatively high, the governments of Scandinavian welfare states have not succeeded in preventing women's poverty. For example, in Sweden a woman headed more than one in three of the households receiving social assistance which were estimated to live below the 'official' poverty line after transfer payments and taxes in 1985. This can be seen from Table 5.4. The share of women among poor families has also been growing fastest in Sweden during the 1980s (Tanninen and Julkunen, 1988).

The figures are rather similar in all the Scandinavian welfare states, except in the case of Finland, where the poverty risk of single men has traditionally been highest among the population. In Finland the

Table 5.4 Households living below the poverty line[a] in Scandinavian countries, by type of household, 1985

	Denmark[b]	Finland	Norway	Sweden
Single man	33.1	39.8	36.6	39.5
Single woman	24.6	20.3	23.7	22.2
Woman-headed households	18.5	12.2	15.5	16.6
Couple, no children	3.8	8.2	6.0	6.0
Couple, with children	15.1	18.5	9.3	14.2
Others	4.9	1.0	8.9	1.5
Total	100.0	100.0	100.0	100.0
Single woman and woman-headed households as a percentage of the total	43.1	32.5	39.2	38.8

Source: Tanninen and Julkunen (1988).
Notes: a Social assistance cases; poverty line measured by one half of average disposable income per household.
    b Figures for 1984.

total number of poor households and the relative share of women among the poor have been declining during the 1980s. But at the same time the living standard of poor households has been worsening relatively. There is also some evidence that the living standards of woman-headed households – all are one-parent households, whereas couples are mostly two-earner households – has been declining in metropolitan areas. In Finland among social assistance cases, woman-headed households are typically in need of permanent assistance for five years or longer, and a great deal of these women are employed in pink-collar jobs or private and public services (Tanninen and Julkunen, 1988).

The main reasons for the feminisation of poverty and the impoverishment of women in other Scandinavian welfare states has been argued to be the sectoral and occupational segregation of labour markets, women's more frequent part-time work, the higher female unemployment rate and lower female earnings. In these countries labour markets are sharply segregated by gender, and women usually work in lower paid sectors: private and public services, and the food and textile industries. Women also work on the lower steps of the occupational hierarchy and have few promotion possibilities.

In many studies it has also been shown that women's 'reproductive breaks' for childbearing and rearing lessen their opportunities and willingness to get on-the-job training and therefore tend to increase wage differentials by gender. Long maternity leave of up to twelve months and additional publicly-subsidised childcare leave of up to three years also decrease women's earning powers and increase their risk of dropping out of the labour market.

These factors partly explain why Finnish women have not been impoverished to the same extent as women in other Scandinavian countries. Although the wage differential by gender in Finland is the largest – female earnings being 77 per cent of male earnings in 1986 – of the Scandinavian countries, Finnish women very rarely engage in part-time work – only 11 per cent of employed women – and the female unemployment rate has traditionally been lower than that of the male population. The labour market status of women is therefore much stronger in Finland than in other Scandinavian and industrialised countries.

5 CONCLUDING REMARKS

The feminisation of poverty and women's poverty is a broad and complex issue. The empirical evidence available confirms that the problem is getting even worse all over the world, irrespective of the level of economic development. The share of women among the poor has been increasing, and there are also reductions in the living standards of women in many countries.

The standard literature on poverty rarely considers the position of women as an issue of importance. Typically, it is thought that poverty strikes at all members of the household. That is why many writers insist on seeing the deprivation of the entire family as the right focus for studying poverty. The systematically inferior position of women inside and outside the family in many societies points to the necessity of treating gender as a force of its own in poverty research.

Because poverty is only one aspect of the living standard, the study of women's poverty should also take account of information other than the distribution of resources, income and other 'quantities'. Every aspect of poverty is not counted in money terms, but rather in the capacity to function in a way that satisfies the 'basic needs' of people. This kind of an approach comes close to the concept of the 'quality of life'.

But most importantly, the intra-family distribution of resources and capabilities comes into focus when studying the gender bias in poverty. Family structures often subordinate women and provide them with fewer economic opportunities and capabilities of functioning.

Note

1. Helpful comments from Nancy Folbre, Bob Rowthorn and the editors are gratefully acknowledged.

References

Boserup, E. (1970) *Women's Roles in Economic Development*, (London: Allen & Unwin).
Clark, M. H. (1986) 'Woman-headed Households and Poverty: Insights from Kenya', in Gelpi *et al.* (eds.) (1986) pp. 103–20.
Corcoran, M., Duncan, G. J. and Hill, M. S. (1986) 'The Economic Fortunes of Women and Children: Lessons from the Panel Study of Income Dynamics', in Gelpi *et al.* (eds.) (1986) pp. 7–24.
Feldberg, R. L. (1986) 'Comparable Worth: Towards Theory and Practice in the United States', in Gelpi *et al.* (eds.) (1986) pp. 163–80.
Gelpi, B. C., Hartsock, N. C. M., Novak, C. C. and Strober, M. H. (eds) (1986) *Women and Poverty* (Chicago, Illinois: University of Chicago Press).
Harriss, B. (1986) 'Intrafamily Distribution of Hunger in South Asia', WIDER conference paper, in Drèze, J. and Sen, A. K. (eds) (forthcoming) *Hunger: Economics and Policy* (Oxford: University Press).
Joekes, S. (1987) Women in the World Economy (Oxford: Oxford University Press).
Kamerman, S. B. (1986) 'Women, Children and Poverty: Public Policies and Female-headed Families in Industrialized Countries', in Gelpi *et al.* (eds.) (1986) pp. 41–64.
Kynch, J. and Sen, A. K. (1983) 'Indian Women: Well-being and Survival', *Cambridge Journal of Economics*, vol. 7, no. 314, pp. 363–80.
Lefkowitz, R. and Withorn, A. (eds) (1986) *For Crying Out Loud. Women and Poverty in the United States* (New York: Pilgrim Press).
Messinger, H., Fedyk, F. and Zeesman, A. (1988) 'The Size and Distribution of the Poverty Gap in Canada: A Micro Analysis of Variations Among Demographic Groups', *Review of Income and Wealth*, vol. 34, no. 3, pp. 275–88.
Meulders, D. and Plassman, R. (1989) *Women in Atypical Employment*. Final Report for the Commission of the European Community; Directorate General: Employment, Industrial Relations and Social Affairs; V/1426–89.

OECD (1988) *Employment Outlook*, September (Paris: OECD).

Pearce, D. (1978) 'The Feminization of Poverty. Women, Work and Welfare', *Urban and Social Change Review*, no. 11.

Peterson, J. (1987) 'The Feminization of Poverty', *Journal of Economics Issues*, vol. 21, no. 1, pp. 329–38.

Peterson, J. (1989) 'The Feminization of Poverty – A Reply to Pressman', *Journal of Economics Issues*, vol. 23, no. 1, pp. 238–44.

Population Crisis Committee (1988) *Poor, Powerless and Pregnant*, Population Crisis Committee, Washington DC.

Pressman, S. (1989) 'Comment on Peterson's "The Feminization of Poverty"', *Journal of Economic Issues*, vol. 23, no. 1, pp. 231–7.

Sawhill, I. V. (1988) 'Poverty in the U.S.: Why is It So Persistent?', *Journal of Economic Literature*, vol. 26, no. 3, pp. 1073–119.

Sen, A. K. (1987a) 'Africa and India: What do We Have to Learn from Each Other?', WIDER Working Papers, no. 19.

Sen, A. K. (1987b) *The Standard of Living* (Cambridge: Cambridge University Press).

Sen, A. K. (1987c) 'Gender and Cooperative Conflicts', WIDER Working Papers, no. 18.

Sen, A. K. and Sengupta, S. (1983) 'Malnutrition of Rural Children and the Sex Bias', *Economic and Political Weekly*, no. 19, pp. 19–21.

Svedberg, P. (1988) 'Undernutrition in Sub-Saharan Africa: Is There a Sex Bias?', WIDER Working Papers, no. 47.

Tanninen, T. and Julkunen, I. (1988) *Utkomststödet i Norden*, (Helsinki: National Board of Social Welfare).

Taylor, C. E. and Faruque, R. (1983) *Child and Maternal Health Services in Rural India: The Narangwal Experiment* (Baltimore Maryland: Johns Hopkins University Press).

World Bank (1988) *World Development Report 1986* (New York: Oxford University Press).

6 Economic Independence of Women in the Netherlands

Marga Bruyn-Hundt
UNIVERSITY OF AMSTERDAM, HOLLAND

1 INTRODUCTION

Women's participation in the labour market in the Netherlands has always been low. But in the 1970s and 1980s the percentage of women, especially married women, performing work in the labour market rose. In 1960 25.6 per cent of the relevant female population of 15–65 years of age participated in the labour market, in 1971 the participation rate was 30 per cent, in 1981 38.6 per cent and in 1987 it reached 50 per cent, at least if a person working for pay for at least one hour a week is counted as economically active (van der Wal, 1985, p. 41; Ministerie van Sociale Zaken en Werkgelegenheid, 1989, p. 11). At first sight one might suppose the economic independence of Dutch women is growing. This supposition leads many policy makers to assume that no further steps are necessary to advance women's economic emancipation. But is women's participation in the labour market a good criterion for measuring their economic independence? What is the difference between labour market participation and economic independence? Why is economic independence important and what criteria can we use to measure it? First and foremost, how do we define economic independence?

2 DEFINITION OF ECONOMIC INDEPENDENCE

Economic independence is the main aim of the second women's movement for emancipation in the Netherlands, a movement which started in 1968. Economic independence is also one of the most important elements of the Dutch Equal Rights Policy Plan, which was accepted by the Dutch Parliament in 1985. Economic indepen-

120

dence is a prerequisite of equal rights, though it is not sufficient on its own to gain an equal position for women in society. Economic independence is a prerequisite for equal positions for women in fields such as political power, living space, free time, knowledge, experience, status, quality of labour, etc.

The Dutch Equal Rights Policy Plan defines economic independence as 'the situation in which all adults whatever their sex, civil status or lifestyle can build up an independent existence. In this context it means they can support themselves and look after themselves. In principle this will be achieved through a growing participation in paid work and, if they are unable to do this, through acquiring (individual) entitlement to benefits. The objective assumes as general as possible participation in paid work but also assumes just as general participation in different types of unpaid work' (Ministry of Social Affairs and Employment, 1985, p. 26). In short, there are two elements in this definition. The first is *financial independence* through paid work. The second is *care independence* through unpaid work, that is doing domestic chores for one's own benefit and possibly for dependent children and sick persons.

The Equal Rights Policy Plan did not translate the definition of economic independence into quantitative targets. In this paper I will try to develop micro- and macro-criteria to measure how many women are economically independent and to what degree.[1] And to measure whether more women are becoming economically independent in the course of time.

What minimum of income and time for care should one have to be economically independent? Who is to decide how much money and time are needed for a decent living? In Holland this question is as difficult to answer as anywhere else. However, Dutch law can be of assistance. All inhabitants of the Netherlands have a right to a minimum subsistence thanks to the General Assistance Law. This minimum is related to the statutory net minimum wage. For someone aged 23 or older and living alone the law provides for a benefit of 70 per cent of the statutory net minimum wage. A single parent receives 90 per cent, people living together married or unmarried 100 per cent, which means a benefit of zero if the partner has an income of 100 per cent or more of the minimum wage. People sharing the same house receive 60 per cent each. In an earlier publication, my colleague Hettie Pott and I chose 70 per cent as the minimum for economic independence, because an independent person should be able to live alone. Economic theory largely ignores unpaid work, such as housework. However, it is obvious that the General Assistance Law presupposes that one should do one's own household chores. The benefit is not large enough to buy household help. People with high incomes can, of course, buy household help, so the higher the income, the less is the need to include unpaid time in the definition of economic independence. How much time should a person living alone spend on his or her own care? Time-budget research shows that a person living alone spends 15 hours a week on average doing household chores (Knulst, 1975 and 1980). We took an income of 70 per cent of the net minimum wage and 15 hours a week spent on household chores as the minimum beneath which one cannot speak of an economically independent person. How about the economic independence of single parents? The General Assistance Law does give single parents a benefit of 90 per cent of the net minimum wage, which, together with the statutory childrens' benefit, should be enough for a single parent. Single parents also need more time for housework and childcare.[2]

These are the minimum conditions for economic independence. Complete economic independence I define as the situation in which women's labour conditions are the same as men's, and women's income distribution is the mirror of men's income distribution. Complete economic independence means that paid and unpaid work is divided equally between men and women, that women as a group not only get the same amount of paid and unpaid work, but have the same distribution of quality of work as men. With these definitions in mind, let us have a look at the position of Dutch women in the labour market.

3   LABOUR MARKET POSITION

There are about 5 million women aged 15–64 in Holland, of whom 2.5 million are not willing to work for pay, because they are still in school or doing unpaid household work (Centraal Bureau voor de Statistiek, 1986). In 1987 the participation rate of all women in this age group was 50 per cent and the participation rate of married women was 43 per cent (Ministerie van Sociale Zaken en Werkgelegenheid, 1989, p. 11); 54 per cent of all women participating in the labour market were working part-time. The percentage of Dutch women participating in the labour market is one of the lowest for women in the industrialised world and the percentage of part-time working women is the highest.

Next let us have a look at another aspect of women's labour market position: their lifetime participation profile. The OECD distinguishes three stages in the age profiles of women participating in the labour market:

1. The first profile shows a peak at 20–4 years of age: women disappear from the labour market when they marry or become pregnant.
2. The second shows two peaks: one at the age of 20–4 years before the first child is born; the other peak at 35 years or older, when mothers return to the labour market. This is a profile with a dip when women are looking after small children.
3. The third profile is the same as the men's profile, namely an upturned U: women enter the labour market after having finished their education and leave the labour market at the pensionable age. In most industrialised countries women are between stages two and three.

Although a growing number of young mothers are staying in the labour market after having their first baby, Holland still has a profile which resembles more the first than the second model. There is one clear peak in the age group 20–4 and a weak second peak in the age group of 30–5 of mothers returning to the labour market after their children are older or grown up. Only one quarter of young mothers having their first baby don't leave their jobs and stay in the labour market. Mothers returning to the labour market after their children are older or grown up are still in the minority. Divorced mothers with small children also stay at home, because child care is only available for about 3 per cent of all children younger than 4 years of age. Most single parents are living on Social Assistance. In fact only one fifth of single mothers are earning a living. Figure 6.1 gives an indication of the percentages of married women of different ages who were participating in the labour market in 1960, 1971 and 1983, as well as the expectations of the Central Bureau of Statistics for the years 1990 and 2000. The growing participation of married women in the second half of the twentieth century is clearly seen. But even in the year 2000 experts think the participation rate will drop from about 80 per cent for the age group 20–4 to about 60 per cent for the childbearing age group. More than three-quarters of mothers having their first baby leave the labour market and do not return, for the second peak is very weak.

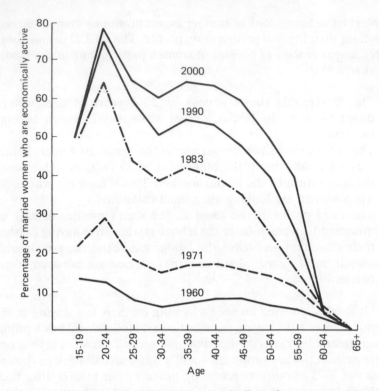

Figure 6.1   Married women who are economically active as a percentage of
the relevant population of 15 years and over in 1960, 1971, 1983,
1990 and 2000

Source: Central Bureau of Statistics, Den Haag.

Registered unemployment as a percentage of the economically
active population has been higher for women than for men since
1975. In 1987 registered unemployment for female employees as a
percentage of the economically active population was 17.4 per cent
for women and 12.6 per cent for men (Centraal Bureau voor de
Statistiek, 1988, p. 168). This percentage does not mean very much,
because many women who would like to have jobs are not registered
as unemployed. Research reveals that if one takes into account
unregistered unemployment as well, total unemployment for women
is twice as high as registered and unregistered unemployment of men
(Ministerie van Sociale Zaken en Werkgelegenheid, 1987, p. 48).

4 INCOME AND INCOME DISTRIBUTION

It is difficult to measure women's economic independence in terms of income. Should one look at gross or net income? If women are treated differently from men in tax and social security regulations, net income is perhaps the better measure. On the other hand, if the aim is to know something about the economic independence women obtain by participating in the labour market, gross labour income would be better.

The second difficulty is of a more practical nature: relatively little data are available. Until 1973 the incomes of man and wife were taxed together. From 1973 the labour income of married women was taxed separately but other items of income are still taxed together, that is counted as the income of married men. So an exact comparison of the income distribution among men and women in the Netherlands is not possible. Research by the Social and Cultural Planning Bureau reveals that in 1985 46 per cent of all Dutch women in the age group 18–64 did not have any income of their own against 5 per cent of all men in this age group. 37 per cent of all women and 70 per cent of all men in this age group earned a labour income; the rest had an income from social security, a pension, other income or were financially dependent. Of all women with labour income only 63 per cent earned the social minimum or more compared to 91 per cent of all men with a labour income. In 1985 the average disposable income (gross income *minus* tax and social security contributions but inclusive of pension contributions) of all women with an income was 52.5 per cent of the average disposable income of men with an income (Centraal Bureau voor de Statistiek, 1988, p. 320). All in all, only 25 per cent of all women between 18 and 64 were financially independent as defined in section 2, compared to 70 per cent of all men (Sociaal en Cultureel Planbureau, 1988, pp. 459 and 460).

5 CRITERIA TO MEASURE THE DEVELOPMENT OF ECONOMIC INDEPENDENCE

If paid and unpaid work were divided equally between men and women, about half of the economically active population would be female. Women's share in the economically active population has grown from 28 per cent in 1975 to 36 per cent in 1988. This development is illustrated in Figure 6.2, which is based on the data in Table

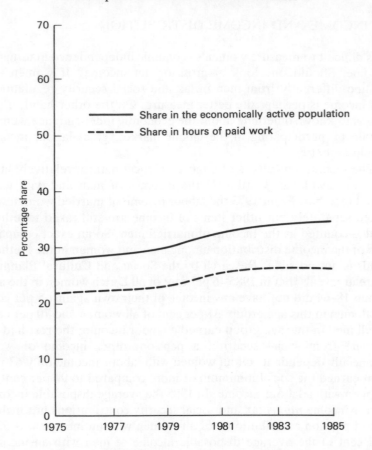

Figure 6.2   Share of Dutch women in the economically active population
and hours of paid work

6.1. Data from the Labour Force Sample Surveys were the basis for
the share in hours of paid labour. The hours men and women worked
during the week the Surveys were taken were multiplied by the
number of men and women working in order to calculate the share of
women in total hours of paid labour. As expected, women's share in
hours of paid labour was considerably lower than their share in the
economically active population. The gap between the two shares is
growing, because more and more women are working part-time or
are having a so called flexible labour contract, that is a temporary
contract or a contract on call, a freelance contract or something
similar. Wages and fringe benefits for part-time work and especially
for flexible contracts are low.

Table 6.1   Women's share in the economically active population, hours of
paid labour and disposable income
(percentages)

	Economically active population	Hours of paid labour	Disposable income
1975	27.7	21.8	20.1
1977	28.5	22.3	21.5
1979	29.7	23.0	22.0
1981	32.5	25.2	23.4
1983	34.1	26.0	24.0
1985	34.8	26.3	26.5

Sources: Centraal bureau voor de Statistiek, *Statistische Zakboeken,
Sociaal-Economische Maandstatistieken, Arbeidskrachtentellingen
and Inkomensstatistieken* for several years.

Women's share in the economically active population and in total
hours of paid labour does not tell us about their share in total income.
As long as men and women do not have the same functions, do not
get equal wages for work of equal value, do not have the same rights
to social security, tax and pensions, women's share in labour income
will be lower than men's. So another indicator of the development of
economic independence is women's share in income. Income data
which can be used to make comparisons between men and women
are very difficult to obtain.[3] Disposable income of all women could be
compared only for the period 1973–85; the figures are given in Table
6.2. Disposable income is gross income from profits, income from
labour, benefits received and other income *minus* tax and social
security contributions.

The total number of women with their own income grew by 107 per
cent from 1973 to 1985 compared to 27 per cent for men. Average
income of women has grown 57 per cent compared to 40 per cent for
men. As a result women's share in total disposable income has risen
from 16.5 per cent to 26.5 per cent. Compared with the women's
share in total hours of paid labour in 1985 of 26.3 per cent this seems
a satisfactory result. One should bear in mind, however, that part of
women's income is a reflection of their role as dependent housewives.
Under Dutch social security law every woman receives an old age
pension when she becomes 65 years of age, whether or not she has
paid contributions. In addition to the old age pensions there are the
pensions for widows from social security and the private pensions for
widows of all ages. In 1985 20 per cent of all women with their own

Table 6.2 Disposable income

	Women		Men		Female share of total (per cent)
	Number (thousands)	Average income (Dutch guilders)	Number (thousands)	Average income (Dutch guilders)	
1973	1 798	8 700	4 262	18 700	16.5
1975	2 353	10 500	4 322	22 800	20.1
1977	2 581	16 100	4 358	26 200	21.5
1979	2 689	13 800	4 435	29 650	22.0
1981	2 893	15 000	4 540	31 300	23.3
1982	2 985	14 300	4 710	27 700	24.6
1983	2 960	14 700	5 041	27 500	24.0
1984	3 285	14 000	5 329	26 200	24.8
1985	3 722	13 700	5 407	26 100	26.5

Source: Centraal Bureau voor de Statistiek, *Inkomensstatistieken* for several years.

income received a pension, but it is impossible to say if they received this pension as a result of their own labour. Nine per cent of all women with their own income were not economically active. If these women are excluded, women's share in total disposable income in 1985 is diminished from 26.5 per cent to 17.9 per cent. If men's incomes from pensions and men's not-active incomes are left out of account, women's share in total disposable income in 1985 becomes 21.8 per cent.[4]

6 OBSTACLES TO ECONOMIC INDEPENDENCE

In everyday reality economic independence is not easy for many women to obtain. There are obstacles to be overcome. First let us take a look at the educational level of boys and girls.

In primary school boys and girls receive the same education. In secondary school more girls than boys opt for a particular course of study consisting predominantly of modern languages and general non-vocational subjects, without mathematics or natural sciences. In vocational education women choose 'women's courses', such as secretarial or domestic science or nursing, courses which give narrower prospects of employment and good labour conditions. The Dutch government is trying by information programmes on television and otherwise to persuade girls to opt for technical and economic vocational training (Van der Wal, 1985, pp. 26–30). So far, the results of these programmes are meagre.

A major obstacle to women's participation in the labour market is the near non-existence of child care for children under 4. Child care which makes it possible for mothers with young children to have a full-time job is available for only 3 per cent of all these youngsters. The Dutch government is planning to give more financial assistance for child care to communities in 1990–94. The government has also proposed unpaid half-time parental leave for a period of six months for both parents.

Another obstacle is the fact that participating in the labour market is financially discouraged because the husband loses financial tax and social security advantages if his wife earns an income. I was invited by the Dutch Organisation for Strategic Labour Market Research to make an inventory of income regulations in Holland and three other countries which encourage or discourage women (Bruyn-Hundt and van der Linden, 1989). I found seven regulations in Holland with breadwinner advantages, *plus* other discouraging regulations, for example in pensions I will summarise the financial consequences of some of these regulations for women, living together married or unmarried.[5] I called 'implicit partner levies' the financial advantages the husband loses because of tax or social security law if his wife is earning her own income. In income tax the tax-free bracket of his income is doubled if his wife has no income. If she enters the labour market and earns f15 000 a year (which is about the average of what married women earn) the implicit partner levy adds 10 to 21 per cent to her individual tax and social security contributions of 23 per cent. So her net addition to family income is only 56 to 67 per cent instead of 77 per cent. If her partner is ill, an invalid, unemployed or pensioned and his social security benefit is a minimum benefit, he loses a supplement if she earns an income. The loss of this supplement means that the levy on her income is 66 to 100 per cent, instead of 23 per cent. Similar effects are found in regulations for a study benefit, housing subsidy, etc.

7 SUMMARY AND CONCLUSION

Policy makers in the Netherlands seem reluctant to take the necessary steps to improve the economic position of women, because they think women's labour market participation will develop as a matter of course. But while the participation rate of women in the labour market has risen, it is still one of the lowest in the industrialised world. More than half of all working women work part-time, so participating in the labour market does not necessarily mean that women are economically independent. Less than one quarter of women stay in the labour market after the birth of their first child. Child care is available for only 3 per cent of all children under 4 years of age. The tax and benefit structure discourages women from paid work, unemployment is high, women take a vocational training with poor employment prospects.

Although comparison of women's share in labour and income poses technical difficulties, clearly further research along these lines is necessary. In my view these comparisons are useful and necessary as a more accurate criterion of women's economic independence than women's participation rate in the labour market. They are a starting point for the analysis of international differences in women's independence. They could also serve as a basis for goal-oriented policy measures on the national and international scale.

Notes

1. The basis for this paper was laid in Bruyn-Hundt and Pott-Buter (1986).
2. The time-budget study of the Social and Cultural Planning Bureau shows that single parents with young children needed on average 27.6 hours a week for housework and childcare.
3. One problem is that the Central Bureau of Statistics uses several definitions in income statistics and often changes them. As already mentioned, the data come from the census. Tax regulations were changed in 1973 and in the years 1983 to 1985. Minor changes in tax regulations occur nearly every year. Another problem is that the non-labour income of married women is counted as the income of the partner with the highest income. But the greatest difficulty is that it is impossible to distinguish between women's own benefits from social security and pensions and the pension and social security benefits they receive as a dependent of their partners or former partners.
4. I would have liked to split up women's share in income in this way for the whole period, in order to be able to make a better analysis. So far the data from the Central Bureau of Statistics has not enabled me to do so.
5. I chose the secondary worker model as a theoretical background. In this neoclassical model labour supply of males is made independently of the labour market decision of females. A woman determines her optimal labour supply given the fact that her partner's earnings are considered to be non-labour income. Her labour market decision depends on what she can add to net family income.

References

Bruyn-Hundt, M. and Pott-Buter, H. (1986) 'Economische zelfstandigheid', in d'Ancona, H. *et al* (eds) *Vrouwen en economische zelfstandigheid* (Amsterdam: SUA) pp. 9–42.

Bruyn-Hundt, M. and van der Linden, Th. (1989) *De invloed van materiële prikkels op het arbeidsaanbod van vrouwen* Werkdocument nr.w 65, Organisatie voor Strategisch Arbeidsmarktonderzoek, Den Haag.

Centraal Bureau voor de Statistiek (1986) *Supplement bij de Sociaal-Economische Maandstatistiek*, nos 6 and 9, Den Haag.

Centraal Bureau voor de Statistiek (1988) *Statistisch Zakboek 1988*, Den Haag.

Knulst, W. (1975) *Een week tijd*, Sociaal en Cultureel Planbureau, Rijswijk.

Knulst, W. and Schoonderwoerd, L. (1980) *Waar blijft de tijd?* Sociaal en Cultureel Planbureau, Rijswijk.

Ministry of Social Affairs and Employment (1985) *Design of an Equal Rights Policy Plan*, Den Haag.

Ministerie van Sociale Zaken en Werkgelegenheid (1987) *Rapportage Arbeidsmarkt 1987*, Den Haag.

Ministerie van Sociale Zaken en Werkgelegenheid (1989) *Kwartaalbericht*, 1e jaargang no. 1, Den Haag.

Sociaal en Cultureel Planbureau (1988) *Sociaal en Cultureel Rapport 1988*, Rijswijk.

van der Wal, E. (1985) *Women on the Move*, Sociaal en Cultureel Planbureau, Rijswijk.

7 The Impact of Demographic Trends in the United Kingdom on Women's Employment Prospects in the 1990s

Lynne Evans[1]

UNIVERSITY OF DURHAM, UK

1 INTRODUCTION

Arguably the most important impact on the UK labour market over the next decade will be the so-called demographic time-bomb – the most salient feature of which is the sharp fall in the number of young people in the population.[2] Allowing for this cohort's increased participation in voluntary education, the labour force aged under 25 is projected to fall by 1.2 million, or approximately 20 per cent, between 1987 and 1995.[3] Not surprisingly, increased labour force participation by women is perceived to be the most likely way to maintain the overall size of the labour force at some sort of steady state.

Recent statements by the government's Department of Employment make their position clear: they project relative stability in the size of the total labour force and stress the need for (i) greater flexibility amongst those in employment and (ii) greater willingness of employers to retrain existing employees to adapt to changes (rather than rely on the market for ready-trained people) and also tap new resources for their recruits. It is in this latter context that there are explicit references to women: the size of the female labour force is projected to increase by some three quarters of a million. The argument runs (Department of Employment, 1988, p. 8):

'Employers must recognise that women can no longer be treated as second-class workers. They will need women employees, and must recognise both their career ambitions and domestic responsibili-

132

ties. This will involve broadening company training policies, much more flexibility of work and hours and job-sharing, to facilitate the employment of women with families and help adapt to their needs.'

Apart from the explicit acknowledgement of second-class worker status for women, something else is worth noting here: the government can be seen to be placing the burden of adjustment on employers by demanding that they change their attitude towards the employment of women.[4] This may demonstrate the belief that women are currently constrained in the labour market by employers' inflexibility and also raises the prospect of firms being frustrated in the labour market of the 1990s unless they make major modifications to their patterns of work organisation. This paper focuses on women's employment prospects in the 1990s and attempts to assess the likelihood of the demographic dip being a 'Golden Opportunity' in which UK women improve their economic status.

Section 2 of this paper describes the projected changes in the demographic composition of the labour force and some general issues related to such changes. Section 3 describes post-war developments in women's economic status in the UK. The following two sections, 4 and 5, identify major features of the labour market of the 1990s together with detailed projections of employment prospects for women. The paper concludes with an assessment of the impact of these changes on women's economic status in the 1990s.

2 PROJECTED LABOUR MARKET CHANGES

The projected changes in the age and sex composition of the UK labour force are summarised in Table 7.1. The two major components of the change are: (i) that between 1987 and 1995, the youth labour supply is projected to fall by 1.2 million – some 20 per cent and (ii) that the prime-age female labour force will rise by 1.26 million, mainly because of a continued rise in activity rates, thereby making the prime-age labour force increasingly female (from 42 to 44 per cent).[5] Given the reduction in young women, the total change in the number of women in the labour market is a projected increase of 0.76 million. The overall size of the labour force remains roughly stable, showing a modest growth of a little over 3 per cent over the whole eight years of the projection period. Of themselves, these changes tell us little about employment prospects for women; for

Table 7.1 Estimates and projections of the civilian labour force in
Great Britain, 1987–95
(thousands)

		Men	Women	Total
Youths	1987	3 349	2 818	6 167
(16–24)	1995	2 669	2 294	4 963
Prime-age	1987	10 138	7 456	17 594
(25–54)	1995	11 088	8 723	19 811
Older	1987	2 178	1 222	3 400
(55 and over)	1995	2 062	1 239	3 301
Total	1987	15 665	11 496	27 161
	1995	15 819	12 256	28 075

Source: 'Labour Force Outlook to 1995', *Employment Gazette*, March 1988.

this, much more information about the demand side of the labour market is required.

First, consider the situation where the aggregate demand for labour is static and where there is complete substitutability across age groups and gender. In this case, the application of simple demand and supply principles predicts an expansion of women's employment sufficient to compensate for the shortfall in young persons and some limited downward pressure on the uniform wage rate. However, there is not complete employment substitutability either across generations or by sex. To the extent that different cohorts and the two sexes have different amounts of work experience and are differentially skilled, there must be differential demands for the separate groups, even in the absence of any sex discrimination. Studies to estimate the degree of substitutability/complementarity across different age-sex groups find that, amongst most pairwise comparisons of young/old, male/female groups, there is evidence of both age and sex segmentation of the labour force.[6] Further, other evidence of the impact of generation size on the earnings of that cohort provides strong evidence of labour market segmentation by age,[7] the cohort size effect rising with the level of schooling. However, significantly, recent studies indicate a move towards substitutability across gender and, most striking in recent UK studies, is the finding that whilst young men are complementary to older men, they are substitutes for women, particularly women who work part-time.[8] These later results, when coupled with Costrell *et al.*'s (1986) finding that older women are substitutable with younger women, indicate that, certainly in the past, employers have been prepared to substitute prime-age women workers for young workers of both sexes. Hence whilst the demographic dip is likely to raise young workers wages relative to those of experienced workers, the rise will be moderated by increased employment of prime-age women workers,[9] but it is important to identify the form this increased employment of prime-age women might take.

3 WOMEN'S PAST EXPERIENCE

Consider first the post-war growth in the employment of women workers: factors on both the supply and the demand side of the labour market have contributed. On the supply side, there has been an increase in the supply of women's labour associated with a decline in fertility and increased non-marriage. Also, there has been a long political struggle to increase women's access to the more remunerative occupations: for example, long before the 1970s there were debates over marriage bars in many occupations. Indeed, one lasting impact has been the withdrawal of the marriage bars on female workers which had been jointly enforced by employers and trade unions in the later half of the nineteenth century. On the demand side, three separate periods are readily identifiable:[10]

1. In the 1950s, labour demand threatened to outstrip the traditional demographic sources of supply; employers responded by employing married women who would otherwise have been out of paid employment, and importantly were not counted as part of the labour force given the customary practice of quitting the labour force on marriage. Not only did women's employment increase, but also the labour force participation increased among all groups of married women irrespective of the number and age of children, a trend which has persisted. Female participation increased from 42 per cent of the female population aged under 60 in 1951 to 50 per cent in 1961, although it is notable that the percentage in full-time employment actually fell by 2 percentage points to 35 per cent (see Table 7.2).
2. During the 1960s the particular mix of industrial and occupational demand for labour, coupled with the gender segregation of occupations, increased the relative labour demand for women so much

that, in the context of an overall reduction in aggregate employment, women's employment continued to grow.

3. In the 1970s, female employment grew and became more stable as the changes in industrial and occupational structure continued and their effect was reinforced by, for example, increased numbers of women heading separate households and the growing tendency for women to delay childbearing.[11] The Equal Opportunities Act supported these developments but it is particularly difficult to isolate the impact of this legislation because of other changes taking place at the same time, including equal pay legislation.

In each of these decades[12] employment of women increased and in that sense the demographic change in the 1950s, the changes in occupational structure in the 1960s and 1970s and the legislation of the 1970s all served to increase women's economic status. However, one should be wary of identifying the increase in the female contribution to UK employment (from 34 per cent in 1959 to 45 per cent in 1987) as emancipatory. Certainly, economic status rests fundamentally upon access to and acquisition of paid employment – ask anyone who has experienced long-term unemployment or any woman who declares that she is 'just a housewife'. But economic status also depends upon the characteristics of the employment contract, for example, full-time/part-time, permanent/temporary, manual/professional and, of course, earnings. Moreover, economic status is also inversely related to the amount of unpaid domestic work carried out.[13]

3.1 Part-Time Work

The most notable feature of the rising trend in women's employment is that the increase in employment is not reflected in an increase in full-time employment. Table 7.2 shows that activity rates for full-time female employment fell over the period 1951–85 (although there was some slight upturn in full-time activity after 1985). By far the bulk of the increase in the activity rate has been in part-time jobs. Many view this as reflecting women's preference for part-time jobs, emphasising that the increased participation rate is made up of a growing number of women re-entering the labour force after a childrearing period, and more recently, also returning to work between children; part-time employment allows them to accommodate the demands of domestic responsibilities and childrearing. However, one should be wary of endorsing the view that women have a 'taste' for part-time

Table 7.2 Labour force participation rates for women under 60,
1951–85, Great Britain
(percentage of population economically active)

	Full-time work	Any paid work	All economically active
1951	37	42	42
1961	35	49	50
1971	33	55	56
1975	33	60	62
1981	33	58	64
1985	33	60	66

Sources: 1951–61, Census of Population; 1971–85, General Household
Survey. The lower age limit is 15 for 1951–71 and 16 for 1975–85.
Table derived from Joshi (1988), Table 1.

jobs which are demonstrably exploitative jobs;[14] it may be that the
'taste' for part-time jobs is actually that of employers and that there is
a degree of underemployment of women who are in part-time jobs.
Certainly there are significant disincentives to full-time work for
women in the UK, on both the supply and the demand side of the
market. For example, the tax structure imposes high marginal rates
on married women who work more than part-time; and when it
comes to employee benefits and insurances, employers enjoy much
lower hourly labour costs with part-time employees than with full-
timers. Thus, in 1984, about 90 per cent of part-time workers were
cut out of pension schemes and about 30 per cent out of sick pay (*The
Economist*, 1984).

In their study of the 1980 Workplace Industrial Relations Survey,
Blanchflower and Corry (1989) address the question of whether
demand or supply effects dominate in the determination of part-time
employment patterns, but are unable to resolve it. However, they do
find evidence of employers identifying part-timers as an extremely
important, if not the most important element of a (desirable) flexible
labour force. This is reinforced by Hakim's study of the UK work
force (Hakim, 1987, p. 551).

3.2 Occupational Segregation

Another major feature of increased female economic activity is
discernable from the fairly sizeable body of research which indicates

that increased female economic activity has not been evenly distributed across industries and jobs; women are disproportionately represented in particular occupations, for example 'clerical and secretarial' and 'personal service' occupations (for example, cleaners and hairdressers).[15] Moreover, most female workers work only with other women: 63 per cent of women were working with others in the 1980 Women and Employment Survey (Martin and Roberts, 1984). But not only are women's jobs generally different from those held by men, they are also less likely to be near the top of occupational ladders.[16] This only serves to reinforce the established differentials between the pay received by men and women.

3.3 Earnings

Through the 1950s and 1960s, the ratio of women's to men's rates of hourly pay was something akin to a Great Constant of 60 per cent. However, the ratio of hourly pay rose sharply during the 1970s,[17] to over 70 per cent in 1977, a level which has been more or less maintained subsequently. The extent to which these differential returns to paid work are attributable to discrimination is notoriously difficult to establish, but the evidence available strongly suggests that discrimination is a force in the labour market and, even if it is diminishing through time, it still represents a cost in forgone earnings attributable to being female.[18] It discourages some women from pursuing career success and within the context of families rationalises the assumption that a husband's career takes priority and, given his higher earnings, gives him the power to resist suggestions that they share more evenly the domestic responsibilities and child care. In its turn of course it is the gendered division of family labour which is offered as another explanation for the lower level of women's pay: in particular, motherhood (which has become increasingly popular)[19] reduces the amount of time (both hours and years) a woman is available for paid work, typically interrupts[20] her employment experience, reduces her geographical mobility and tends to provoke downward occupational mobility.[21] These interrelated, and reinforcing, issues seem to have ensured that despite women's increased employment, their economic status has not improved substantially.[22] More than this, where women are not part of a two adult, male and female household partnership, they will continue to receive pay commensurate with being a woman, with its associated relative financial hardship.[23]

4 THE 1990s LABOUR MARKET

We therefore turn to the labour market for the 1990s knowing that it has a legacy of differential treatment of men and women. Additionally, it is a labour market which has recently experienced very high levels of unemployment,[24] leading some commentators to view the sharp reduction in new young entrants as something of a godsend. However, the scale of the reduction is so great that maintenance of a roughly static labour force can only be achieved by a marked increase in the participation rate of prime-age women and it should also be borne in mind that a virtually static labour force creates its own difficulties for the economy as a whole.[25] With a relatively static labour force, adjustment to structural change requires relatively greater mobility of the labour force, yet in the 1990s the changes in the labour force will be unfavourable to both geographical and occupational mobility: people in their 20s are the most mobile, yet this is the group which is shrinking, and many of the prime-age women will have limited geographical mobility (because of the limitations imposed by their family responsibilities and the growing number belonging to two career households) and limited upward occupational mobility (attributable to their relative age, which discourages their participation in further skill acquisition, even if the training opportunities are present). The relative tightness of the labour market portrayed may of itself bring about a slow growth economy with its attendant disadvantages and opportunities.[26] Any projections of future employment prospects are likely to be in the context of a slow growth economy.

Moreover, for the past 40 years there have been some marked changes in the way in which labour services have been utilised and all the indications are that these will continue into the future. Specifically, there has been a changing balance between the 'traditional' system of full-time jobs of indeterminate duration and more flexible types of work, favouring the latter. The sheer magnitudes involved have made this change seem most dramatic in the 1980s. The division of the whole labour force into just two sectors termed 'traditional' and 'flexible' oversimplifies the differences, but the distinction does make sense in terms of British labour law. The three most important – and overlapping – groups within the 'flexible' workforce are, in decreasing order of size: part-time work, self-employment and temporary work.

By 1986 about a quarter of the men and half the women in work were in 'the flexible workforce', which means that women contributed two-thirds of the total flexible workforce and one-third of the traditional. An important shift in the 1980s was that flexible work is now viewed in terms of its benefits to employers whereas in previous decades the focus was on benefits to workers (especially women). This is important when assessing the employment prospects for the future. Already employers' organisations are emphasising the need for change. Changes in the pattern and organisation of work are actively promoted by the Confederation of British Industry (CBI) (1985a, b) and the Institute of Directors (1985) following their own employer surveys and the results of a European Commission study which indicated that almost three-quarters of European industrial companies were dissatisfied with their working time arrangements (see Hakim, 1987), perhaps not least because the benefit costs were so much lower for employers of a flexible labour force.

5   PROJECTED EMPLOYMENT PROSPECTS FOR WOMEN

The general picture which is emerging is that of a labour market in which employers face recruitment difficulties because of the limited expansion of the labour supply. Moreover, they will need seriously to assess their willingness to substitute other groups of labour market participants for those they would in other circumstances have chosen to employ. This is true whatever the occupational post to be filled, whatever the industry in which they operate.

Some indication of the scale and directions of change required can be inferred from one of the richest sources of information on future employment prospects, both by industry and by occupation – the regular *Review of the Economy and Employment* produced by the Institute for Employment Research at the University of Warwick. The Institute has a good track record in employment projections for the UK economy. Their projections of the UK economy to 1995 are developed in the context of a model which predicts a downturn in the rate of growth of GDP from the almost 5 per cent achieved during 1987 to less than 2.5 per cent per annum to 1995. The Institute for Employment Research projects that aggregate employment will increase by 1.7 million (7 per cent) between 1987 and 1995.[27] This expansion of employment is greater than the projected (900 000) increase in the labour force over this period, giving some indication of the extent to which previously unemployed persons will be drawn into employment.

Table 7.3 Change in employment by broad industrial sector,
UK, 1954–95
(thousands)

	Production industries			Service industries			Whole economy		
	Male	Female	Total	Male	Female	Total	Male	Female	Total
1954–71	− 610	−192	− 802	+189	+1571	+1760	− 421	+1379	+ 958
1971–81	−1494	−592	−2086	+389	+1509	+1898	−1105	+ 917	− 188
1981–87	− 952	−289	−1241	+986	+ 885	+1871	+34	+ 596	+ 630
Projections:									
1987–95	− 108	− 18	− 126	+923	+ 926	+1849	+ 815	+ 908	+1723

Source: Derived from *Review of the Economy and Employment*, Institute for Employment Research, 1988/89, vol. 1, Table 4.

The structure of the projected employment is based upon detailed analysis of the industrial and occupational effects for males and females separately. Information on the way occupational structure has changed and is projected to develop up to 1995 is contained in Volume 2 of the *Review* (IER, 1989b) which is a collection of careful assessments of projected developments for each of the individual occupational groups. Over two-thirds of the additional jobs are projected to be part-time; and about 60 per cent of the additional jobs are projected to be filled by women. Compared with the experience of the past thirty years, this gender distribution of the increased employment is markedly less favourable to women: since the mid 1950s, women have obtained increases in total employment while, in aggregate, men have lost jobs (see Table 7.3).

5.1 Industrial Structure

The final row of Table 7.3 summarises the projected impact of changing industrial structure on employment needs for the period 1987 to 1995. The trend of rising service sector employment, apparent since the 1950s, seems set to continue, albeit with a roughly balanced gender distribution of the new jobs (which is in sharp contrast to the pre-1981 experience when over 80 per cent of the growth in service sector jobs went to women). The decline in overall production sector employment is projected to be modest relative to previous decades, with men gaining sufficient new employment opportunities in the construction sector to compensate for the losses in manufacturing. Over half of the new employment opportunities for

women are projected to be in the business and miscellaneous services
sector.

5.2 Occupational Changes

Some changes in occupational employment are attributable to
changes in industrial structure (industry effect) but others are due to
technical and organisational changes which affect the ways in which
goods and services are provided (occupational mix effect). The three
major trends which prompt change in occupational requirements are:
mechanisation, an increase in organisational complexity, and an increase in non-price competition. The first leads to capital substitution
and particularly affects the demand for manual occupations, but also
for clerical and secretarial. The other two tend to increase the
demand for managerial and marketing/sales occupations. Evidence
of strong occupational mix effects has been found in the growth of
managerial and administrative employment of men in the 1971–81
period and in the growth of female employment in sales occupations
in the period 1981–87.[28]

Yet, turning to the projections for the period 1987–95, it can be
seen from Figure 7.1 that increased employment of women is projected to occur in almost all the major occupational groups; the
exceptions being 'craft and skilled manual' and 'plant and machine
operatives'. Most of the growth is expected in the 'associate professional and technical' and 'clerical and secretarial' occupations, two
groups where females are expected to benefit disproportionately.
Over 20 per cent of the enhanced opportunities for female employment are predicted to be in the 'associate professional and technical'
occupations, largely in health care, to which the industry and occupational effects contribute roughly equally. But almost as many
opportunities will be in the 'clerical and secretarial' occupations
where the occupational effect of, for example, capital substitution is
expected to reduce employment, but the industry effect will more
than outweigh it. However, the gender composition of the associate
professional group shows that women are concentrated in the lower
paid, lower status jobs such as laboratory technicians, nurses and
social welfare associated professionals (Green, Baker and Owen,
1989). Moreover, women constitute the majority of the sub-group
'health and associated professionals' for whom increases in pay have
not only consistently lagged behind that for the occupational group as
a whole but have also lagged behind that of the secretarial and
clerical occupational groups.[29]

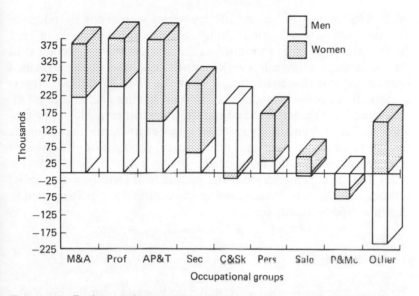

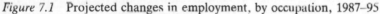

Figure 7.1 Projected changes in employment, by occupation, 1987–95

Source: Institute for Employment Research, Warwick.
Note: Occupational groups:

M&A	Managers and administrators
Prof	Professional occupations
AP&T	Associate professional and technical occupations
Sec	Clerical and secretarial occupations
C&Sk	Craft and skilled manual occupations
Pers	Personal and protective service occupations
Sale	Sales occupations
P&Mc	Plant and machine operatives
Other	Other occupations

For a full enumeration of occupations assigned to each occupational group see *Review of the Economy and Employment*, Institute for Employment Research, 1988/89, vol. 1, Table A6.

5.3 Occupational Segregation

Data on women's employment rates in major occupational groups for the period 1971–87 provides evidence of persistent occupational segregation, as measured by the percentage of women in each occupational group.[30] Also, there is evidence that over time there is greater segregation, rather than integration, of the sexes in employment. For example, in 1971, 45 per cent of supervisors were women;

yet by 1987 almost 70 per cent of supervisors were women. Indeed of the nine occupational groups designated as strongly female in 1971 (in that the percentage of women in the occupation was greater than the percentage women in employment), only one of them (skilled operatives) lost this characteristic over the 1971–87 period. Nevertheless, there is some evidence of women having gained ground in, for example, managerial and administrative positions,[31] lower professions and most dramatically in sales representatives positions; but the overall picture is of persistent occupational segregation with women over-represented in the lower grades of work.

By 1995 it is projected that the picture will look broadly similar although the literary, artistic and sports occupations are expected to become predominantly female.

6   ASSESSMENT

To assess whether women will make relative gains over the 1990s, it is first useful to note some crude estimates of market pressure in the 1990s labour market. Interpreting the IER projections as a rough proxy for demand over the period 1987–95, the total increase in demand for workers exceeds the projected increase in the labour force by about three-quarters of a million (see Table 7.1). As already indicated, this gives some indication of the likely reduction in unemployment which in mid 1987 stood at 2.8 million. If one considers separate markets for men and women workers, the IER projected increase in the demand for women exceeds the increase in the female labour force by approximately one quarter of a million; the projected increase in the demand for men exceeds their increase in the labour force by approximately one half a million. The mid-1987 stock of registered unemployed women and men stood at 0.8 million and 2 million respectively.

If employers seeking new recruits (for 'male jobs') look to the pool of unemployed men more readily than they will overcome traditional gender segregation, then the market pressure to achieve change is relatively modest. This is important as claims that women will do well from the conditions of the 1990s labour market are in part based upon the assumption that employers with recruitment difficulties will turn to women workers and not to the unemployed. This is not to say that the outlook is pessimistic for women: it is not.

By the mid 1990s, women will be more heavily represented in paid work than ever before and this represents some gain in their economic status. Yet, of itself, increasing the female contribution to UK employment does not necessarily imply greater emancipation of women. It matters what kind of work these women do. Research findings confirm both unequal treatment of women and men in the labour market and marked effects of family responsibilities on women's experiences in work. Over the past 40 years, despite growing access to paid work, women continue to do segregated jobs; there is little evidence of any significant breakdown in occupational segregation, indeed the evidence suggests the reverse and that vertical segregation seems to have increased. Also, despite the improvement in the late 1970s, there has been no marked improvement in the relative hourly earnings of women workers; indeed, there is now some sign of erosion. Thus, entry of more women into paid employment has not been accompanied by any lessening of inequalities between women and men once in employment.

In order to further women's equality with men it is necessary to demand not only the right to work, but also the right to work in conditions which are compatible with women's continued domestic responsibilities and, in particular, work in conditions which are compatible with motherhood. In the 1990s, projections are that over 80 per cent of women who have reached childbearing age will be mothers and, in the UK, it is full-time employment which is difficult to combine with motherhood, not part-time.[32]

The climate of the 1990s is right to see an expansion of this type of employment opportunity; what has already become clear in the 1980s is that employers have increasingly displayed a desire to employ workers part-time and on other flexible arrangements (see, for example, CBI, 1985a and 1985b; Hakim, 1987). The demographic dip has pushed the focus on women as the largest single source of new recruits and there will be some matching of increased employment opportunities with the kind of work that women find compatible with domestic responsibilities. For some women, simply the opportunity to secure paid work on this basis will be a major advance, but to view the 1990s as a great opportunity for women in a more general sense there needs to be some indication that significant numbers of women will be securing paid work which offers equal pay and equal status for equal work, and equal opportunities for career ambitions.

It is helpful to identify three categories of women in the 1990s labour market: young skilled women with high levels of educational attainment, older (prime-age) unskilled women and older skilled women. In general terms, employers will face relative difficulty in recruiting the young people they demand – a demand based either on the fact that young people are relatively cheap labour or because they are to become long-term employees. In the former case, unskilled, older women may well prove to be a good substitute and therefore this group of women will gain jobs they would not otherwise have secured. However, they will constitute a group with little bargaining power to secure higher wages or other attractive elements of a remuneration package. To the extent that these women will work part-time, there is likely to be an overall shift from full-time jobs held by the young to part-time jobs held by older women.

Where employers choose young workers because they have long-term employment objectives, the situation will be different. Often the objective is to train people on the job, thereby creating a career track within the sector. This would be typical in certain professional occupations where profession-specific qualifications are acquired on the job, for example accounting and banking.[33] In this case employers will have a strong preference for the young worker, competition for this young cohort will therefore be strong and employers will have to make better job offers to secure the young people they want. Young women should find themselves in high demand, but what constitutes a good job offer to a young person is important here: in general, young people's perceptions of a good job offer are likely to be dominated by the level of pay offered (see Sandell and Shapiro, 1980). We might therefore predict that the young, highly-skilled women of the 1990s will take their gains from being part of a small cohort in the form of higher pay.

The final group of women – the older skilled women – are the group most likely to gain non-pecuniary benefits[34] – especially in the short-term. For this group of women, a good job offer will place more emphasis on their ability to combine motherhood and other domestic responsibilities with paid work. Employers trying to attract this group of workers will need first and foremost to respond to this requirement. To the extent that they face further recruitment difficulties they will need to respond further with higher pay offers.

In analysing the effects on these different groups, two factors should be remembered. First, the decline in the number of young people is much less marked amongst the professional, managerial, senior administrative and skilled, non-manual occupations which, historically, exhibit higher participation rates in voluntary education

(16 plus).[35] Secondly, whilst the proportion of young people staying on in voluntary schooling has been increasing for both males and females over the past 20 years, the female participation rate has exceeded the male since the early 1970s. One outcome of this is that, for females, the percentage of the relevant age group attaining 2 or more A-levels (a basic requirement for degree-level higher education) has risen to equal that for males. These changes point to there being a rising proportion of highly educated women in the population as a whole. Thus, younger women will do much better than they have done in the past simply because they have the potential to move into new occupations; most older women are already locked into relatively low-paying occupations.

In summary, in the labour market of the 1990s, young skilled women will gain money, older unskilled women will gain the opportunity to be in paid work (but with no obvious improvements in conditions of that type of paid work) and older skilled women may gain a return for paid work which has the potential to become employment with equal pay and status to that received by men. These changes could set the pattern for the future: once older women have secured improved economic status, future generations may be afforded similar status. But the general prospect for change should not be exaggerated. This paper has suggested that the degree of pressure to bring about change may not be that great. Employers facing recruitment difficulties may turn to the pool of male unemployed in preference to women and, to the extent that more flexible jobs (which favour women's employment prospects) become available, there will be new participants in the labour force like students who wish to combine wage-earning activities with other activities.[36] Women could face more competition for paid employment opportunities than has been officially recognised and will need to be pro-active, not simply reactive, in their fight for equal economic status in the 1990s.

This will of course come as no surprise to those who have consistently argued that the labour market itself constitutes an important source of economic inequality. Feminists will be among the first to stress that the relative size of age cohorts is not the primary determinant of the gender distribution of employment; and to insist that public policies must remain the focus of attention. If women are to improve their economic status in the labour market of the 1990s they will need to continue the fight for changes in the tax and benefit provisions which disadvantage women and part-time workers; and campaign for the type of child care policies and facilities which have contributed to the more equal female labour force participation observable in, for example, France and Sweden. They will need to break down the barriers to the appointment of women to certain occupational positions, encouraging organisations to adopt good practice in making appointments and defining work conditions – for example, conducting equal opportunity audits, adopting equal opportunity targets and objective assessment criteria, dropping age limits on jobs, offering career break schemes, paternal leave and child care vouchers.[37] The demographic influences on the labour market of the 1990s offer an opportunity for change. However, unless existing barriers are rapidly dismantled, women will continue to be denied equal access to many occupational positions.

Notes

1. In preparing the final version of this paper, I have greatly benefited from both the comments and the editorial advice given by Nancy Folbre. She is, of course, not responsible for any errors or misinterpretations.
2. For example, the numbers aged 16–19 in the population will have fallen by almost 1 million, or approximately 25 per cent, between 1983 and 1993 (Population Projections, Series PP2 no. 13, Office of Population Censuses and Surveys, London).
3. *Employment Gazette*, March 1988, pp. 118–19. The labour force is defined as people in employment and unemployed people. Also known as the working population or the economically active population.
4. This is not to suggest that the Government is abdicating all responsibility: its own contribution is largely through training initiatives undertaken by the Training Agency.
5. The rise in the prime-age female labour force is strongly influenced by an increased activity effect; 44 per cent of the increase in women's participation is attributable to an increased activity effect (and not a population effect) (*Employment Gazette*, March 1988). The reasons for the projected increased activity effects are set out in detail in Joshi and Overton (1988). For studies of the post-war increase in women's participation rates (from 42 to 66 per cent for women aged under 60, in the period 1951 to 1985), see Joshi, Layard and Owen (1985) and Sprague (1988).
6. See Costrell *et al.* (1986), Hamermesh and Grant (1979) and Freeman (1979).
7. See Bluestone and Harrison (1988), Welch (1979) and Ermisch (1988).
8. See Levine and Mitchell (1988), Pike (1985) and Ermisch (1983, pp. 145–52).
9. It could therefore be anticipated that the highly educated subset of young workers will gain most from the demographic dip, although young

women may well not fare as well as young men (see Dolton and Makepeace (1986)).

10. Of course, during the second World War, women took jobs which were once the prerogative of men and indeed constituted a large fraction of the labour force. But these changes were largely temporary: after the war, most women gave up their paid jobs. The post-war changes, notably since the 1950s, show no signs of being temporary.

11. The increase in employment was most marked amongst women with dependent children. Roughly the same proportion (69 per cent) of women without dependent children were in employment in 1979 as in 1973; however, the percentage of mothers of dependent children in employment rose from 47 to 52 per cent over the same period (General Household Survey reports published by HMSO). For evidence on the stability of women's employment see Tzannatos and Zabalza (1985).

12. For a more detailed account, see Ermisch (1983), Chapter 4 'The evolution of the UK labour market'.

13. See Blau and Ferber (1986, pp. 304–32) for a discussion of criteria which could be used to measure economic status.

14. The Department of Employment, in their submission to the House of Lords Select Committee investigating part-time employment, expressed the view that 'while there are clearly disadvantages which part-timers suffer in relation to full-timers, it is possible to see this as a price which part-timers are prepared to pay for the opportunity to fit work into other commitments', House of Lords Select Committee on the European Communities, *Voluntary Part-Time Work*, House of Lords Paper no. 216, Session 1981–82, 19th report, quoted in Walsh (1989). However, the issue is not whether or not part-time work is an attractive part of an employment package for which one pays a 'price', but how high a 'price' is placed upon this element of the package. See Hurstfield (1978) for a clear demonstration of the exploitative nature of part-time work; and Walsh (1989) for evidence that some employers take the view that their provision of part-time work meets individuals' own circumstances and therefore justifies less favourable treatment of the workers.

15. See Hakim (1979) and Joseph (1983). At the 1981 Census, three-quarters of all women workers were in just four of the 16 occupational orders, where they outnumbered men: personal services, clerical, professional workers in education and health and welfare (mainly school teachers and nurses) and selling (predominantly shop assistants) (Joshi, 1989).

16. Miller (1987) shows that gender wage differentials derive largely from wage differences *within* occupations.

17. This coincided with the implementation of the Equal Pay Act which was probably the explanation; see, for example, Zabalza and Tzannatos (1985).

18. It is important to recognise that the question is not about whether discrimination is totally absent, but whether it represents an important influence on returns to women's labour efforts. Recent work on the 1946 birth cohort in the UK, found 'there was an unexplained excess of men's pay over women's pay worth about 30 per cent of that received by the average 32 year old female employee in early 1978' (Joshi, 1989, p. 168).

Interpreting this unexplained gap as some measure of discrimination, the scale of discrimination was found to be markedly high for women with no educational qualifications and low occupational attainments and again for women graduates, reinforcing the findings of Dolton and Makepeace (1986).

19. For every 10 women born around the turn of the century, about three never bore any children. For the post-World War II generations over eight in 10 are projected to become mothers themselves (Ermisch, 1983; Joshi, 1988). Also, families are on average becoming smaller, the most likely number of children is now two (Central Statistical Office, 1989, p. 46). The average age at which women give birth to their first and subsequent children has been rising since the early 1970s and this trend has contributed to the historically low levels of overall fertility rates experienced during the period (see Werner, 1987).

20. The number of women who work continuously is a very small minority which has not increased in 20 years despite the statutory provision of maternity leave (Daniel, 1980; Martin and Roberts, 1984).

21. Several studies of British data have found evidence of occupational downgrading after childbearing (Dex, 1987; Stewart and Greenhalgh, 1984; Martin and Roberts, 1984; and Joshi and Newell, 1987).

22. For example, Greenhalgh and Stewart (1985) conclude that while single women have gained some ground in the labour market 'as a consequence of society's reassessment of men's and women's roles', married women have been inhibited by family responsibility from gaining access to higher occupations.

23. It should be remembered that this must be viewed in the light of an increasing proportion of women (one in four households) being in the role of main breadwinner (Coyle, 1988, p. 5).

24. The annual average unemployment in the UK from 1981 to 1988 was always in excess of 2 million (8 per cent), and was over 3 million in 1985 and 1986. (*Employment Gazette*, Historical Supplement, no. 1, April 1989).

25. See Ermisch (1982) for an analysis of the economic problems associated with a relatively static labour force.

26. Kindleberger (1967) and Schmitt (1977) have both attributed the slow growth of the post-war UK economy, relative to other European countries, to the UK's slow rate of labour force growth.

27. The results have been subjected to sensitivity analysis and the IER reports a relative lack of sensitivity of the overall occupational structure of employment to fairly large variations in some of the key exogenous assumptions underlying the macroeconomic and industrial employment scenario (IER, 1989, p. 29).

28. See Tables in the Annex to IER (1989); or, for summarised data, see Evans (1990) and the tables therein. The occupational groups now used by the IER are based upon the Standard Occupational Classifications being developed for the Department of Employment and the Government Statistical Service. These are summarised in the *Employment Gazette*, April 1988, pp. 214–21.

29. One special point to be made about the secretarial and clerical group is

that there are good reasons for anticipating that the projected expansion in employment for this occupational group may not reflect a corresponding expansion in hours worked. For example, in the period 1979–86, while part-time secretarial jobs increased by 33 per cent, full-time jobs declined by around 9 per cent (Whitfield, Baker and Owen, 1989) possibly indicating a creation of part-time job opportunities filled by women returners at the expense of full-time opportunities which might have been taken by young women. This is of course a general issue. Given that the vast majority of the expansion in women's employment has been part-time, the full-time equivalent female input to the paid economy is less than that indicated by rising activity rates.

30. See *Review of the Economy and Employment*, Institute for Employment Research, 1985/6, vol. 2; and *Review of Economy and Employment, Occupational Update*, 1988. Summarised data are to be found in Table 5 of Evans (1990).

31. This is consistent with Beller's evidence that any observed decline in occupational segregation has been most pronounced for new and recent entrants to the labour market and for managerial and professional jobs. (Beller, 1984, 1985). It should be made clear that Beller's findings of reductions in occupational segregation in the 1970s are in contrast to findings for earlier periods (Dex and Sloane, 1988).

32. See evidence in Wright and Hinde (1988). It may also be relevant to point out here the evidence on the gender distribution of unpaid work: Gershuny *et al.* estimate that women averaged 16 hours per week more than men in 1983–84, somewhat less than the 26 hour finding in 1961 (evidence quoted in Joshi, 1989). Clearly, a continued change in male attitudes to their domestic responsibilities is also a mechanism through which women might achieve greater labour market equality. Moreover, public policies such as those relating to child care have important implications here: for example, in France, a large percentage of women work full-time, facilitated by appropriate child care arrangements.

33. This is not to suggest that this is only a characteristic of professional occupations: certainly, old-style apprenticeships have similar characteristics.

34. When Myrdal and Klein (1956) were making a case for women's right to paid work they regarded part-time work as a mechanism by which women could combine their dual roles. Since then, part-time work has come to be used rather more to the advantage of employers as an effective way to obtain a flexible workforce. This is, of course, not surprising but it should serve to remind us that only if employers find it to their advantage will they provide for women's child care needs.

35. As a percentage of all live births, those occurring to families in the professional, managerial, senior administrative and skilled, non-manual occupations – social classes I, II and IIIN (non-manual) – remained fairly constant (at around 27 per cent) between 1959 and 1965. Since then the proportion has risen, reaching 40 per cent in 1980, largely reflecting movements in occupational structure, not differentials in fertility by social class. (Royal Society, 1983, Table 1.10; Department of Education and Science, 1984, p. 3).

36. In the UK the move to student loan financing must increase the search for flexible employment by students.
37. For a recent public declaration of the need to institute such changes, see Hansard Society Commission (1990).

References

Beller, A. (1984) 'Trends in Occupational Segregation by Sex and Race, 1960–81', in Berskin, B. (ed.) *Sex Segregation in the Workplace* (Washington DC: National Academy Press), pp. 11–26.

Beller, A. (1985) 'Changes in the Sex Composition of US Occupations, 1960–1981', *Journal of Human Resources*, vol. 20, pp. 235–50.

Blanchflower, D. and Corry, B. (1989) *Part-time Employment in Great Britain. An Analysis Using Establishment Data*, Research Paper no. 57, Department of Employment, London.

Blau, F. D. and Ferber, M. A. (1986) *The Economics of Women, Men and Work* (Englewood Cliffs, NJ: Prentice-Hall).

Bluestone, B. and Harrison, B. (1988) 'The Growth of Low-wage Employment: 1963–86', *American Economic Review*, vol. 78, pp. 124–8.

CBI (1985a) *Change to Succeed: The Nationwide Findings* (London: Confederation of British Industry).

CBI (1985b) *Managing Change: The Organisation of Work* (London: Confederation of British Industry).

CSO (1989) 'Households and Families', *Social Trends*, vol. 19 (London: HMSO), pp. 35–49.

Costrell, R. M., DuGuay, G. E. and Treyz, G. I. (1986) 'Labour Substitution and Complementarity Among Age-sex Groups', *Applied Economics*, vol. 18, pp. 777–91.

Coyle, A. (1988) 'Introduction – Continuity and Change: Women in Paid Work', in Coyle, A. and Skinner, J. (eds) *Women and Work: Positive Action for Change* (London: Macmillan), pp. 1–12.

Daniel, W. W. (1980) *Maternity Rights: The Experience of Women*, PSI Report no. 596 (London: Policy Studies Institute).

Department of Education and Science (1984) *Demand for Higher Education in Great Britain 1984–2000*, Report on Education no. 100 (London: HMSO).

Department of Employment (1988) *Employment for the 1990s* (London: HMSO).

Dex, S. (1987) *Women's Occupational Mobility* (London: Macmillan).

Dex, S. and Sloane, P. J. (1988) 'Detecting and Removing Discrimination under Equal Opportunities Policies', *Journal of Economic Surveys*, vol. 2, pp. 1–28.

Dolton, P. J. and Makepeace, G. H. (1986) 'Sample Selection and Male–female Earnings Differentials in the Graduate Labour Market', *Oxford Economic Papers*, vol. 38, pp. 317–41.

Economist, The (1984) 'Part-timers: The Market at Work', *The Economist*, 29 September.

Ermisch, J. (1982) 'The Future Operation of the Labour Market', in Eversley, D. and Kollman, W. (eds) *Population Change and Social Planning* (London: Edward Arnold), pp. 210–69.

Ermisch, J. (1983) *The Political Economy of Demographic Change* (London: Heinemann).

Ermisch, J. (1988) 'Fortunes of Birth: The Impact of Generation Size on the Relative Earnings of Young Men', *Scottish Journal of Political Economy*, vol. 35, pp. 266–82.

Evans, L. (1990) 'The "Demographic-Dip": A Golden Opportunity for Women in the Labour Market?', *National Westminster Bank Quarterly Review*, February, pp. 48–69.

Freeman, R. B. (1979) 'The Effect of Demographic Factors on Age-Earnings Profiles', *Journal of Human Resources*, vol. 14, pp. 289–318.

Green, A. E., Baker, M. and Owen, D. W. (1989) 'Associate Professional and Technical Occupations', Occupational Study 3 in *Review of Economy and Employment, Occupational Studies*, Institute for Employment Research, University of Warwick.

Greenhalgh, C. and Stewart, M. B. (1985) 'The Occupational Status and Mobility of British Men and Women, 1965–75', *Oxford Economic Papers*, vol. 37, pp. 40–71.

Hakim, C. (1979) *Occupational Segregation*, Research Paper no. 9, Department of Employment, London.

Hakim, C. (1987) 'Trends in the Flexible Workforce', *Employment Gazette*, November, pp. 549–60.

Hansard Society Commission, The (1990) *The Report of The Hansard Society Commission on Women at the Top*, The Hansard Society for Parliamentary Government, London.

Hamermesh, D. S. and Grant, J. H. (1979) 'Econometric Studies of Labor Substitution and Their Implications for Policy', *Journal of Human Resources*, vol. 14, pp. 518–42.

Hurstfield, J. (1978) *The Part-Time Trap*, Low Pay Unit, London.

IER (1989) *Review of the Economy and Employment. Occupational Assessment*, 1988/89 – vol. 1, Institute for Employment Research, University of Warwick.

Institute of Directors (1985) *Labour Market Changes and Opportunities: New Patterns of Work* Institute of Directors, London.

Joseph, G. (1983) *Women at Work. The British Experience* (Deddington: Philip Allan).

Joshi, H (1988) 'Changing Roles of Women in the British Labour Market and the Family', Birkbeck College Discussion Paper in Economics, 88/13.

Joshi, H. (1989) 'The Changing Form of Women's Economic Dependency' in Joshi, H. (ed.) *The Changing Population of Britain* (Oxford: Basil Blackwell), pp. 157–76.

Joshi, H., Layard, R. and Owen, S. (1985) 'Why are More Women Working in Britain?' *Journal of Labour Economics*, Supp., vol. 3, pp. S147–76.

Joshi, H. and Newell, M.-L. (1987) 'Job Downgrading after Childbearing', in Uncles, M. (ed.) *London Papers in Regional Science 18. Data Analysis: Methods and Applications* (London: Pion), pp. 89–102.

Joshi, H. and Overton, E. (1988) 'Forecasting the Female Labour Force in

Britain', *International Journal of Forecasting*, vol. 4, pp. 269–85.

Kindleberger, C. P. (1967) *Europe's Post-War Growth – The Role of Labor Supply* (Cambridge, Massachusetts: Harvard University Press).

Levine, P. B. and Mitchell, O. S. (1988) 'The Baby Boom's Legacy: Relative Wages in the Twenty-first Century', *American Economic Review*, vol. 78, pp. 66–9.

Martin, J. and Roberts, C. M. (1984) *Women and Employment: A Lifetime Perspective* (London: HMSO).

Miller, P. W. (1987) 'The Wage Effect of the Occupational Segregation of Women in Britain', *Economic Journal*, vol. 97, pp. 885–96.

Myrdal, A. and Klein, V. (1956) *Women's Two Roles* (London: Routledge and Kegan Paul).

Pike, M. (1985) 'The Employment Response to Equal Pay Legislation', *Oxford Economic Papers*, vol. 37, pp. 304–18.

Royal Society, The (1983) 'Demographic Trends and Future University Candidates', Working Paper, April, The Royal Society, London.

Sandell, S. H. and Shapiro, D. (1980) 'Work Expectations, Human Capital Accumulation and the Wages of Young Women', *Journal of Human Resources*, vol. 15, pp. 336–53.

Schmitt, H. O. (1977) 'Labor Shortage, Excess Demand Hindered Postwar Growth of UK', *IMF Survey*, June, pp. 162–4.

Sprague, A. (1988) 'Post-war Fertility and Female Labour Force Participation Rates', *Economic Journal*, vol. 98, pp. 682–700.

Stewart, M. B. and Greenhalgh, C. (1984) 'Work History Patterns and the Occupational Attainment of Women', *Economic Journal*, vol. 94, pp. 493–515.

Tzannatos, Z. and Zabalza, A. (1985) 'The Effect of Sex Anti-discriminatory Legislation on the Variability of Female Employment in Britain', *Applied Economics* vol. 17, pp. 1117–34.

Walsh, T. (1989) 'Part-time Employment and Labour Market Policies', *National Westminster Bank Quarterly Review*, May, pp. 43–55.

Welch, F. (1979) 'Effects of Cohort Size on Earnings: The Baby Boom Babies' Financial Bust', *Journal of Political Economy*, vol. 87, pp. 565–97.

Werner, B. (1987) 'Fertility Statistics from Birth Registration in England and Wales, 1837–1987', *Population Trends*, vol. 48, pp. 4–10.

Whitfield, K., Baker, M. and Owen, D. W. (1989) 'Clerical and Secretarial Occupations', in Occupational Study 4 in *Review of the Economy and Employment, Occupational Studies*, Institute for Employment Research, University of Warwick.

Wright, R. E. and Hinde, P. R. A. (1988) 'The Dynamics of Female Labour Force Participation in Great Britain', Centre for Population Studies Research Paper 88–3, London School of Hygiene and Tropical Medicine.

Zabalza, A. and Tzannatos, Z. (1985) 'The Effect of Britain's Anti-discrimination Legislation on Relative Pay and Employment', *Economic Journal*, vol. 95, pp. 679–99.

8 Union Density and Women's Relative Wage Gains

Jean Fletcher and Sandra Gill

GETTYSBURG COLLEGE, USA

1 INTRODUCTION

The drive to improve wages and working conditions which accompanied the industrial revolutions in democratic countries has primarily been a men's movement. In virtually all countries, the vast majority of strikes have been in industries in which men predominate and union leadership has tended to be a male prerogative. In part this is explicable in terms of the greater importance of wage work to men than to women since the early stages of the industrial revolution. In a number of countries women's employment was crucial in the early stages of industrialisation, yet many women tended to see wage work as occupying brief periods in their lives rather than as a lifetime commitment.

This view of women as sporadic participants in the labour force has been rapidly changing as more and more women work for pay throughout their lives. Clearly women who do work for pay in the labour force are faced with problems similar to those which led many men to organise into unions. Working women seek to improve wages and working conditions. Over the past two decades occupational segregation and the wage differential between men and women have received considerable attention. So has the movement to make working conditions more compatible with women's reproductive and family roles and to allow men to take a larger share in these roles. The question we address here is whether labour unions are a viable vehicle for improving the relative wages of women.

2   UNION TRADITIONS

The issues of women's wages and working conditions have a clear impact on men's positions. Women have historically been paid lower wages for their work than have men in all countries for which such data are available, so it is not surprising that larger numbers of women working for longer periods would be perceived as a threat to men's jobs. Unions have generally tried either to discourage women from working, at least in the jobs in which men predominate, or to gain for women the wages men receive, thereby reducing their attractiveness as employees.

Historically, examples of both types of responses to women's lower wages can be found; however, unions' responses tended toward excluding women workers from direct competition with men.[1] As far back as 1919, the constitution of the International Labour Organisation (ILO) incorporated the idea that women and men should get equal pay for work of equal value (ILO, 1987, p. 266). Cook *et al.* (1984) note that early union efforts to establish equal pay were often intended to protect the jobs of men: 'They made demands on employers for equal pay for equal work in the expectation that under these circumstances employers would prefer to hire men and therefore women would be employed less and less' (Cook *et al.*, 1984, p. 13).

In Sweden the labour movement has played a central role in improving women's wages and working conditions. With approximately 90 per cent of workers in unions or employee associations, Sweden has perhaps the highest rates of unionisation in the world (ILO, 1987). Sweden is also the model country which illustrates the potential for equal wages for women and for working conditions which allow both parents to maintain employment when they have children. The wage gap in Sweden is lower than in any other country for which data are available. Women's average hourly wage in manufacturing was 87 per cent of that of men in 1977 (OECD, 1980). In addition, Sweden has been a leader in shaping working conditions through contract negotiations and legislation to facilitate parenting. For example, new parents may share up to nine months of parental leave at full pay. A parent may take up to sixty days off each year to care for sick children and may reduce work hours to six hours per day until a child is 8 (OECD, 1980, pp. 245–68). Sweden's National Labour Market Board supervises the public Employment Service and is the central planning and advisory group for national labour market issues. The board is composed of union, employer and government representatives. This board has as a specific task promoting equality between men and women in the labour market.[2]

Steinberg and Cook (1988) point out that women in Sweden and other highly unionised countries have higher relative earnings and argue that increasing the unionisation of women as well as increasing the role of women in union leadership are critically important steps towards achieving equality in labour markets. A systematic approach to assessing modern unions' position in the struggle for gender equality would examine women's wages and working conditions in highly unionised countries in contrast with less unionised countries.

Women's labour force participation has been increasing rapidly, and women are becoming a larger share of union membership. Thus, unions acting rationally should be working towards wage equality. In countries such as the United States and the Netherlands where union membership has been declining for some time, women represent a potential for union growth. Freeman and Medoff (1984) cite survey data showing that non-unionised women are more likely than non-unionised men to vote for union representation; they attribute the low fraction of women in unions in the United States to the lower unionisation in industries where women's jobs are clustered. As women become a larger fraction of the voting members, union leaders wishing to maintain their positions would place greater emphasis on issues of interest to women.[3] Also, gender wage equality ensures that men will not be replaced by cheaper female labour. Unions in many countries are highly committed not only to economic unionism – winning gains for their own members – but also to social unionism – winning gains for all working people whether organised or not.

Despite growing participation in the labour force and in unions in many countries, we know of no nation in which women hold anything close to a proportional share of union leadership positions.[4] While this may improve in the future, in the short run men will continue to dominate. Can women work within a predominantly male hierarchy to improve their wages and working conditions?

Labour unions and their effectiveness in influencing public policy vary tremendously. Type of national government, the nature of union political association, type and density of union coverage, cultural and social factors, and collective bargaining legislation are but a few of the variables that affect the role of trade unions in improving working conditions and earnings for women and men.

Recognising the complexity of the relationship between union membership and earnings, an examination of aggregate union density and relative earnings over the past decade was undertaken to determine whether a discernible pattern could be found of greater wage equality for women in nations with strong union traditions.

3   RELATIVE WAGES AND UNION DENSITY

Grouping countries by degree of unionisation or union density (the percentage of the economically active population holding union membership), the ratio of women's to men's average hourly earnings (F/M wage ratio) is shown for 19 countries in Table 8.1. These countries were selected only because data were not readily available for other countries.

Sweden and several other highly unionised countries have high relative earnings for women, but there are numerous inversions – cases of countries with lower unionisation rates having higher relative earnings for women (such as the comparison of France and Belgium). This is not surprising, as there are many other determinants of relative wages. Scandinavian countries seem to have higher ratios in general; they also have governments with explicit commitments to enhancing social equality. Overall, the wage ratio is positively correlated with union density.

Also interesting is the rate of change of relative earnings over the last decade. The last column of Table 8.1 shows the percentage change in the ratio of female to male hourly earnings from 1970 to 1980. With very few exceptions, those countries with 50 per cent or greater unionisation have higher, usually much higher, percentage increases in women's relative earnings than those countries with less than 50 per cent union density. Also striking is the fact that those nations where unions are explicitly linked to political parties – such as Denmark, Sweden, Australia, and the United Kingdom[5] – have much higher than average gains for women over the decade.

Figure 8.1 is a plot of the average annual growth rate of the F/M wage ratio by union density for the 13 countries for which union density percentages are shown in Table 8.1. Shown in Figure 8.2 are the averages (noted by black circles) and standard deviations (dispersion of the averages) for the annual growth rates of the relative wage from 1970 to 1980 for all of the countries in Table 8.1 grouped by union density category.

As with any international comparison, these results are only

Table 8.1 Comparison of the degree of unionisation and women's relative earnings in selected industrialised countries, early 1980s

Country	Union density (per cent)		Women's LF share (per cent)	F/M wage ratio (per cent)	Percentage change in wage ratio, 1970–80
Sweden		87	46	90	12
Belgium		73	38	69	4
Denmark	> 70	72	44	85	17
Finland			47	75	7
Austria		65	39	72[a]	5[a]
Norway		62	40	82	9
Australia		57	36	86	32
United Kingdom	50–70	56	39	70	16
Ireland			28	69	22
Italy			33	83	12
Luxembourg			30	65	14
German Federal Republic		41	38	72	5
Netherlands		41	30	78	6
Canada	30–50	35	41	63[b]	8[b]
Switzerland		33	35	67	7
Greece			32	68	3[c]
New Zealand			34	77	4[d]
France		19	39	79	2[e]
United States	< 30	25	42	64[f]	3

Sources: Union density: For Sweden, Austria, FRG and France ranges of trade union membership as percentage of economically active population from ILO (1987) p. 112. Other figures are for 1981 (1978 for Austria and Norway) from Windmuller *et al.* (1987), page 19; for Switzerland and France from Troy and Sheflin (1985); Australian figure is for 1976 from Bain and Price (1980) p. 124.

Women's LF share: Calculated from economically active population by sex in ILO (1987) pp. 278–82. Figures are for 1981 except for Netherlands (1979) and Italy, United Kingdom, and Switzerland (all 1980). Data for Greece (1980) and Australia, Norway, and Austria (1977) are from OECD (1985), p. 14. Years are chosen as close as possible to year for union density figure.

F/M wage ratio: Ratio of women's to men's average hourly earnings in non-agricultural activities, from OECD (1985), p. 70.

Notes: [a] Based on 1979 data, 1980 unavailable.

[b] Data from *Women in the Workplace*, Statistics Canada, 1987, p. 68.

[c] Calculated using 1968 and 1977 data from OECD (1980) p. 32.

[d] Based on 1975 and 1982 data, 1970 unavailable.

[e] Based on 1973 and 1981 data, 1970 unavailable.

[f] Calculated from median weekly earnings of full-time wage and salary workers by sex from BLS (1982) for 1970 and BLS (1989) for 1980.

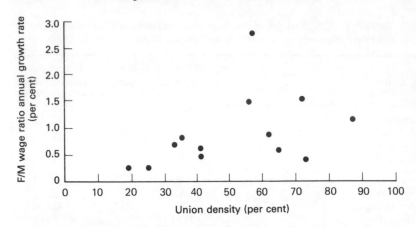

Figure 8.1 Annual growth rate in F/M wage ratio, 1970–80, by union density

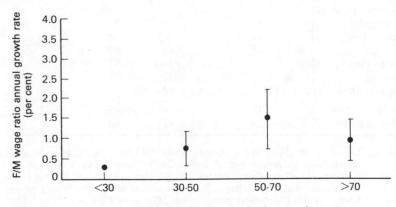

Figure 8.2 Average and standard deviation of annual growth rate in F/M wage ratio by union density range

suggestive, given the inconsistencies in the data. Even data collected by the same organisation in the same series may have variations in definitions across countries (such as the age of the relevant working population, the basis on which earnings are reported, the types of unions included in union density figures, and the years in which data are available). However, we have tried to be as consistent as possible in comparing wage ratios and their changes over time. These results are indicative of a relationship between unionisation and trends toward greater equality for women.

An obvious question is whether women represent a larger fraction of union members in those countries where relative wages are high and/or relative wage gains have been large. Table 8.2 displays information on women as a proportion of union membership. The highest proportions of women union members occur in Scandinavian countries (apart from Norway). Women's share of union membership grew during the 1970s in most of the countries reporting such data.[6] As noted earlier, women's proportion of union leadership has not grown as rapidly as women's proportion of membership.

The last two columns in Table 8.2 display women's union density (the fraction of women in the labour force who are union members) and the ratio of women's union density to men's union density. These values are calculated from the union density and women's labour force share information in Table 8.1 and the fraction of union members who are women from Table 8.2. For the 13 countries with union density measures in Table 8.1, the annual growth rate of the relative wage ratio is plotted against women's union density in Figure 8.3. For the 17 countries with women's union membership share in Table 8.2, the annual growth rate of the relative wage is plotted against the ratio of women's to men's union density in Figure 8.4. While these are only rough approximations, since the underlying data come from several different sources, they show a pattern of large relative wage growth for women in the 1970s in countries where women's union density was large, and large relative to men's.

4 RECENT US DATA

After a decade of little, if any, progress toward aggregate wage equality, women's earnings as a percentage of men's began to rise in the United States in the early 1980s.[7] This occurred despite the election and re-election of a President whose administration placed a low priority on the achievement of greater equality for women. The increasing lengths of women's careers, the change in the composition of jobs with economic restructuring, women's increasing representation in professional fields, and many other factors contributed to these modest gains for women in the 1970s and 1980s. Most importantly, social attitudes continued to change, and overt discrimination

Table 8.2   Women's participation in unions, early 1980s

Country	Women's share of union members' (per cent)	Women's union density (per cent)	F/M union density ratio
Sweden	46	87	1.0
Belgium	32	61	0.8
Denmark	43, 56[a]	74	1.0
Finland	53	n.a.	1.3
Austria	30	50	0.7
Norway	33	51	0.7
Australia	30	47	0.8
United Kingdom	34	49	0.8
Ireland	32	n.a.	1.2
Italy	33	n.a.	1.0
Luxembourg	8	n.a.	0.2
German Federal Republic	21	23	0.4
Netherlands	15	20	0.4
Canada	27	23	0.5
Switzerland	12	11	0.3
Greece	n.a.	n.a.	n.a.
New Zealand	n.a.	n.a.	n.a.
France	30	15	0.7
United States	27	16	0.5

Sources: Women's share of union membership: Information for Australia, Canada, the United Kingdom, and the United States from ILO (1987), p. 117. For the remaining countries the information was obtained from *Women's Representation in Trade Unions*, European Trade Union Institute, 1983.

Women's union density calculated as union density (from Table 8.1) multiplied by women's share of union membership (from Table 8.2)) divided by women's labour force share (from Table 8.1).

F/M union density ratio is the ratio of women's to men's union membership share divided by the ratio of women's to men's labour force share, using men's union membership share as (1 *minus* women's union membership share) and men's labour force share as (1 *minus* women's labour force share).

Notes: [a] Data for Denmark are given separately for the two major union groups in the European Trade Union Institute publication; no aggregate figure was given. In the calculations of women's union density, a weighted figure of 45 per cent was used.

n.a. = not available.

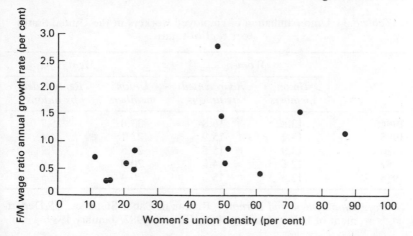

Figure 8.3 Average annual growth rate in F/M wage ratio, 1970–80, by women's union density

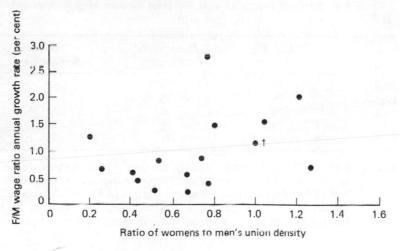

† Two points superimposed

Figure 8.4 Average annual growth rate in F/M wage ratio, 1970–80, by ratio of women's to men's union density

diminished. Union activity supporting women's pay equity became a factor in negotiating labour agreements, especially in the public sector.[8]

Overall, union influence in the USA declined during the 1980s, yet recent data show that unionised women received significantly higher relative earnings than women who were not represented by unions.

Table 8.3 Union affiliation of employed workers in the United States
(per cent of total)

	Women		Men	
	Union members	*Represented by unions*	*Union members*	*Represented by unions*
1984	13.8	16.8	23.0	25.7
1985	13.2	15.9	22.1	24.4
1986	12.9	15.5	21.5	23.7
1987	12.6	14.9	20.9	22.9
1988	12.6	15.0	20.4	22.5

Source: *Employment and Earnings*, Bureau of Labor Statistics, US Department of Labor, January 1985, January 1987, January 1989.

Table 8.4 Ratio of female to male full-time median weekly earnings[a]
(per cent)

	Union members	*Represented by unions*	*Non-union*
1984	74	74	69
1985	75	75	68
1986	76	76	70
1987	79	78	71
1988	80	79	72

Source: Calculated from median weekly earnings of full-time wage and salary workers by age, sex, race, Hispanic origin, and union affiliation in *Employment and Earnings*, Bureau of Labor Statistics, US Department of Labor, January, 1985, January 1987, January 1989.
Note: [a] Figures for employed, full-time workers over 16 years of age.

Table 8.3 displays the pattern of union representation in the USA over the past five years. Women have continued to increase their fraction of union membership over the 1980s, but this is only because the decline in men's union membership rates has been larger than the decline in women's membership rates.

Table 8.4 suggests that unionised US women had higher relative earnings and greater relative earnings growth than their non-union counterparts. Previous econometric studies of union wage effects have typically found that unions do increase wages and that wage benefits of union representation are roughly equal for women and men (Freeman and Medoff, 1984). The comparison of the ratios of union women's to union men's earnings and the ratios of non-unionised women's to non-unionised men's earnings in Table 8.4 shows that women represented by unions are closer to wage equality. Thus in the 1980s, it appears that unions, even in their declining state, were of value to women workers.

5 SUMMARY

An overview of the relative earnings gains of women in the last decade has shown that women have made more progress towards wage equality in those countries with strong union traditions. No causal link has been proved, and it may be that the social and political attitudes which favour unionism are also associated with greater concern for pay equality. However, commitment by unions to wage equality appears to have had a large impact in several countries, and potential gains for women from greater participation in unions appear promising. Even within the USA, a country with relatively low union density, relative earnings gains for women who are union members and/or are represented by unions are consistently higher.

Notes

1. For examples from various countries, see country chapters in Cook, Lorwin and Daniels (1984).
2. Information on the Swedish National Labour Market Board comes from 'Equality Between Men and Women in the Labour Market: The Swedish National Labour Market Board', by Berit Rollen in Ratner (1980).
3. Freeman and Medoff (1984), chapter 14, present evidence that union members in the United States have considerable voice in determining union leadership and policies.
4. For specific data on women's share of leadership roles in European countries, see Karlsson (1983).
5. The explicit relationship between labour unions and political parties is described in International Labour Organisation (1987).
6. Bain and Price (1980) provide data showing this for Australia, Canada, and the United Kingdom. US data are given in Blau and Ferber (1986).
7. Calculations using median full-time weekly earnings by sex from BLS (1989) show that the ratio of women's to men's earnings in the United States rose from 0.64 in 1980 to 0.70 in 1988.

8. See Wertheimer in Cook, Lorwin and Daniels (1984) for a description of the Coalition of Labor Union Women. See Bergmann (1986) for a discussion of the activities of public sector unions supporting pay equity.

References

Bain, G. and Price, R. (1980) *Profiles of Union Growth* (Oxford: Blackwell).
Bergmann, B. (1986) *The Economic Emergence of Women* (New York: Basic Books).
Blau, F. and Ferber, M. (1986) *The Economics of Women, Men and Work* (New Jersey: Prentice-Hall).
Bureau of Labor Statistics (1982) *Labor Force Statistics Derived From the Current Population Survey: A Databook, Volume 1*, US Department of Labor, September 1982.
Bureau of Labor Statistics (1989) *Handbook of Labor Statistics*, US Department of Labor, August 1989.
Cook, A. Lorwin V. and Daniels, A. K. (eds) (1984) *Women and Trade Unions in Eleven Industrialised Countries* (Philadelphia: Temple University Press).
Freeman, R. and Medoff, J. (1984) *What Do Unions Do?* (New York: Basic Books).
International Labour Organisation (1987) *World Labour Report 1–2* (Oxford: Oxford University Press).
Karlsson, G. (1983) *Women's Representation in Trade Union's* (Brussels: European Trade Institute).
OECD (1980) *Women and Employment. Policies for Equal Opportunities* (Paris: Organisation for Economic Cooperation and Development).
OECD (1985) *The Integration of Women into the Economy* (Paris: Organisation for Economic Cooperation and Development).
Ratner, R. (1980) *Equal Employment Policy for Women* (Philadelphia: Temple University Press).
Steinberg, R. and Cook, A.H. (1988) 'Policies Affecting Women's Employment', in Stromberg, A.A. and Harkness, S. (eds) *Women Working: Theories and Facts in Perspective*, 2nd edn. (California: Mayfield).
Troy, L. and Scheflin, N. (1985) *U.S. Union Sourcebook*, Industrial Relations Data and Information Service, West Orange, New Jersey, USA.
Windmuller, J. P. (ed.) (1987) *Collective Bargaining in Industrialised Market Economies: A Reappraisal* (Geneva: International Labour Organisation).

Part III

Part-Time Market Work: Causes and Consequences

9 The Effects of Japanese Income Tax Provisions on Women's Labour Force Participation

Aiko Shibata[1]

TEZUKAYAMA UNIVERSITY, JAPAN

1 INTRODUCTION

At a session of the Congress of the International Institute of Public Finance in Istanbul in the summer of 1988, a gentleman from a small oil-producing country in the Middle East asked me: 'Was there any effective governmental means of keeping wives at home?' I was taken by surprise and didn't know how to respond. However, I later realised that Japanese tax laws implicitly do just that. Designed to give a tax break to married taxpayers, they discourage housewives from taking jobs. Further, many private companies have adopted wage structures that also discourage housewives from working outside their homes.

2 THE FEMALE LABOUR FORCE IN JAPAN

I shall now explain the situation of the Japanese working woman (Department of Female Labour, 1989). In 1987, the rate of participation in the labour force was 48.6 per cent for women, and 77.3 per cent for men. The number of Japanese women and men employed in 1987 was 16.5 million and 28.13 million, respectively. Among female employees, the number of part-time employees was 3.65 million, representing a 72.1 per cent share of overall part-time employment.[2] Here, a part-time employee means one who works less than 35 hours a week. In 1987, monthly earnings of a female worker averaged 209 063 yen, or 52 per cent of the average monthly earnings of a male worker. One of the main reasons for this difference was the larger

169

proportion of female employees than of male employees working part-time. In 1987, the hourly wage for a full-time female employee averaged 866 yen and that for a part-time female employee, 623 yen. Therefore, among female employees, the average part-time worker earned only 72 per cent of the hourly wage of the average full-time worker. According to an estimate by the Japanese Ministry of Labour, one-third of all female employees earned less than the minimum taxable income. The labour participation rate for females between the ages of 40 and 50 was the highest for all age groups of women and a large proportion – 40 per cent – of all female workers in that age range worked part-time. As might be expected, wages for part-time female employees do not increase much with increasing age: in 1987, the average hourly wage for a part-time female employee between the ages of 35 and 39 was 605 yen; between 40 and 45, 614 yen; between 50 and 54, 634 yen; and between 55 and 59, 631 yen.

Among married male employees, 48 per cent had wives who were also employed. Among married women, their husbands levels of income strongly influenced labour force participation: 53 per cent of wives whose husbands earned less than 1.99 million yen, and 55 per cent of wives of those who earned more than 2 million yen but less than 2.99 million yen were employed, while only 35 per cent of wives of those who earned more than 7 million yen worked outside the home. Thus, the general tendency is that the higher the husband's income, the smaller the proportion of wives working.

3   JAPANESE INCOME TAX LAW

Many factors discourage Japanese housewives from taking jobs. Japanese income tax law, reformed to a great extent in April 1989, allows an employee very large deductions for a spouse. This affects the labour participation rate of housewives in two ways. First, the spouse deductions lower the net marginal wage rate in comparison with the market wage for a housewife. Second, the spouse deductions increase disposable income for some families. Both effects work to reduce female labour force participation. Research has shown that the wage rate does not have much effect on the supply of labour of male employees between the age of 30 and retirement (Pencavel, 1986). However, the wage rate has a statistically significant effect on the labour supply of women, the elderly and the young (Higuchi and

Table 9.1 National and local personal income taxes in Japan

National income tax		Local income tax	
Taxable income (10,000 yen)	Rate (per cent)	Taxable income (10,000 yen)	Rate (per cent)
Less than 300	10	Less than 120	5
300–	20	120–	10
600–	30	500–	15
1 000–	40		
2 000–	50		

Income tax deductions[a]		
Deduction	Amount of deduction (10,000 yen)	
	National	Local
Basic exemption	35	30
Spouse deduction	35	30
Spouse special deduction	35	30
Deduction for dependent	35–45	30–35
Special disability deduction	35	28
Head of household deduction	27	26

Source: Japanese Treasury Department (1989) Japanese Tax Code (Tokyo: Japanese Treasury Department Press).

Note: [a] Income tax deductions other than those shown in this Table are also available.

Hayami, 1984). Therefore, if the income tax system lowers the wage rate, it creates a disincentive effect for these groups of people.

Certain sections of Japanese income tax regulations which must be understood for this analysis are set out in Table 9.1. In Japan, there are three different levels of income taxes levied on a wage earner. They are the national income tax, the income tax levied by the prefectural government and that levied by the city, town or village. Following the convention in Japan, I have combined the last two taxes and called them the local government tax. As seen in Table 9.1, both national and local income taxes have similar deductions, but the local tax rates are lower than the national tax rates. There are no joint returns for a married couple in either tax system; thus, if a husband and wife have separate incomes, they must file separate income tax returns.

Let us now examine how a wage earner calculates his or her taxable income. First, a wage earner can deduct an employee's standard deduction from wage income (not shown in Table 9.1). The marginal rate of an employee's standard deduction starts from 40 per cent of wage income and is gradually reduced to 5 per cent. The employee's minimum standard deduction is 570 000 yen. Second, an employee is permitted to take the deductions shown in Table 9.1 if they apply to him or her. Any employee is entitled to a basic exemption of 350 000 yen per person. Then, if married, he or she can take two spouse deductions called the spouse deduction and the spouse special deduction, each of which is 350 000 yen. The employee's income ceiling for a spouse special deduction is 12.2 million yen, which is so high that most married workers do not exceed this limitation. These spouse deductions are reduced by the amount of spouse income over 570 000 yen, which is the minimum employee's standard deduction. The spouse special deduction was added to the pre-existing spouse deduction in 1987.

However, there is not much difference between the two spouse deductions. The spouse special deduction is reduced first, and then the spouse deduction. Thus, when spouse earnings exceed 1 270 000 yen, both spouse deductions, 700 000 yen in total, are lost. Since the Japanese tax system requires separate returns from a married couple, a spouse has to pay income tax on earnings in excess of 920 000 yen, which is the sum of the employee's minimum standard deduction plus the basic exemption.[3]

4 EARNINGS AND CONTRIBUTIONS TO HOUSEHOLD INCOME

Since these regulations make the marginal wage rate for a housewife lower than the market wage rate, and also increase disposable income to some households, they discourage a housewife from working outside the home. If the hourly wage for a woman is given as W, her earnings, Y_w, after working H hours are given as:

$$Y_w = W \times H \tag{1}$$

If a housewife earns less than the employee's minimum standard deduction of 570 000 yen, she does not need to pay income tax on it and her husband can deduct two spouse deductions worth 700 000 yen from his income; thus, Y, the benefits a wife can bring to the household, are given as follows:

If $0 \leqslant Y_w \leqslant 570\ 000$,

$$Y = (W \times H) + 700\ 000t_h \tag{2}$$

where t_h is the marginal tax rate for a husband.[4] Then, the wife's total contribution to disposable household income, Y, is the sum of the wife's wage earnings and her husband's tax savings by taking two spouse deductions. Here the marginal contribution in terms of H, M_{h1}, is given as:

$$M_{h1} = dY\ /\ dH = W \tag{3}$$

If a wife earns wages in excess of 570 000 yen, the spouse deductions are reduced by the amount of the wife's earnings between 570 000 yen and 1 270 000 yen, the point at which all spouse deductions are used up. Thus,

if $570\ 000 < Y_w \leqslant 920\ 000$,

$$Y = (W \times H) + (1\ 270\ 000 - [W \times H])t_h \tag{4}$$

Then the marginal contribution M_{h2} is given as:

$$M_{h2} = W(1 - t_h) \tag{5}$$

Earnings over 920 000 yen are taxable for a wife as stated above. If the tax rate for a wife's income is given as t_w, we obtain,

if $920\ 000 < Y_w \leqslant 1\ 270\ 000$,

$$Y = (W \times H) + (1\ 270\ 000 - [W \times H])t_h$$
$$- ([W \times H] - 920\ 000)t_w \tag{6}$$

Then, the marginal contribution M_{h3} is given as:

$$M_{h3} = W(1 - t_h - t_w). \tag{7}$$

When a wife's earnings are greater than 1 270 000 yen, the contribution she makes to disposable household income is reduced to only her net of tax earnings, as her husband loses the entire spouse deduction.

If $1\ 270\ 000 < Y_w$,

$$Y = (W \times H) - ([W \times H] - 920\ 000)t_w \tag{8}$$

Then, the marginal contribution M_{h4} is given as:

$$M_{h4} = W(1 - t_w) \tag{9}$$

The relationships between the hours worked and the contribution a wife makes are shown in Figure 9.1. The vertical axis of Figure 9.1 indicates the yen value of the wife's contribution, Y, and the horizontal axis indicates the numerical value of the wife's wage earnings, X, which is given by:

$$X = W \times H \tag{10}$$

Thus, if there are no tax savings for a husband due to spouse deductions and no income taxes paid on the wife's earnings,

$$Y_w = X \tag{11}$$

Equation (11) is expressed as line OM in Figure 9.1, which has a slope of 45°. (Note that the unit for both X and Y axes is 10 000.)

Using equations (10) and (11), the net of tax contributions to household income, Y, and the marginal contribution in terms of X, M_x, are obtained from equations (2) to (9) as follows:

If $0 \leqslant Y_w \leqslant 570\ 000$,

$$Y = X + 700\ 000t_h \tag{12}$$

$$M_{x1} = 1 \tag{13}$$

If $570\ 000 < Y_w \leqslant 920\ 000$,

$$Y = X(1 - t_h) + 1\ 270\ 000t_h \tag{14}$$

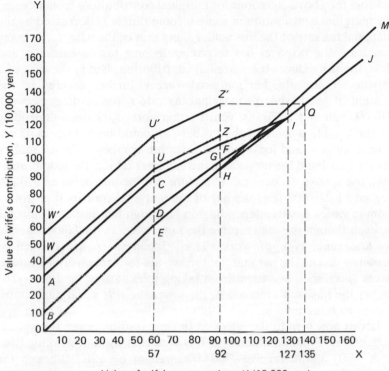

Figure 9.1 Earnings lines

$$M_{x2} = 1 - t_h \tag{15}$$

If $920\,000 < Y_w \leqslant 1\,270\,000$,

$$Y - X(1 - t_h - t_w) + 1\,270\,000t_h + 920\,000t_w \tag{16}$$

$$M_{x3} = 1 - t_h - t_w \tag{17}$$

If $1\,270\,000 < Y_w$,

$$Y = X(1 - t_w) + 920\,000t_w \tag{18}$$

$$M_{x4} = 1 - t_w \tag{19}$$

From the above equations for marginal contributions from women, the marginal contribution in some income ranges is decreased by the marginal tax rate of the husband, t_h, and that of the wife, t_w. In many countries, the taxpayer has to pay an income tax on earnings, and thus, the tax reduces the marginal contribution. But in the case of a Japanese housewife, her marginal wage is further lowered by the amount of her husband's marginal tax rate t_h for earnings between 570 000 yen and 1 270 000 yen. Furthermore, t_h changes depending on the taxable income of the husband: it could be as high as 45 per cent if national and local income taxes are combined, or it could be zero if a husband has no taxable income after taking deductions other than the spouse deductions. Therefore, for income between 570 000 yen and 1 270 000 yen, the net of tax marginal contribution from a woman varies greatly, depending on how high her husband's income is, even though she may receive the same wage in the labour market for the same type of work. Thus, Japanese spouse deductions seriously distort the net marginal wage rate for some working housewives and discourage them from taking jobs outside the home. The higher the husband's income is, the lower the wife's marginal contribution to household income.

Let us now turn to the effect on income resulting from two spouse deductions. From equation (12) it is seen that without working (that is $X = 0$) a wife receives $700\ 000t_h$ yen of benefits, although the household actually receives the benefits, rather than the wife personally. This amount increases if t_h increases. For example, if t_h is 45 per cent, tax benefits a wife receives without working equal 315 000 yen. This amount is very large if compared with the approximately 230 000 yen, which represents the income taxes to be paid by a standard wage earner in 1989 (Nihon Keizai Shinbun Sha, 1989), and the average monthly earnings (before tax) of a female worker, 209 063 yen in 1987, as mentioned above. If t_h is not zero, the $700\ 000t_h$ yen of tax benefits that a wife receives raises her income. This increased income would discourage her from working. Again, the higher the husband's income, the more income a household receives from two spouse deductions. The effects of two spouse deductions are stronger for a wife if her husband's earnings are larger. The statistics to which I referred above, namely, the smaller the percentage of working women in a group of households, the larger the earnings of the husbands in that group, appear at least in part to represent a rational response by households to the tax law.

I shall now illustrate my analysis using actual numbers for some specific groups of women in Figure 9.1. Let us choose three representative groups of women based on their husbands' taxable incomes: namely, the poor, the middle class and the rich.[5] If the husband's taxable income without two spouse deductions is zero, his wife is in the low income group. If a woman is single, she belongs to this group because our standard for classification is the husband's taxable income. If the husband's taxable income is greater than zero, but not greater than 1 200 000 yen, his wife is in the middle income group. Over 20 per cent of average wage earners' households belong to this group (Miyachi, 1989). As seen from Table 9.1, the national income tax rate for this taxable income bracket is 10 per cent and the local income tax rate is 5 per cent; thus, the marginal income tax rate for the husband, t_h, is 15 per cent. A woman in the high income group has a husband whose taxable income is greater than 6 000 000 yen but not greater than 10 000 000 yen. The national marginal income tax rate for this group of men is 30 per cent and the local marginal income tax rate, 15 per cent; thus t_h is 45 per cent.

In Figure 9.1, line *OEHIJ* expresses the relationship between earnings and the wife's corresponding net of tax contribution to household income (the sum of net of tax earnings and tax savings) for the low income group. I will call this line the 'earnings line'. The earnings line for the middle income group is line *BDGIJ*, and that for the high income group, line *ACFIJ*. Any woman with earnings over 1 270 000 yen is taxed at the starting rate of 10 per cent as shown by the identical section of the lines, *IJ*. Figure 9.1 shows that two spouse deductions give the household of a wife in the high income group the largest contribution by the wife to household income, but at the same time the marginal contribution is the lowest among the three groups for earnings greater than 570 000 yen but not greater than 1 270 000 yen.

5   COMPANY WAGE STRUCTURES

Let me now examine the aspect of the customary method of setting the wages for an employee in a private company, as this also discourages a woman from participating in the labour force, although the intention of the company is said to be one of helping the employee by giving extra wages if he has a wife whose income is small. A common practice among Japanese companies in determining wages for its employees is explained below. Seventy-seven per cent of private companies give their employees extra payments called spouse benefits (Japanese Ministry of Labour, 1986). Of these companies, 41 per cent require a spouse to satisfy certain conditions to qualify for this spouse benefit. Normally, a spouse is required to have an independent income of less than 920 000 yen so that an employee can take a spouse deduction on his national tax return. This type of requirement becomes more common as the company becomes larger, and thus the average wage of the employee becomes larger. For example, among companies with over 1000 employees, 61 per cent have limitations on income for spouses as a criterion for determining eligibility for spouse benefits. The average spouse benefits paid by companies were 86 400 yen a year; the larger the company, the greater the amount of such payments. For example 4 per cent of companies with over 1000 employees paid an average of 480 000 yen a year per employee in spouse benefits.

These private spouse benefits shift the earnings line for a housewife further upward. This is demonstrated in Figure 9.1 by adding those payments to the earnings line for a woman in the high income group. Line WUZ is obtained by adding 47 520 yen (86 400 [1–0.45]) to the earnings line ACF. Line $W'U'Z'$ is also obtained from line ACF by adding 264 000 yen (480 000 [1–0.45]). Private companies' spouse benefits cause special problems regarding the supply of female labour. These spouse benefits, as stated above, are often cut off at spouse earnings of 920 000 yen. This is indicated by the earnings line having a valley, $Z'ZFIQ$. The vertical line, $Z'ZF$, indicates that the implicit tax on a wife's earnings over 920 000 yen is over 100 per cent. A wife at point Z' earning 920 000 yen would not receive the same net of tax benefits unless she earns 1 350 000 yen. Thus, it is economically irrational for many women to work within this earnings range.

6   CONCLUSION

Income tax deductions are regressive in the sense that the higher the marginal income tax rate is, the larger the benefits from deductions. Thus, income tax deductions make a progressive income tax structure less progressive. However, if the deductions are given in such a way that the taxpayer and his or her family can easily adjust their economic position, the deductions place an extra burden on society. As we have seen, a household receives greater spouse benefits as the marginal tax rate of the husband increases. Thus, in a certain earnings range, the tax rate on the wife's earnings is the sum of the two tax rates, that is the wife's marginal income tax rate and the husband's marginal income tax rate. Therefore, this tax policy tends to reduce the supply of female labour to the market and is detrimental to the achievement of long-term equality of employment opportunities and pay between the sexes.

If we return to the question put by the gentleman from an oil-producing country, Japanese income tax law and also the Japanese companies' customary method of setting wages could be an answer for his government. These methods have the advantage of appearing to help the family and are less explicit about the fact that they are discouraging wives from working outside the home.

Notes

1. The author wishes to acknowledge the detailed comments and valuable suggestions of Professor Nancy Folbre and the generous support of Tezukayama University Research Foundation.
2. Over the years 1985-87, the annual growth rate of part-time female employment averaged 5 per cent and that of full-time female employment 1.4 per cent.
3. A person could have other deductions such as social security payments and insurance payments. Other deductions for a female worker are assumed to be zero in this analysis, in order to limit this analysis to spouse deductions. The amount of other deductions allowed would be small compared to the spouse deductions.
4. For simplicity, it is assumed throughout this paper, that the marginal tax rate for a husband does not change in the range of spouse deductions.
5. We assume that the husband is a wage earner.

References

Department of Female Labour, Japanese Ministry of Labour (1989) *Fujin-rodo no Jittai 63* (Tokyo: Japanese Treasury Department Press).

Higuchi, Y. and Hayami, H. (1984) 'Joshirodokyokyu no Nichibe Hikaku', *Mitashogaku Kenkyu*, vol. 27.

Japanese Ministry of Labour (1986) *Chingin Rodojikan Seidonado Sogochosa* (Tokyo: Japanese Treasury Department Press).

Miyachi, S. (1988) *Shohizei o Kensho Suru* (Tokyo: Chuou Keizai Sha).

Nihon Keizai Shinbun Sha (ed.) (1989) *Q & A Shohizei* (Tokyo: Nihon Keizai Shinbun Sha).

Pencavel, J. (1986) 'The Labour Supply of Men', in Ashenfelter, O. and Layard, R. (eds) *Handbook of Labour Economics* (New York: North Holland).

10 Women and Part-time Work: France and Great Britain Compared

Marie-Gabrielle David and
Christophe Starzec[1]
CERC, PARIS

1 INTRODUCTION

A brief comparison of the female labour force participation rates in France and Great Britain shows that their level and evolution are very similar. Nevertheless, this similarity conceals substantial differences between the two countries in the structure of female employment and its distribution between full-time and part-time work. Almost one half of working women in Great Britain work part-time compared with one fifth of French working women. This widespread part-time work in Great Britain is primarily attributable to young married people, especially those who have dependent children (Leicester, 1982). Two surveys initiated at about the same time (1980–81) in Great Britain and in France, and covering similar samples (women with dependent children), made it possible to compare the employment situations of mothers of families in the two countries, specifically the socio-demographic characteristics of their family and their economic situation. The results of these two surveys lead us to conclude that the considerable differences in the labour force participation patterns of women in the two countries are due mainly to differences in social and economic policies.

The two national surveys were the Women's Employment Survey (WES) in Britain (Martin and Roberts, 1984) and the Vie Familiale et Vie Professionnelle (VFP) in France (David *et al.*, 1985). Both obtained their sample from a survey of households. A single interview was carried out with all respondents. The interview dates were May–July 1981 in France and April–July 1980 in Britain. The questionnaires contain a set of questions which are directly comparable and others which are almost comparable. Both surveys contain information, based on recall, of the employment histories of these women.

The French VFP sample consisted of women aged 18–60 in 1981 who were mothers of at least one child under 16. A total of 3935 women were interviewed. This sample had to be weighted to give a sample representative of all such women in French households, giving a weighted sample size of 4461 women. The sample was then adjusted to contain only mothers aged 18–54, reducing the weighted sample size to 4366 women.

The British WES sample contained 5588 women between the ages of 16 and 59, 49 per cent of whom had a child under 16. This sample was representative of all households in Britain and did not need weighting. As for the French sample, the sample was then adjusted to contain only mothers aged 18–54 with at least one child under 16, giving a sample of 2631 women.

2 SIMILARITIES AND DIFFERENCES

The economic participation of women has evolved differently in France and Great Britain. Since the 1950s, part-time work among women has expanded very rapidly in Great Britain (Dale and Glover, 1990). In France, on the other hand, full-time work has accounted for most of the increase in female participation in the labour force (INSEE, 1987). However, this trend has altered since the mid-1980s primarily because unemployment rates have increased, making part-time work less a choice than a constraint 'for lack of something better' (Belloc, 1986; Heller, 1986).

In Great Britain, the proportion of part-time workers among women engaged in paid labour is 45 per cent, whereas in France, it is hardly over 23 per cent (SOEC, 1986). This difference may appear surprising if we take into account the similarity of the evolution of the female labour market and its structure in both countries:

- Women working part-time are concentrated in the service sector: 75 per cent in France, 86 per cent in Great Britain, in 1983. They are very much over-represented amongst shop employees and under-represented amongst office employees (Dale and Glover, 1990).
- The proportion of women employed in the service sector has increased: from 48 per cent in 1970 to 59 per cent in 1983 in France

Table 10.1 Full- and part-time labour force participation rates of mothers
with dependent children[a]
(per cent)

	Great Britain (1980)		France (1981)	
Employed in paid labour	51.3		51.2	
of which full-time		32.6		83.0
part time		67.4		17.0
Not employed in paid labour	48.7		48.8	
Total	100.0		100.0	

Sources: Women's Employment Survey (1980) (WES); Vie familiale et Vie
professionnelle (1981) (VFP).
Note: [a] Women aged between 18 and 54 with at least one child under 16.

and, over the same period, from 53 per cent to 64 per cent in Great
Britain (Garnsey, 1984).

• Women with at least one dependent child under 16 are subject to
greater family constraints than other wage earners, and these
constraints greatly influence their participation in the labour force.
The VFP and WES survey results show that almost the same
percentage of mothers of dependent children in France and in
Great Britain participate in paid labour, about 51 per cent. However in France only 17 per cent of these women worked part-time,
whereas in Great Britain, 67 per cent did (see Table 10.1).

The designation of employment status in these surveys is based on
the self definition of the interviewed women. If the actual number of
hours employed is taken into account, even larger differences in the
paid work-time in both countries can be observed: 40 per cent of
British women employed part-time worked less than 16 hours a week
compared to only 27 per cent of those in France. The same tendency
can be observed amongst full-timers: 77 per cent of women employees in France worked at least 40 hours compared to only 32 per
cent in Great Britain.

Although the presence of dependent children discourages paid
work among women in both countries, the impact of increasing
numbers of children is far more significant in France than in Great
Britain. In Great Britain, the birth of the first child prompts the

major reduction in women's economic participation in paid labour; in France, this reduction takes place gradually under the pressure of the increasing difficulties encountered by the mother in combining full-time work with family responsibilities which increase with each additional child. In Great Britain the presence of dependent children also encourages part-time paid work and the fall in the proportion of women working full-time is much greater than in France. In France the arrival of children is not associated with an increase in the proportion of women working part-time, but with a continuing fall in the proportion working full-time (see Table 10.2).

The proportion of British working mothers who work part-time remains practically the same whatever the mother's age (see Table 10.3). There is a slight peak that we observe for the youngest mothers (under 34) that corresponds to the demands of looking after young children, which women in England encounter more frequently. In France, on the other hand, the proportion of women working part-time increases with the age of the mother, as the overall participation rate declines.

The women who work part-time exhibit employment and training characteristics which are very different in France and in Great Britain. In France, the proportion working part-time is particularly high amongst the professional occupations and it is especially low in Great Britain for those with higher levels of education (A level or above). It is, in both countries, relatively low in the intermediate categories (see Table 10.4); the proportion working part-time is reduced in Great Britain when the level of women's training increases. This is also the case in France, but only up to the secondary level. Beyond this, the part-time participation rate increases and reaches its highest value (36 per cent) amongst women with a higher education diploma. Although very high in France, this rate is below that in Great Britain for those with A-level or higher qualifications (54 per cent).

In France, an intermittent career is, to a greater extent than in England, associated with part-time employment (Table 10.5). The more frequent the breaks in activity (of 6 months or more) in the working past of women, the more likely these women are to be employed part-time. Of those with three or more breaks, 46 per cent worked part-time, and of those who had never taken a break only 14 per cent were employed part-time. Part-time paid work appears in Great Britain to be a frequent form of employment for women

Table 10.2 Full-time and part-time employment among women, by number of children (per cent)

Number of children	France				Great Britain			
	Not in paid employment	In paid employment		Total	Not in paid employment	In paid employment		Total
		Full-time	Part-time			Full-time	Part-time	
0	40.0	48.6	11.4	100.0	19.0	59.1	21.9	100.0
1	34.3	57.1	8.6	100.0	56.6	17.0	26.4	100.0
2	45.4	45.2	9.4	100.0	46.0	16.0	38.0	100.0
3	67.4	25.9	6.7	100.0	44.9	17.6	37.5	100.0
4 and over	80.0	10.4	9.6	100.0	45.1	18.0	36.9	100.0
Total for those with children	48.8	42.5	8.7	100.0	48.2	16.9	34.9	100.0

Sources: VFP and WES surveys.
Enquête Emploi for those with no children in France.

Table 10.3 Full-time and part-time employment among mothers by age (per cent)

Age of mother	France			Great Britain			Overall participation rates	
	Full-time	Part-time	Total	Full-time	Part-time	Total	France	Great Britain
20–24	87.3	12.7	100.0	32.7	67.3	100.0	71.0	68.9
25–29	86.1	13.9	100.0	23.1	76.9	100.0	72.2	56.5
30–34	85.1	14.9	100.0	27.4	72.6	100.0	69.8	56.1
35–39	81.3	18.7	100.0	38.0	62.0	100.0	68.3	64.4
40–44	77.2	22.8	100.0	34.4	65.6	100.0	66.7	70.2
45–49	77.5	22.5	100.0	36.2	63.8	100.0	63.2	70.8
50–54	66.7	33.3	100.0	30.6	69.4	100.0	56.2	63.8
Total	83.0	17.0	100.0	32.6	67.4	100.0	67.3	64.4

Sources: VFP and WES surveys.
Eurostat, Labour Force Survey, 1983 for overall participation rates.

Table 10.4 Full-time and part-time work among mothers by level of education
(per cent)

Level of education	France			Great Britain		
	Full-time	Part-time	Total	Full-time	Part-time	Total
No diploma	76	24	100			
Primary						
CEP (general)	82	18	100			
CAP (professional)	87	13	100			
Secondary						
BEPC (first level)	88	12	100			
BAC (second level)	91	9	100			
University level						
Undergraduate	83	17	100			
Degree graduate	64	36	100			
Total	83	17	100			
No diploma				27	73	100
CSE (primary)				30	70	100
O–level (second)				37	63	100
A–level (higher)				46	54	100
Total				33	67	100

Source: VFP and WES surveys.

irrespective of the number of breaks in their career. In France, full-time and unbroken activity appear to be the norms for working mothers, whereas in Great Britain an unbroken career is unusual.

3   THE EFFECTS OF ECONOMIC AND SOCIAL POLICIES

These differences in patterns of female labour force participation between France and Great Britain are largely attributable to differences in economic and social policies between the two countries including social insurance, taxation, family benefits and child care.

In Great Britain, employers (like employees) do not pay social security contributions if the gross remuneration does not exceed a certain limit (£39 = 430 French francs per week, in 1987). Beyond this threshold the contribution rates increase progressively with the

Table 10.5   Full-time and part-time work among mothers by number of
paid work interruptions
(percentages)

Number of breaks (6 months and more)	France			Great Britain		
	Full-time	Part-time	Total	Full-time	Part-time	Total
0	86	14	100	49	51	100
1	79	21	100	29	71	100
2	75	25	100	35	65	100
3 and over	54	46	100	36	64	100
Total	83	17	100	33	67	100
	Percentage of total					
0	64	49	62	7	4	5
1	29	38	31	44	53	50
2	6	9	6	31	28	29
3 and over	1	3	1	18	16	16
Total	100	100	100	100	100	100

Source: VFP and WES surveys.

level of gross remuneration. Thus the employer, by multiplying the
number of jobs with reduced time, can considerably diminish his
social security contributions. This measure encourages the multipli-
cation of offers for part-time jobs to the detriment of full-time ones,
whatever the activity of the business: in 1981, the share of social
security contributions in total labour costs was about 25 per cent on
average. In France, until 1981 both employers and employees paid
social security contributions for part-time as well as full-time work
since there was no incentive in the taxation (social security contributions) for reduced work time as compared to 'normal' work time. On
the contrary, in some cases, notably for wages exceeding the ceiling
for the contributions, two part-timers could cost more in contributions to the employers than one full-time equivalent of these two
part-timers. This relative disadvantage was abolished in 1981 and the
law became neutral: social security contributions are identical in both
cases whatever the wage level (Memento Pratique Francis Lefebvre
Social, 1981); in 1981, the share of social security contributions in
total labour force costs was about 39 per cent on average. The

pre-1981 legislation had the effect of limiting part-time jobs to certain businesses with special labour requirements on hours operation, such as supermarkets.

In Great Britain the unit of taxation is either the married couple or the adult.[2] The couple can decide on separate taxation of the sole activity incomes of each of the parties. In the case of a common declaration two deductions are possible: the 'couple' deduction and the deduction with respect to the income from the woman's activity (which applies to the whole of the household's income). These deductions are fixed (and not proportional as in France) and are all the more significant when the incomes are low. The English system is featured by a broad 'basic' tax band (in 1980–81 with a 30 per cent tax rate) of great amplitude which applies to the great majority of tax payers. As a result, the average rate for taxable income is equal to the marginal rate for most tax households. Compulsory social security contributions are not deductible from the taxable income which encourages tax payers (especially the women) not to exceed the social security contributions relief threshold (of £39 per week in 1987). For those who exceed the relief threshold the rate of compulsory social security contributions rapidly surpasses 20 per cent. In practice the English system encourages the woman's working participation but this participation should remain limited owing to the highly progressive taxation beyond the threshold. Thus low wages or limited activities are encouraged at the expense of full-time participation which suffers from a highly progressive income tax and social security contributions.

In the case of high incomes, separate taxation becomes more advantageous than combined taxation, especially when the difference between the incomes of the wife and those of the husband is considerable. The loss of the fixed deduction is more than compensated for by the reduction in the marginal rate of taxation. This helps to explain the relatively greater participation of women with high incomes: the relative significance of the fixed deduction is in this case slight and other possibilities of tax shelter are open.

In France, the system of taxation is different. It is based on the notion of a tax household and takes its demographic structures into account. In this system, the family is typically the tax unit for which many possibilities of deduction and tax arbitration are available. The variations of the tax according to the number of children and more generally according to the number of dependent persons (family quotient) is its most unique feature. In this system, with constant total income, the tax is lower when the number of dependents is higher. Deductions from earned incomes are proportional (28 per cent) and cumulative within the household (they are calculated separately for each employment income). The taxable income is calculated by household (all the incomes of the household are added together) and the tax bands are applied to this income. These bands feature a high tax relief threshold and are highly progressive beyond this threshold. This system taxes low and medium incomes very lightly (per member of the family) and becomes highly progressive only for relatively high incomes. Thus for all people whose potential family incomes are low or medium, tax disincentives to increased participation in the labour force are slight, especially when the number of dependents is large. Only families with a high potential income have an incentive to reduce partially their employment incomes in response to the marginal tax rate. When the husband has a very high income and the wife a relatively low one, her contribution (if considered as marginal) is heavily taxed at the margin and she therefore has every interest in reducing it.

In Great Britain, the 'child benefit' is distributed to each family with children, with equal amounts per child and is not progressive for children of different birth order and without any means test. Another benefit, the Family Income Supplement (FIS) is provided to families whose income is below a certain level. This benefit is not very high and a large percentage of families are eligible for it. This system is not a strong disincentive to female labour force participation, but does compensate for the possible reduction of earnings resulting from female labour force withdrawal as a response to child care demands.

In France, family benefits are paid only for the second and subsequent children. The size of the benefit is determined by birth order (benefits for the third child onwards are distinctly higher): they are increased with the child's age and eligibility is universal. Family benefits with a means test are relatively low and depend on the number (beyond the third), or age (under three) of the child.

Despite the relative scale of the transfers, (4 and 12 per cent of family disposable income or 8 and 17 per cent of the average net woman's salary respectively for families with and without the woman in paid employment) this system has little discouraging impact on women's labour supply in France. The French system, more pro-children than redistributive, disregarding the first child, at the same time disregards the changes involved by the birth of a child for the life of a couple. In fact, as from the first child the family has to deal with constraints due to the presence of children (availability of child care, work-family reconciliation, economic costs . . .) in spite of the provision of a large number of facilities. This change in life style first takes place without the aid of family benefits and under an increased economic constraint. In this context the system encourages the woman to keep working with her one child and can encourage her to have others, given that many of the necessary adaptations to reconcile family life and professional life have already been made. The birth of a second or third child does not necessarily require a considerable reduction in the work time or even a cessation of full-time employment.

Child care facilities in Great Britain are extremely limited as compared to France. Day nurseries and crèches are more widely available for French children under the age of 3 and the organisation of pre-school (3 to 5 years old) and school life (6 years and over) is far more conducive to child care. The mother in France can count on the whole of the scholastic and para-scholastic system to take charge of her child throughout the day without interruption. This system encourages women to take up or to keep a full-time job whatever the age of their children.

In Great Britain the child care system for young children is relatively weak and the school attendance patterns are different – school days are far shorter than in France. Thus the organisation of child care for young children presents a real problem to those women who wish to reconcile a professional life with their family life.

Questioned as to their degree of satisfaction with their employment situation and particularly the length of their hours of work, women in both France and Great Britain gave very similar answers (see Table 10.6). Generally speaking, they were satisfied, although British part-timers expressed more satisfaction than French and French full-timers more than British. How can it be explained that in situations as different as these, women find the same level of satisfaction? The survey answers are instantaneous and reflect preferences at the moment of the survey. There is a real need for part-time work in both countries to cope with child care problems. The difference is in the long-term behaviour and preferences. In France, part-time is considered as a temporary solution. Moreover, the lack of flexibility in working time in France means that a large part of the demand for part-time work remains unsatisfied. On the other hand, the economic incentives to paid employment encourage women to change into full-time as soon as possible. In Britain similar family constraints are

Table 10.6   Preferences for changing working hours by full-time or part-time work
(per cent)

Preference	France		Preference	Great Britain	
	Full-time	Part-time		Full-time	Part-time
			More working hours	1.0	12.8
Part-time	25.8				
No change	70.1		Less working hours	39.4	6.6
No answer	4.1				
			Happy with number of working hours	59.7	80.7
Total	100.0				
			Total	100.0	100.0
Full-time		11.0			
No change		61.8			
No answer		27.2			
Total		100.0			

Source: VFP and WES surveys.

very often associated with a strong economic disincentive to paid employment which makes a woman's decision to work part-time almost irreversible.

4   CHANGING ROLES OF MEN AND WOMEN

The level of women's labour force participation influences men's labour force decisions. The French survey data suggest that greater female professional involvement is associated with relatively lower husband's earnings. In the French case, for the same education level and social category, especially for higher education levels where the career effects are significant, the husbands' incomes were up to 18 per cent lower in those cases where their wives had been working without interruptions when compared to those of husbands whose wives do not work (see Table 10.7).

Some substitution effects are at work inside the family (between husband and wife) in terms of labour supply and professional involvement. These effects tend to equalise men's and women's contributions to family income. Thus the prevalence of part-time work for

Table 10.7   Husband's wage difference by employment status of the wife
(per cent)

Husband's profession	Wage differential between husbands with employed wives and those whose wives are not employed	Wage differential between husbands with continuously employed wives and those whose wives are not employed
Senior executive	−15.5	−18.1
Professor	−18.0	−20.0
Middle level executive	−13.8	−17.1
Teacher	− 7.7	−10.2
Office clerk	+10.1	+ 7.2
Shop employee	+ 6.5	+12.4
Skilled worker	+ 2.8	+ 3.8
Unskilled worker	−10.7	− 8.9
Service personnel	−14.9	− 9.9
Other (army, police, etc)	− 6.2	−10.8
Total	− 5.7	− 7.7

Source: VFP survey.

women may be an obstacle to the greater parity of men's and
women's position in the family as well as in the economy.

5   CONCLUDING REMARKS

Simple consideration of trends in rates of female labour force participation in France and Great Britain suggests a trend towards their
convergence. However, consideration of the distribution of women's
paid labour between full-time and part-time reveals a remarkable
divergence between the two countries. However flexible, the British
system discourages full-time work for women and therefore has a
negative impact on their working status. In France, part-time work is
less available and considered as a situation 'for lack of something
better' or as a substitute for not working rather than for working
full-time. As a result, relatively more women work full-time at
continuous careers. These differences in patterns of female labour

force participation can be largely explained by state policies regarding income tax, social security contributions, family allowances and child care.

Notes

1. This paper is based on a study made in collaboration with Shirley Dex (Keele University) and Patricia Walters (Salford University).
2. This was the position until 1990–91 when married couples began to be taxed separately as a matter of course.

References

Baroin, D. (1982), 'Le travail à temps partiel en France', in Jallade, J. P. (ed.) (1982).

Barrère-Maurisson, M. A., Letablier, M. T., Daune-Richard, A. M. (1987) 'Activité, Emploi et Travail des femmes- Jalons pour une comparaison France-Grande-Bretagne', Association d'Economie Sociale, Conference communication, Aix-en-Provence, 1987.

Belloc, B. (1986) 'De plus en plus de salariés à temps partiel', *Economie et Statistiques*, no. 193–4, pp. 43–50.

Dale, A. and Glover, J. (1990) 'An Analysis of Women's Employment Patterns in the UK, France, and the USA; The Value of Survey Based Comparisons', Research Paper no. 75, Department of Employment, London, UK.

David, M. G., Euvrard, F. and Starzec, Ch. (1985) 'Mères de famille: Coûts et revenus de l'activité professionnelle', Documents du Centre d'Étude des Revenus et des Coûts (CERC), no. 75.

Dex, S. (1987) *Women's Occupational Mobility: A Lifetime Perspective* (London: Macmillan)

Dex, S. (1988) *Women's Attitudes Towards Work* (London: Macmillan)

Garnsey, E. (1984) 'The Provision and Quality of Part-time Work; The Case of Great Britain and France', Report of the European Community, Brussels.

Heller, J. L. (1986), 'Emplois précaires, stages: des emplois "Faute de mieux"', *Economie et Statistiques*, no. 193–4, pp. 27–36.

INSEE (1987) 'Population active, emploi et chômage depuis 30 ans', les Collections de l'INSEE, Série D, no. 123, Paris.

Jallade, J. P. (ed.) (1982) *L'Europe à temps partiel* (Paris: Economica).

Jallade, J. P. (1984) *Towards a Policy of Part-time Employment* (Maastricht: European Centre for Work and Society).

Leicester, C. (1982), 'Le travail à temps partiel en Grande-Bretagne' in Jallade, J. P. (ed.) (1982).

Martin, J. and Roberts, C. (1984) *Women and Employment: a Lifetime Perspective* (London: HMSO)

Memento Pratique Francis Lefebvre Social (1981), Editions Francis Lefebvre, Paris.

SOEC (1986) Enquête Forces de travail 1986.

11 Differential Returns to Human Capital in Full-time and Part-time Employment

John F. Ermisch[1]
NIESR, LONDON

and

Robert E. Wright[1]
BIRKBECK COLLEGE, LONDON

1 INTRODUCTION AND BACKGROUND

In Britain, part-time employment is very important among women, but in such employment they tend to receive lower hourly pay. For example, according to the 1980 Women and Employment Survey (WES) reported on by Martin and Roberts (1984), 44 per cent of employed women worked part-time (their own assessment), and the mean hourly wage for part-time women workers was £1.60 compared wtih £1.90 for women in full-time jobs. In the late 1980s, a similar percentage of women were in part-time employment, and it continues to attract lower average pay than full-time employment. One purpose of the analysis in this paper is to estimate whether the lower average pay in part-time employment arises primarily because women who take part-time jobs have less human capital, or because wage offers are lower for part-time jobs, thereby giving women a lower return on their human capital in these jobs. A second purpose is to measure the contribution of differential returns in part-time employment to the average pay gap between men and women.

In the conventional labour supply model, a woman receives an hourly wage offer, and given other family income and family responsibilities, she chooses the number of hours to work (see, for example, Smith, 1980; Killingsworth and Heckman, 1986; and Mroz,

1987). When tax and benefit systems are taken into account, her marginal net hourly wage may vary with the number of hours, but it is almost always assumed that her gross hourly wage offer is invariant to hours worked, with the possible exception of 'overtime hours'.[2] An important exception is Moffitt's (1984) model in which the hourly wage offered depends on the number of hours worked. His estimation method accounts for the endogeneity of hours worked and wage offers, and he finds that wage offers to American women rise over the part-time range of hours, peaking at about 34 hours per week.[3]

This paper presents evidence that the assumption of a constant gross wage is also questionable in the labour market for British women, in which part-time employment is much more common than in the USA. For instance, in a sample of British women of comparable ages to those in the US sample analysed by Moffitt, 56 per cent of British employed women worked 30 hours or less compared to about a quarter in the US sample.[4] We show that a woman with given education and employment history generally receives a lower wage offer in part-time employment than in a full-time job. Lower wage offers at fewer hours would tend to bias upwards estimates of the wage elasticity in conventional models of working hours, as Moffitt's (1984) results confirm.

Jones and Long (1979), in a study of American women's pay in part-week and full-week jobs, also find lower wage offers to part-timers. By distinguishing whether each employment spell was part-time or full-time, the work history data used in the analysis that follows is superior to that used in their study, and they did not address the endogeneity of work status in their estimates of the impact of part-time employment on hourly pay. Canadian research (Simpson, 1986) addresses the endogeneity issue and also suggests lower wage offers in part-time jobs, but the estimated wage offer equations omit employment history information, as do Moffitt's (1984).

2   WHY WAGE OFFERS DIFFER IN FULL-TIME AND PART-TIME EMPLOYMENT

One reason why wage offers in part-time jobs may be lower is primarily a compositional one. Montgomery (1988) shows that the cost of recruiting and training is a significant impediment to hiring part-time workers. To the extent that positions offering higher pay and better opportunities for advancement are also jobs which involve more recruiting and training costs to the firm, such jobs are less likely to be filled by part-time workers. Even when part-time jobs are offered, these fixed costs of employment would entail lower wage offers at fewer hours of work (Rosen, 1976). Barzel (1973) also calls attention to factors generating rising marginal product and wage offers with daily hours worked.

Another reason may lie in the segmented nature of the market for part-time workers. Women primarily seek part-time employment because of their home responsibilities. They want jobs with working hours that mesh with these responsibilities, such as while the children are at school or when their husband is at home to look after the children.[5] The supply function for part-time workers tends, therefore, to be distinct from that for full-time workers. Employers who can offer these sorts of working hours are in a good bargaining position concerning the other aspects of the pay and employment conditions package, particularly pay. In other words, compensating wage differentials may emerge, with these attributes of part-time jobs being substitutable for wages.[6]

Segmentation in the supply of part-time workers may also have a geographical dimension because of spatial constraints on their labour supply. Not only would part-time workers be less willing to pay commuting costs than full-timers, because of the smaller number of hours worked, but they would find it much easier to combine paid employment with the demands on their time from home if the employer is easily accessible from their home. Because of the restricted mobility of women seeking part-time work relative to those seeking full-time jobs, their labour supply is likely to be less elastic than the supply of full-timers. If, therefore, employers exercise a degree of monopsony power in local labour markets, profit maximisation entails paying part-time workers a lower wage.

On the demand side there is, of course, scope for substitution between part-timers and full-timers. Employers can alter the employment mix of part-timers and full-timers according to the supply conditions in a local labour market. In areas where there is an abundant supply of women seeking part-time employment, because of a concentration of women with children or older women, employers would use part-time labour to a greater extent because it can be obtained at a lower cost, while in areas lacking such a supply, employers would compete on a larger geographical scale for full-time workers. Thus, even in the absence of monopsony power, because of their less elastic labour supply, part-timers are rarely observed earning more than full-timers, but often less, causing an average differential in favour of full-timers.[7]

Tax rules could also reduce the pay of part-timers. Part-timers earning less than the income tax threshold (47 per cent of part-timers in 1980) would be more willing to supply additional hours at each gross hourly wage than full-timers, thereby tending to depress part-timers' gross hourly pay, which is what we measure. In other words, this tax advantage is partly passed on to employers. But there is an opposing effect on the demand side of the market. The earnings of 40 per cent of part-timers (in 1980) were below the national insurance threshold, exempting the employer as well as employee from national insurance contributions. Employers would be more willing to hire additional hours from such part-timers at each gross wage than from full-timers, thereby tending to increase part-timers' pay. Part-timers' pay would be lower if the supply side effects of these tax rules dominated the demand side effect.

3 METHODS AND MATERIALS

3.1 Human Capital Wage Equations

The econometric analysis is based on Mincer and Polachek's (1974) extension of the human capital model of earnings to workers with interruptions in their employment history. Optimal life-cycle investment plans have no clear implications about whether human capital investments increase or decrease with experience in paid employment or even with the duration of a particular employment spell. A reasonable approximation, particularly for short spells in and out of employment, is the following earnings function

$$\log W_t = \log E_0 + \log (1 - k_n) + rS + \sum_{i=1}^{n} rk_i e_i \qquad (1)$$

where W_t = earnings *net* of on-the-job investment in human capital in period t, which occurs during the most recent (the nth) work history segment;

E_0 = initial (before any investment) gross earnings;

k_i = the ratio of *net* investment to gross earnings in segment i of a woman's work history;

e_i = the duration of segment i;

S = the duration of education; and

r = the rate of return to human capital.

In view of the lack of theoretical guidance for a more concise parameterisation, we made some special assumptions. The analysis groups the segments of a woman's work history into durations of full-time employment, part-time employment and periods out of employment, and it allows the *net investment ratios* to differ among these types of segment, but assumes that they are the same for each segment of a given type:

$$\log W = \log E_0 + \log (1 - k_n) + rS + rk_F \sum_F e_i$$

$$+ rk_P \sum_P e_i + rk_N \sum_N e_i, \tag{2}$$

where F, P and N designate whether a work history segment is full-time, part-time or a period not in employment respectively, and $\sum_j e_i$ indicates summation over all segments of type j ($j = F$, P or N).

We allow for the net investment ratios to vary with the total time in each type of segment:

$$k_j = a_j + b_j \sum_F e_i + c_j \sum_P e_i, \qquad \text{for } j = F \text{ and } P. \tag{3}$$

For periods out of employment:

$$k_N = a_N + b_N \sum_N e_i. \tag{4}$$

It is plausible to expect that there is less on-the-job investment in part-time jobs because of fewer hours on the job, their shorter expected pay-off period and more depreciation of skills (Jones and Long, 1979), so that $k_P < k_F$, and during periods out of employment, the depreciation of acquired skills is likely to outweigh human capital investment, making it likely that $k_N < 0$. Different wage offers in part-time and full-time employment would correspond to different values of r and/or a different E_0 in equation (2).

Allowing for different offered wages in full-time and part-time employment, equations (2), (3) and (4) imply wage offer equations of the following form:

$$\log W_i = \gamma_i X + \varepsilon_i, \qquad i = F \text{ and } P, \tag{5}$$

where W_i is the hourly wage; X is a vector of human capital attributes; and ε_i is a random variable representing unmeasured influences on offered wages.

We do not, however, observe wage offer functions (5), but only accepted offers (observed wages). Thus, in order to obtain consistent estimates of (5), the endogeneity of accepted offers (that is, work status) must be addressed. This is done by extending the procedures to correct for sample selection bias, originally developed by Heckman (1979), to the three-way decision of whether to work full-time, part-time or not at all.[8]

3.2   Data and Estimates of Wage Offer Equations

Our sample consisted of 4075 women from the 1980 Women and Employment Survey (WES), of which 1512 were employed full-time and 1084 were employed part-time at the time of the survey. The WES is a nationally representative sample of women in Great Britain; complete demographic and work histories were collected of 5320 women, as well as information about their earnings and other income, including husband's earnings, in 1980. The means and standard deviations of the variables included in the wage equations are shown in Table 11.1.

In addition to the work experience variables and amount of time not in paid employment, the equations contain two education variables: the number of years of post-compulsory education and educational qualifications (that is A-levels and above, O-levels and other qualifications). Because the choice of work status depends on a woman's pay in full- and part-time employment, the sample selection equation includes the wage equation variables as well as demographic, childbearing and marital status variables thought to influence employment decisions. This specification follows very closely the labour force participation model suggested by Joshi (1986). The estimates of the wage offer equations are shown in Table 11.2.[9] A statistical test allows us to accept the hypothesis that the work experience variables are exogenous in the wage equations;[10] thus ordinary least squares (with the sample selection bias correction) are used to estimate the wage equations.

The *t*-statistic on the sample selection variable, λ, allows us to accept the hypothesis of no selection bias in the part-time wage equation, but this hypothesis is rejected for full-time employees.[11] The positive and statistically significant coefficient on λ for full-timers suggests that women having unobservable characteristics (for

Table 11.1 Means and standard deviations of variables for British women, 1980

Variable	All women		Full-time women		Part-time women		Married men	
	Mean	Standard deviation	Mean	Standard deviation	Mean	Standard deviation	Mean	Standard deviation
Work experience (years)								
Full-time	7.631	8.16	12.103	9.94	8.953	6.26	23.190	1.09
(Full-time)^2	160.930	281.57	245.27	361.32	119.290	202.84	660.64	562.54
Part-time	3.107	5.15	1.634	3.72	7.175	6.24		
(Part-time)^2	36.174	99.08	16.499	57.63	90.414	148.10		
Not working	7.731	8.16	3.783	5.87	8.983	6.52		
(Full-time)(Part-time)	29.868	56.96	21.618	53.05	62.318	68.30		
Education:								
Post-compulsory (years)	1.309	1.93	1.675	2.19	1.007	1.65	[a]	
Qualifications:								
A-level(s) and above	0.171		0.240		0.133		0.259	
O-level(s)	0.199		0.259		0.146		0.191	
Other	0.153		0.169		0.142		0.173	
λ			0.512	0.52	0.091	0.61		
N	4075		1512		1084		1868	

Source: 1980 Women and Employment Survey.
Note: a Measure of years of post-compulsory education is truncated for men.

Table 11.2   Parameter estimates of wage equations for British women, 1980

	Full-time	Part-time
Qualifications:		
A-level(s) or above	0.216	0.117
	(7.36)	(2.56)
O-level(s)	0.104	–0.040
	(4.84)	(1.20)
Other	0.052	0.019
	(2.30)	(0.59)
Years of:		
Post-compulsory education	0.0716	0.072
	(14.42)	(7.79)
Full-time experience	0.0466	0.0157
	(17.58)	(2.51)
(Full-time experience)^2	–0.000907	–0.000294
	(13.00)	(1.87)
Part-time experience	0.0374	0.0160
	(5.35)	(2.37)
(Part-time experience)^2	–0.00088	–0.00031
	(2.62)	(1.42)
(Full-time)(Part-time)	–0.001614	–0.000696
	(5.40)	(1.85)
Non-employment	–0.0115	–0.0045
	(6.49)	(2.48)
Constant	0.051	0.238
	(1.95)	(4.68)
λ_i	0.0464	–0.0192
	(2.24)	(0.94)
σ_i	0.282	0.343
R^2	0.482	0.172
F	126.87	20.31
N for wage equation	1512	1084
N for total sample size	4075	4075
Mean log w_i	0.595	0.430
Standard deviation log w_i	0.391	0.375

Notes: Absolute values of t-statistics in parentheses. The dependent variable is the logarithm of the hourly wage rate.

example, ability, motivation) which give them a higher full-time wage are also more likely to be employed full-time at the time of the survey. The full-time equation accounts for 48 per cent of the variation in the logarithm of hourly wages. In contrast, only 17 per cent of the variation in the logarithm of part-time hourly wages are accounted for by the model.

Table 11.3 Comparison of the rates of return to work experience and education between full-time and part-time employment, for British women, 1980

Effect on logarithm of hourly wage rate	*Full-time employment*	*Part-time employment*
Work experience:		
Full-time experience	0.036	0.012
Part-time experience	0.028	0.012
Not working	−0.011	−0.005
Education:		
Post-compulsory	0.072	0.072
A-level(s) or above	0.216	0.117
O-level(s)	0.104	−0.040
Other qualifications	0.052	0.019

Notes: Derived from parameter estimates given in columns 1 and 2 of Table 11.2. Rates of return evaluated for a one year increase in work experience with the mean number of years of full-time experience equal to 9.751, part-time experience equal to 3.107 and not working equal to 7.631. These estimates assume that an additional year of work experience of either type entails one less year not employed.

3.3 Rates of Return to Human Capital

Table 11.3, which is based on the parameter estimates in Table 11.2, compares the effects of work experience and education on full-time and part-time hourly wages for a 'typical' woman with full-time and part-time experience equal to their means in the full sample (that is, including women not employed at the time of the survey). Full-timers gain more from an additional year of full-time or part-time work experience than part-timers, indicating a lower return to on-the-job human capital investments in part-time jobs. Our estimates suggest that the rate of return to these investments is about 60 per cent lower in a part-time job. While a full-timer's wage is enhanced more by full-time than part-time experience, the rewards from each type of experience are similar for part-timers. Full-timers are penalised more for a year out of employment than part-timers (that is 1.1 per cent compared to 0.5 per cent). While an additional year of education appears to have a very similar effect on a woman's full-time and part-time wage, she is rewarded more for her formal qualifications (A-level, etc.) in full-time work.[12] These results imply that this 'typical' woman would be offered about 8.5 per cent less in a part-time job than in a full-time job.

In terms of the human capital model, the estimates of the wage offer equation for full-time jobs suggest that there is more on-the-job investment in human capital in full-time jobs; that is, $k_F > k_P$ in equation (2). This confirms the estimates of Jones and Long (1979) for American women, which had to rely on poorer work history data than ours. Both wage offer equations suggest that on-the-job investment in human capital diminishes with employment experience, either full-time or part-time (that is, b_j and c_j are negative in equation (3)) and that there is net depreciation of human capital while a woman is not employed ($k_N < 0$). The estimated impact of an additional year of education suggests a rate of return on human capital (r) of 7.2 per cent (see equation (2)). There is also a gradient according to the type of qualifications received in full-time jobs.

4   DECOMPOSITION OF FULL-TIME/PART-TIME WAGE DIFFERENTIAL

Using a method similar to that developed by Oaxaca (1973), when augmented by their selection bias variables, equations (5) suggest the following decomposition of the difference between the average log hourly earnings of full-timers and part-timers:

$$\overline{\log W_F} - \overline{\log W_P} = \hat{\gamma}_F(\bar{X}_F - \bar{X}_P) + (\hat{\gamma}_F - \hat{\gamma}_P)\bar{X}_P$$
$$+ [(\hat{\varrho}_F\hat{\sigma}_F)\bar{\lambda}_F - (\hat{\varrho}_P\hat{\sigma}_P)\bar{\lambda}_P] \qquad (6)$$

where the bar represents a mean value and the symbol ^ represents the estimate of the respective parameter vector in Table 11.2. The first term on the right hand side of equation (6) shows the contribution to the observed wage differential of the difference in average human capital attributes between full-time and part-time employees, evaluated using the wage equation for full-time jobs; the second term shows the contribution of differences in the remuneration of these attributes in the two types of employment, evaluated at the average attributes of a part-time worker; and the third term shows the contribution of selection bias in the samples of women in full-time and part-time employment to the observed wage differential. An

Table 11.4 Decomposition of full-time/part-time hourly wage differential for British women, 1980

Component	Logarithm
(a) Observed hourly wage differential	
$\overline{\log W_F} - \overline{\log W_P}$	0.165
(b) Differential attributable to differences in average selection bias	
$(\hat{\varrho}_F \hat{\sigma}_F)\bar{\lambda}_F - (\hat{\varrho}_P \hat{\sigma}_P)\bar{\lambda}_P$	0.029
(c) Difference in average log wage offers: (a)–(b)	0.136
(1) Differential attributable to differences in human capital	
(a) using wage equation for full-time employment:	
$\hat{\gamma}_F(\bar{X}_F - \bar{X}_P)$	0.116
(b) using wage equation for part-time employment:	
$\hat{\gamma}_P(\bar{X}_F - \bar{X}_P)$	0.058
(2) Differential attributable to different remuneration of human capital attributes	
(a) for a woman with the average characteristics of a part-time worker:	
$(\hat{\gamma}_F - \hat{\gamma}_P)\bar{X}_P$	0.020
(b) for a woman with the average characteristics of a full-time worker:	
$(\hat{\gamma}_F - \hat{\gamma}_P)\bar{X}_F$	0.078

alternative decomposition would use the wage equation in part-time jobs $(\hat{\gamma}_P)$ and the average attributes of full-time workers $(\bar{X}_F)$ respectively in the first two terms of the decomposition.

Table 11.4 shows these two alternative decompositions of the observed differential in average log hourly earnings between full-time and part-time workers in the survey. Of the observed mean log wage differential of 0.165, 0.029 is accounted for by a difference between full-timers and part-timers in average selection bias; in particular, women choosing full-time employment have, on average, unobserved attributes that give them a higher wage in full-time jobs, thereby contributing to the observed pay differential between full-timers and part-timers. Because equations (5) are *wage offer* functions, if this selection bias effect is subtracted from the observed wage differential, the difference in average *wage offers* between full-timers and part-timers is obtained (compare equations (5) and (6)).

Of the difference in average log wage offers of 0.136, 0.116 (or 85 per cent) is accounted for by differences between the observed human capital attributes of these women (that is work experience, education, etc.) when the returns to these are those received by full-timers. When part-timers' returns are used to evaluate the impact of these human capital differences, only 0.058 of the offered log wage differential (or 43 per cent) is accounted for by differences in human capital. Therefore, an average full-timer switching to part-time work would be penalised by an 8 per cent reduction in her hourly wage, while an average part-timer would receive a premium of 2 per cent if she switched to a full-time job. This difference reflects the self-selection of women into these two types of jobs.

5   DECOMPOSITION OF MALE/FEMALE WAGE DIFFERENTIAL

In accounting terms, the importance of part-time work among women in conjunction with lower average pay in part-time employment contributes to the gender log pay gap (G), as equation (7) shows:

$$G = (\overline{\log W_M} - \overline{\log W_F}) + p(\overline{\log W_F} - \overline{\log W_P}) . \qquad (7)$$

In order to determine the contribution of differential returns between women in full-time and part-time jobs to the gender pay gap, we substitute equation (6) into equation (7). We also substitute into (7) the following equation for the decomposition of the observed pay differential between married men and women in full-time jobs,

$$\overline{\log W_M} - \overline{\log W_F} = \hat{\delta}(\bar{X}_M - \bar{X}_{F1}) + (\hat{\delta} - \hat{\gamma}_{F1})\bar{X}_{F1}$$

$$- \hat{\gamma}_{F2}\bar{X}_{F2} - (\hat{\varrho}_F\hat{\sigma}_F)\bar{\lambda}_F, \qquad (8)$$

where X_{F2} is the subset of variables in X involving part-time employment experience and time not in employment and X_{F1} is the remaining variables in X; γ_{F2} and γ_{F1} are the corresponding parameter vectors; and δ is the vector of parameters in the man's earnings function.

The latter was estimated under the assumption (as is usual) that a man's employment experience is equal to the difference between his age at the survey and his age when he left full-time education, and we have also assumed that all employment experience was in full-time jobs (as the percentage of men working part-time is very low). Data on hourly earnings, education and experience is from the husbands of women in the WES.

The restriction of the male sample to married men suggests that a better male/female comparison would be obtained from a comparable sample of women. For instance, a sample of married women would cover a more comparable age range to that of married men than the entire female sample. Furthermore, other recent decompositions of the gender wage gap in Britain, which have not distinguished between full-time and part-time employment, have focused on married men and women. Thus, we re-estimated the full-time and part-time wage offer equations on a sample of married women, 55 per cent of whom were in part-time employment.

As these estimates led to conclusions about differential returns to education and employment experience in part-time jobs similar to those in Table 11.3, they are not presented. It is, however, noteworthy that they indicate that the difference in returns to human capital between full-time and part-time jobs is larger among married women than single women.

The decomposition of the gender pay gap, based on these estimates and equations (6), (7) and (8), is given in Table 11.5. Four different decompositions are possible, two for each component of the right hand side of (7). We use the men's earnings function to evaluate the difference in human capital between men and women in full-time jobs and the characteristics of women in full-time jobs to evaluate differences in the remuneration of human capital between men and women full-timers. Both of the decompositions of the part-time/full-time pay differential described above are used in Table 11.5.

Differences in the remuneration of human capital attributes between full- and part-time jobs accounts for about one-fifth of the gender pay gap (6.4–8.5 percentage points of the log differential). The dominant component is the differences in remuneration between men and women in full-time jobs, which is the last row of Table 11.5. This is the component that is associated with measures of

Table 11.5 Decomposition of the male/female wage differential for Britain, 1980

Component	Logarithm	
(a) Observed log wage differential (G):	0.398	
(b) Sample selection effects:		
$p[(\hat{\varrho}_F \hat{\sigma}_F)\bar{\lambda}_F - (\hat{\varrho}_P \hat{\sigma}_P)\bar{\lambda}_P] - (\hat{\varrho}_F \hat{\sigma}_F)\bar{\lambda}_F$	0.010[a]	
(c) Difference in wage offers: (a)–(b)	0.388	
Differential attributable to:		
(1) Differences in human capital between men and women in full-time employment:		
$\hat{\delta}(\bar{X}_M - \bar{X}_{F1})$	0.052	
(2) Differences in human capital between women in full- and part-time employment:		
$p\hat{\gamma}_F(\bar{X}_F - \bar{X}_P)$	0.062	(0.041)[b]
(3) Differences in remuneration between full-time and part-time employment:		
$p(\hat{\delta}_F - \hat{\delta}_P)\bar{X}_P$	0.064	(0.085)[c]
(4) Effects of non-employment and part-time employment among women in full-time jobs:		
$-\hat{\gamma}_{F2}\bar{X}_{F2}$	0.126	
(5) Differences in remuneration of human capital between men and women in full-time jobs ('discrimination'):		
$(\hat{\delta} - \hat{\gamma}_{F1})\bar{X}_{F1}$	0.172	

Notes: a. Sample selection effects are slightly negative for the sample of married women.
      b. Component is based on $p(\hat{\gamma}_F - \hat{\gamma}_P)\bar{X}_F$.
      c. Component is based on $p\hat{\gamma}_P(\bar{X}_F - \bar{X}_P)$.

pay 'discrimination'. It suggests that married women's pay in full-time jobs would be 19 per cent ($e^{0.172} \times 100$) higher in the absence of 'discrimination'. This is almost identical to the estimate of pay discrimination in Wright and Ermisch (1990), which also compares married men and women, but does not make the full-time/part-time distinction.

6 CONCLUSIONS

The analysis presents strong evidence that wage offers to British women are lower in part-time jobs than full-time ones. This finding is supported by American research by Jones and Long (1979) and Moffitt (1984) and Canadian research by Simpson (1986), but these earlier studies had to rely on data inferior to that used in the present study. This wage offer differential means that there is a substantial component of the hourly wage differential between full- and part-time employment left unexplained by differences in human capital attributes of women in these two types of employment. More specifically, the rates of remuneration for both full- and part-time work experience are clearly lower for part-time employment. In addition, educational qualifications are differentially rewarded with full-time employment yielding a higher rate of return for a given educational qualification. However, part-time workers appear to lose less from time spent out of the labour force.

Ignoring this variation in wage offers tends to produce an upward bias in estimates of the wage elasticity in labour supply equations. Lower wage offers in part-time jobs also produce a non-convexity in the budget constraint in the neighbourhood of the threshold hours for full-time employment, which has implications for modelling women's labour supply (see Moffitt, 1984).

Significant sample selection bias was discovered for full-timers. This implies that it is important to treat the decision whether to work full-time or not as endogenous in the empirical analysis of women's earnings in Great Britain and that part of the observed differential between the hourly pay of full-timers and part-timers arises because of self-selection of women who can command higher pay in full-time employment.

Finally, the lower rate of return to human capital in part-time employment in conjunction with the larger proportion of women than men in part-time jobs makes a relatively small contribution to women's lower pay relative to men's. The primary reason for women's lower pay is smaller remuneration for human capital attributes in full-time jobs; if women's human capital was remunerated at the same rate as men's, their hourly pay in full-time employment would be substantially – of the order of one fifth – higher.

Notes

1. This research was supported by a grant from the Economic and Social Research Council for research on 'Income Inequality, Gender and Demographic Differentials'. All correspondence should be addressed to Robert E. Wright.
2. Burtless and Hausman (1978) show how overtime premia, taxes and welfare benefit systems affect net marginal wages and derive the implications for modelling labour supply.
3. Rosen's (1976) estimates also suggest that offered wages increase with hours worked, although the estimates of the wage offer equation could suffer from sample selection bias, and Larson's (1979) analysis suggests his estimates are not very robust.
4. Moffitt's (1984) sample is from the 1972 wave of the National Longitudinal Survey of Older Women, while the comparable British sample is of women aged 35–59 from the 1980 Women and Employment Survey, which is described further below. The average ages of women in these two surveys are 44.4 and 46.3 respectively, and the mean hours of employed women are 35.1 and 27 respectively.
5. The husband is by far the most important source of child care outside of school, particularly among women working part-time, the majority of whom rely on the husband as the primary source of care (Martin and Roberts, 1984, pp. 38–40).
6. This raises modelling issues similar to those for heterogeneous jobs, see for example Killingsworth (1986).
7. Ermisch and Wright (1988) develop this argument more fully.
8. Our method uses an ordered probit model, but similar results are obtained using a method suggested by Nakamura and Nakamura (1983). See Ermisch and Wright (1988) for details.
9. See Ermisch and Wright (1988) for the selection equation estimates. The coefficient of the square of time spent out of employment was insignificant in the wage equation and was dropped from the wage equation.
10. Conditional on the education, childbearing and marital status variables being exogenous (that is, uncorrelated with ε_F, ε_P and the error term in the selection equation), we tested whether the six work experience variables in the wage equations (see Table 11.2) are exogenous using a Wu-Hausman test (see Hausman, 1978). The F-statistics in the full-time and part-time equations are 0.98 and 1.81 respectively, compared with a 5 per cent critical value of 2.09.
11. Simpson (1986) found the same with Canadian data, although with a very limited set of variables in the wage equation.
12. The simple human capital model of equations (2), (3) and (4) ignores the possibility that the tenure of the current job may affect earnings differently from other experience in part-time or full-time employment because of returns to 'firm-specific human capital'. We omitted a job tenure variable because of the questionable exogeneity and interpretation of its coefficient (see Abraham and Farber, 1987). When a job tenure variable is included in wage equations like those in Table 11.2, the estimated effect of the *net return to job tenure* (years) is 0.0067 for full-time jobs

and 0.0063 for part-time jobs. Not surprisingly, its inclusion reduces the impact of full-time experience in the full-time equation and of part-time experience in the part-time equation, but the other coefficients were hardly affected.

References

Abraham, K. G. and Farber, H. S. (1987) 'Job Duration, Seniority, and Earnings', *American Economic Review*, vol. 77, pp. 278–97.

Barzel, Y. (1973) 'The Determination of Daily Hours and Wages', *Quarterly Journal of Economics*, vol. 87, pp. 220–38.

Burtless, G. and Hausman, J. A. (1978) 'The Effect of Taxation on Labor Supply: Evaluating the Gary Negative Income Tax Experiment', *Journal of Political Economy*, vol. 86, pp. 1103–30.

Ermisch, J. F. and Wright R. E. (1988) 'Differential Returns to Human Capital in Full-time and Part-time Employment: The Case of British Women', Birkbeck College Discussion Paper in Economics no. 14, Birkbeck College, London.

Hausman, J. A. (1978) 'Specification Tests in Econometrics', *Econometrica*, vol 46, pp. 1251–72.

Heckman, J. J. (1979) 'Sample Selection Bias as a Specification Error', *Econometrica*, vol. 47, pp. 153–61.

Jones, E. B. and Long, J. E. (1979) 'Part-Week Work and Human Capital Investment by Married Women', *Journal of Human Resources*, vol. 13, pp. 563–78.

Joshi, H. E. (1986) 'Participation in Paid Work: Evidence from the Women and Employment Survey', in Blundell, R. and Walker, I. (eds) *Unemployment, Search and Labour Supply* (Cambridge: Cambridge University Press), pp. 217–42.

Killingsworth, M. R. (1986) 'A Simple Structural Model of Heterogeneous Preferences and Compensating Wage Differentials', in Blundell, R. and Walker, I. (eds) *Unemployment, Search and Labour Supply* (Cambridge: Cambridge University Press), pp. 303–17.

Killingsworth, M. R. and Heckman, J. J. (1986) 'Female Labor Supply', in Ashenfelter, O. and Layard, R. (eds) *Handbook of Labor Economics* (Amsterdam: North Holland), pp. 103–204.

Larson, D. (1979) 'Taxes in a Labor Supply Model with Joint Wage-Hours Determination: Comment', *Econometrica*, vol. 47, pp. 1311–13.

Martin, J. and Roberts, C. (1984) *Women and Employment: A Lifetime Perspective* (London: HMSO).

Mincer, J. and Polachek, S. (1974) 'Family Investments in Human Capital: Earnings of Women', *Journal of Political Economy*, vol. 82, pp. S876–918.

Moffitt, R. (1984) 'The Estimation of a Joint Wage–hours Labor Supply Model', *Journal of Labor Economics*, vol. 2, pp. 550–66.

Montgomery, M. (1988) 'On the Determinants of Employer Demand for Part-time Workers', *Review of Economics and Statistics*, vol. 70, pp. 112–17.

Mroz, T. A. (1987) 'The Sensitivity of an Empirical Model of Married Women's Hours of Work to Economic and Statistical Assumptions', *Econometrica*, vol. 55, pp. 765–99.

Nakamura, A. and Nakamura, M. (1983) 'Part-time and Full-time Work Behaviour of Married Women: A Model with a Doubly Truncated Dependent Variable', *Canadian Journal of Economics*, vol. 16, pp. 229–57.

Oaxaca, R. (1973) 'Male–Female Wage Differentials in Urban Labor Markets', *International Economic Review*, vol. 14, pp. 693–709.

Rosen, H. S. (1976) 'Taxes in a Labor Supply Model with Joint Wage–Hours Determination', *Econometrica*, vol. 44, pp. 485–507.

Simpson, W. (1986) 'Analysis of Part-time Pay in Canada', *Canadian Journal of Economics*, vol 19, pp. 798–807.

Smith, J. P. (ed.) (1980) *Female Labor Supply: Theory and Estimation* (Princeton: Princeton University Press).

Wright, R. E. and Ermisch, J. F. (1988) 'Gender Discrimination in the British Labour Market: A Reassessment', Discussion Paper no. 278, Centre for Economic Policy Research, London.

12 Part-time Work in Sweden and its Implications for Gender Equality

Marianne Sundström
SWEDISH CENTRE FOR WORKING LIFE,
STOCKHOLM

1 INTRODUCTION

Following the steep rise in female labour force participation over the last 20 years, part-time employment has increased in most Western countries.[1] This paper compares Sweden and the EC countries with respect to the trends in female part-time work and the extent of job security and social benefits for part-time workers. For Sweden I report my findings and explanations for the trends and discuss the effects on women's economic position. This comparison is of interest since Sweden has had, for a long time, a high proportion of part-time workers who work rather long hours and enjoy full social benefits, and because Sweden aspires to a closer association to the EC.

2 THE DEVELOPMENT OF PART-TIME WORK AMONG SWEDISH WOMEN

During the last 20 years labour force participation rates of Swedish women have risen strongly, from 55 per cent in 1967 to 80 per cent in 1987 (see Table 12.1), a rate unrivalled in the OECD area.[2] This rise was associated with a rapid increase in the proportion of part-time employed women, from 36 per cent in 1967 to 47 per cent in 1982 when it reached its peak[3] (see also Table 12.2). In the same period the proportion of part-time workers increased from 3 per cent to 6 per cent among employed Swedish men. But as almost 90 per cent of part-time workers are women and the main part of the growth in

213

Table 12.1   Female labour force participation rates[a] in EC countries and
Sweden, 1973–87
(per cent)

	1973	1979	1983	1987[b]
Belgium	42.5	47.4	49.8	51.3[c]
Denmark	61.9	69.9	74.2	76.5[c]
France	50.1	54.2	54.4	55.8
Germany	49.6	49.6	49.7	51.8
Greece	n.a	32.8	40.4	41.7[c]
Ireland	34.1	35.2	37.8	37.2[c]
Italy	33.7	38.7	40.3	43.2
Luxembourg	35.9	39.8	42.0	44.3[c]
Netherlands	n.a.	33.4	40.5	41.1[c]
Portugal[d]	32.1	57.3	60.1	57.7
Spain	33.4	32.3	33.0	37.5
Sweden	62.6	72.8	76.6	79.5
United Kingdom	53.2	58.0	57.2	62.0

Source: OECD (1988) *Employment Outlook*, p. 200.
Notes: a. Defined as total female labour force divided by all women aged
15–64 in the population at mid-year.
  b. The rates for 1987 have been estimated by the OECD secretariat.
  c. The rate in 1986.
  d. Data include a significant number of persons aged less than 15
years.
  n.a. = not available.

part-time work has been amongst women this paper will focus on the
latter.

Factors on both the supply side and the demand side of the labour
market contributed to the growth in part-time work among women.
On the supply side, rising female wages, separate taxation of married
couples (from 1971), expanded public child care and parental leave
encouraged women to take up paid work. Also, the attractiveness of
part-time work as compared to full-time was increased through rising
marginal tax rates and full social benefits (see section 4 below) as well
as through reforms broadening employee opportunities for reduced
hours (see section 5 below).[4] Consequently, a high proportion of
labour force entrants were mothers of pre-school children who if
employed worked part-time in higher proportions than other employed women.[5] On the demand side, continuous high levels of
labour demand which could not be met from traditional sources –

Table 12.2 The proportion of female employment working part-time[a] in the EC countries and Sweden, 1973–86 (per cent)

	1973	1979	1983	1986
Belgium	8.2	16.5	19.7	22.6
Denmark	40.3	46.3	44.7	41.9
France	11.2	17.0	20.1	23.2
Germany	20.0	27.6	30.0	29.8
Greece	n.a.	n.a.	12.1	10.4
Ireland	n.a.	13.1	15.7	14.2
Italy	8.5	10.6	9.4	9.5
Luxembourg	13.9	17.1	18.8	15.4
Netherlands	15.5	31.7	50.5[a]	55.2[a,b]
Portugal	n.a.	n.a.	n.a.	6.6
Spain	n.a.	n.a.	n.a.	n.a.[c]
Sweden	38.8	46.0	45.9	42.8[d]
United Kingdom	38.3	39.0	42.4	45.0

Sources: For 1973, OECD (1983) *Employment Outlook*, p. 44; for 1979–86, OECD (1988) *Employment Outlook*, p. 149,

Notes: a. Part-time workers are those who declare themselves to be part-time workers or those who usually work less than 35 hours per week, except for the Netherlands from 1983 where they are those who worked less than 35 hours per week; see OECD (1985) p. 131 and OECD (1988) p. 21.

    b. The figure is for 1985.

    c. 0.37 per cent of the total Spanish labour force worked part-time in 1984 but the proportion has risen since the passing of a new law in 1984 ('Part-time work in 15 countries').

    d. The figure is from Statistics Sweden, *The Labour Force Survey 1986*, recalculated to obtain comparability over time.

    n.a. = not available.

males, unmarried women or immigrants – raised women's wages and made employers more willing to employ part-time workers.[6]

Since 1982 the proportion employed part-time among Swedish women has declined and the proportion employed full-time has increased (see Table 12.2). Possible explanations for this break in the trend are the cuts in marginal tax rates in 1983 and following years and the reduced level of income replacement in the partial pension (Sundström, 1987, p. 111). Further, hours worked among female part-time workers have increased continuously: 57 per cent worked 20–34 hours per week in 1967, 79 per cent in 1982 and 83 per cent in

1987. By contrast, part-time workers in the EC countries tend to work fewer hours. Thus, in 1985 two-thirds of all part-time workers, male and female, worked less than 21 hours per week in Belgium, Great Britain, Germany and the Netherlands (Maier, 1989). In Sweden only 19 per cent of all part-time workers worked less than 20 hours per week in 1985.

3   THE DEVELOPMENT OF PART-TIME WORK IN THE EC COUNTRIES

In the EC countries female labour force participation also increased between 1973 and 1987, when it ranged from about 77 per cent in Denmark to 37 per cent in Ireland. Swedish experience leads us to expect that countries with high female labour force participation rates, that is where mothers of pre-schoolers also have paid work, will have a higher proportion of women working part-time. Comparing Tables 12.1 and 12.2 we see that this expectation is largely confirmed.[7] Denmark, the EC country with the highest female labour force participation rate, has the highest proportion of women employed part-time, while Italy and Ireland which have the lowest rates, also have the smallest proportions in part-time work. The Netherlands is an exception to this pattern, since the low female labour force participation rate is combined with a high proportion of women working part-time.[8] Further, in the 1980s the proportion of employed women working part-time can be seen to have risen rapidly in the UK, Germany, France and especially in the Netherlands. Denmark, on the other hand, displays a trend similar to Sweden: part-time work has declined since 1979, although participation has remained high, possibly also due to a tax reform cutting the marginal tax rates. As to the Netherlands, the dramatic increase in part-timers was due partly to a change in definition and partly to rapidly rising levels of unemployment in the early 1980s (Kranenburg, 1985).

4   JOB SECURITY AND SOCIAL BENEFITS FOR PART-TIME WORKERS

For some years it has been recognised at the European Community level that part-time workers are disadvantaged in terms of basic employment and social security rights (see, for example, *European*

Industrial Relations Review, 1980, and Robinson, 1979a, 1979b). With the aim of improving these rights, the EC Commission submitted a draft Directive on voluntary part-time work to the EC Council in 1981 and an amended proposal was submitted in 1983 (see *European Industrial Relations Review*, 1984). The preamble of the Directive establishes that

'although . . . the number of part-time workers is increasing, measures have yet to be taken to guarantee part-time workers the same rights as full-time employees while taking into account the special features of part-time work.'

To that end, Article 2 of the Directive stipulates that

'part-time workers shall receive the same treatment as full-time workers in the same situation, except where the difference in hours of work itself objectively justifies differences in treatment. . . . The remuneration, holiday pay and redundancy and retirement payments of part-time workers shall be calculated on the same basis as and in proportion to those of full-time workers in the same situation' (*European Industrial Relations Review*, 1984).

In Sweden, the treatment of part-time workers has been in line with this principle for many years.

4.1 Job Security

All Swedish employees who have been employed with the same employer for at least six months, regardless of the number of hours worked, are protected against unfair dismissal. Seniority rules and notice periods apply equally to part-time and full-time workers. Similarly, part-time workers enjoy the same rights with regard to job protection, notice periods and redundancy pay as do full-time workers in all EC countries except Ireland, Italy and the United Kingdom (see *European Industrial Review*, 1985). In Ireland the legislation on minimum notice, redundancy pay and unfair dismissal applies only to employees working more than 18 hours a week, and Italy has no provisions relating to the rights of part-time workers to notice periods, redundancy pay, etc. In the UK, on the other hand, the employment protection legislation applies only to employees working at least 8 hours a week, and for those who have less than five years' service with their employer only to those working at least 17 hours a week.

4.2 Social Security Benefits

All statutory social benefits apply equally to part-time and full-time workers in Sweden, but as for example with sick pay, in proportion to earnings. However, the right to one year of parental leave and at least five weeks' paid holiday apply to all employees irrespective of hours worked. But holiday and parental pay are, of course, *pro rata* to earnings. Also, to be eligible for a partial pension one must work at least 22 hours a week at the time of its application – normally at the age of 60 – since one must reduce hours of work by at least five hours a week and after the reduction work at least 17 hours per week (see section 5 below).

When it comes to employee benefits and insurances guaranteed through collective agreement between the central employers organisation and the central trade unions the terms are less favourable for those part-time workers who work less than 16 hours a week (which, as already mentioned, very few do). To those who work 16 hours or more benefits apply equally but *pro rata* to earnings. Thus, those working less than 16 hours a week will get reduced redundancy pay, group life insurance and special supplementary pension (Folksam, 1986, p. 126). Further, one must work at least 17 hours a week to belong to the unemployment fund (managed by the unions) and one must also be willing to work that many hours to obtain unemployment benefits. It should, however, be observed that employers' social security contributions amount to the same percentage of the total wage for workers who work less than 17 hours a week as for those working more hours. Thus, hourly labour costs are not lower for employers with employees working few hours as is the case, for example, in the United Kingdom and West Germany.

In all EC countries employers are obliged to insure against industrial injury and occupational disease for all employees irrespective of hours worked or earnings. But when it comes to any social security above this basic level, practices vary widely (see *European Industrial Relations Review*, 1985; and Hörburger and Rath-Hörburger, 1988, Chapter 3). In Denmark, Greece, Spain, Italy and, with one minor exception, Luxembourg and the Netherlands, all employees enjoy coverage on the same basis as full-time employees but *pro rata* to their hours or earnings. In other EC countries this is not the case, however. For example, in Belgium those working only two hours per day or less are excluded from the social security system. In Ireland, on the other hand, only employees working at least 18 hours a week are covered by the Social Welfare Acts and only those working at least 120 hours a month have a right to a paid holiday. Similarly, in the United Kingdom employers do not have to pay social insurance contributions for employees earning less than a specified minimum (in 1988 £35.50 a week) who do not qualify for all benefits. Thus, in 1984 about 90 per cent of British part-time workers were cut out of pension schemes, about 70 per cent cut out of training and about 30 per cent out of sick pay (*The Economist*, 1984). In Germany, those working less than 10 hours a week, earning below 400 DM (in 1988) or employed on a short-term basis (less than two months or 50 working days per year) are excluded from the social security system. In France, there are earnings thresholds for various schemes which apply to all employees regardless of hours worked.

5 WIDER OPPORTUNITIES IN SWEDEN FOR REDUCED HOURS OF WORK

With the aim of enabling those wishing to work less than full-time to take up paid work, several reforms which widened the opportunities for reduced hours were introduced in the 1970s. Thus, in 1970 government employees obtained the right to work part-time or reduce their hours of work through partial (unpaid) leave for reasons of education, service in parliament and care of children under the age of 12.[9]

Public policies regarding parenthood have a significant impact on women's labour force participation. In Sweden, employed women have had the right to maternal leave at childbirth with some pay since 1931 (enhanced in 1937, 1955 and 1962). In 1974 Sweden was the first country in the world to introduce a system of parental leave, which gave mothers and fathers the right to six months of benefits to share as they preferred. Benefits were raised to the level of sick pay (90 per cent of the pre-tax wage) and could be used on a full-time or part-time basis any time before the child was 8. Leave benefits were further extended to seven months in 1975 and to 12 months in 1980 (of which three were replaced with a *per diem* allowance equal for all). Finally, in 1989 the Swedish parliament decided to extend the paid leave to fifteen months, with the last three at the flat rate.

In addition to the parental leave, all full-time employed parents of pre-school children in 1979 were guaranteed the right to reduce their hours to 75 per cent of full-time (that is normally to 30 hours a week) until the child is 8, provided that they have been employed full-time for at least six months with the same employer prior to the reduction.

In 1974, union shop stewards throughout the whole economy were guaranteed the right to unpaid, full or partial leave of absence from work for discharge of their duties within the unions. Also, all employees were given the right to work part-time or to have a full or partial leave of absence from work for vocational training or university studies.

Moreover, the partial pension reform, introduced from 1 July 1976, gave employees (and from 1980 the self-employed too) between 60 and 65 years old with ten years of pensionable income after the age of 45, the right to reduce their weekly hours. As mentioned, weekly hours must be reduced by at least 5 hours and after the reduction at least 17 hours must still be worked. Up to 1981 the partial pension replaced 65 per cent of pre-tax earnings lost through the reduction but in 1981–87 only 50 per cent was replaced. Thus, in the early years the number of partial pensioners rose steeply to about 68 000 (of which 21 000 were women) in 1980, but owing to the 50 per cent rule the number fell to 32 000 (of which 13 600 were women) in 1986. However, as the replacement level was restored to 65 per cent in 1987, the number of partial pensioners rose again to 38 500 (of which 15 000 were women) in 1988.[10]

6   IMPLICATIONS FOR ECONOMIC EQUALITY

As mentioned, Swedish part-time work has grown mainly at the expense of the number of women not employed. This has occurred not only through non-employed women taking up paid work but also through a decrease in the number of women dropping out of the labour force, for example when they have children. According to my research, women to an increasing extent work full-time up to the birth of their first child and remain (and are counted as) full-time employed while on parental leave.[11] At the return to work from parental leave, an increasing proportion of first-time mothers have shifted from full-time employment to part-time work.[12] That is, they make use, *inter alia*, of the wider opportunities for reduced hours described above. Thus, continuous part-time employment has replaced work interruptions during child-rearing years for women.[13] More generally, I have found that women's part-time work has taken the form of continuous part-time employment and that the pattern whereby part-time work is alternated with periods of non-employment or periods of full-time work, common in the EC countries, has been reduced.[14]

Further, my research has shown that the growth in part-time work has not been followed by increasing difficulties for women working part-time to shift to full-time. On the contrary, the proportion of women who increased their hours from part-time to full-time has grown in the 1980s and is particularly high among women with children aged 7–16.[15]

All these changes, along with the rise in hours worked among female part-time workers mentioned above, have strengthened and increased the continuity of women's attachment to the labour force. Significantly, the proportion of women who earn an income of their own has grown, as well as their level of earnings and their social security. Thus, women's economic dependency has been reduced. According to another study conducted at the Swedish Centre for Working Life, in 1984 married women in Sweden earned 39 per cent of after-tax family income, while German wives only earned 12 per cent (Gustafsson, 1989). Thus, although further evidence is needed to assess the total effects on equality, it can be concluded from the Swedish experience that the economic position of women can be improved through the introduction of an option to work part-time, and not only full-time, with *pro rata* social security benefits.

Notes

1. In this paper a part-time worker is defined as a person who ordinarily works 1–34 hours per week.
2. See OECD (1988) p. 131. The Swedish rate is sometimes said to be exaggerated, since employed mothers who are on parental leave are included among the participants. However, if these absent mothers are deducted the rate would be 77 per cent, still the highest in the OECD area, given that employed women on parental leave are also included in the Danish rate.
3. Here and subsequently the data source is the Swedish Labour Force

Surveys, if no other source is given. Reports on these surveys are published by Statistics Sweden, Stockholm.

4. Nevertheless, a breakdown of the 1968–81 growth in female part-time workers into the contributions due to (i) increased proportions employed, (ii) higher proportions part-time of the employed and (iii) population changes, showed that two-thirds was due to increased proportions employed. That is, the rise in the proportion employed was larger among groups of women with above average proportions employed part-time (Sundström, 1987, pp. 83–7).

5. As early as 1968, 62 per cent of employed mothers of pre-school children worked part-time, compared to 39 per cent of all employed women (Sundström, 1987, pp. 84–5).

6. The introduction of separate taxation of married couples could be seen partly in the light of this shortage of labour. It is labour demand that has adjusted to the full-time/part-time composition of the labour supply, rather than *vice versa* (Sundström, 1987, ch. 7).

7. This pattern has also been discussed in OECD (1983), p. 48.

8. Finland also deviates from the observed pattern, since it has a high female labour force participation but a low proportion of part-time workers (OECD, 1988, p. 200 and p. 149).

9. In the fiscal year 1976–77 more than 9000 women and 200 men in government service worked part-time or reduced hours for care of children according to this right (Edsta, 1978, p. 72), out of a total of 158 300 women and 263 900 men in government service.

10. See National Insurance Board (1989). For a review of the Sweidsh partial pension system, see Ginsburg (1985).

11. The proportion of all first-time mothers who worked full-time for eight calendar quarters in a row increased from 25 per cent in 1970–72 to 39 per cent in 1984–85, including those on parental leave (Sundström, 1987, p. 109). Compare also note 2 above. Parental benefits are higher if the mother works full-time prior to birth and leave.

12. In eight consecutive calendar quarters during 1970–72, 12 per cent of all first-time mothers reduced their hours from full-time to part-time, while in the period 1981–83 the corresponding figure was 20 per cent.

13. The proportion of first-time mothers interrupting work, that is changing from full-time work to non-employed, fell from 18 per cent in 1970–72 to less than 6 per cent in 1984–85, and among mothers of pre-school children the proportion that were non-employed for eight calendar quarters in a row fell from 23 per cent in 1970–72 to only 5 per cent in 1984–85, while the proportion that worked part time for eight calendar quarters in a row increased from 10 per cent in 1970–72 to 32 per cent in 1984–85 (Sundström, 1987, pp. 105–9).

14. The proportion of all women aged 16–64 years employed part-time for eight consecutive calendar quarters rose from 12 per cent in 1970–72 to 26 per cent in 1982–84 when it peaked; in 1984–85 it was 24 per cent. The proportion changing more than once between non-employed and part-time fell from 9 per cent in 1970–72 to 3 per cent in 1984–85 (Sundström, 1987, p. 95).

15. Among women aged 16–64 the proportion who increased their hours

from part-time to full-time rose from 2.5 per cent in 1970–72 to 4.6 per cent in 1984–85, while among those with children aged 7–16 years it increased from 4.2 per cent to 7.4 per cent over the same period (Sundström, 1987, pp. 98 and 101).

References

Economist, The (1984) 'Part-timers: the Market at Work', 29 September.
Edsta, B. (1978) *Inför jämställdheten 1978* (Stockholm: Liber).
European Industrial Relations Review (1980) 'Part-time Workers: Rights and Obligations', no. 82, pp. 16–32.
European Industrial Relations Review (1984) 'Voluntary Part-time Work', Amended Proposal for an EEC Council Directive on Voluntary Part-time Work, no. 130, p. 31.
European Industrial Relations Review (1985) 'Part-time Work in 15 Countries', no. 137, pp. 21–8.
Folksams sociala råd (1986) *Vår trygghet* (Stockholm: Folksam).
Ginsburg, H. (1985) 'Flexible and Partial Retirement for Norwegian and Swedish Workers', *Monthly Labour Review*, vol. 108, pp. 33–43.
Gustafsson, S. (1989) 'Income Taxes and Women's Economic Dependency', Working papers, Swedish Centre for Working Life, Stockholm.
Hörburger, H. and Rath-Hörburger, F. (1988) *Europas Frauen gleichberechtigt? Die Politik der EG-länder zur Gleichberechtigung der Frau im Arbeitsleben* (Düsseldorf: Wi-Verlag).
Kranenburg, M. (1985) 'Part-time arbeid', *NRC-Handelsblad*, 2 Oct.
Maier, F. (1989) *Part-Time Work, Social Security Protections and Labour Law: An International Comparison*, Mimeo. (West Berlin: Wissenschaftzentrum).
National Insurance Board (1989), 'Delpensioneringen 1976–1988', *Statistisk rapport Is-R 1989:9* (Stockholm: National Insurance Board).
OECD (1983) *Employment Outlook* (Paris: OECD).
OECD (1985) *Employment Outlook* (Paris: OECD).
OECD (1988) *Employment Outlook* (Paris: OECD).
Robinson, O. (1979a) 'Part-time Employment in the EEC – a Marginal Labour Force?', *The Three Banks Review*, no. 122, pp. 61–75.
Robinson, O. (1979b) 'Part-time Employment in the European Community', *International Labour Relations Review*, May–June, pp. 299–314.
Sundström, M. (1987) *A Study in the Growth of Part-time Work in Sweden* (Stockholm: Swedish Centre for Working Life and Almqvist and Wicksell International).

Part IV

Education and Family Policy

13 Re-entrance into the Labour Market of Women Graduates in Greece: The Results of an Experimental Training Programme

Athena Petraki Kottis[1]
ATHENS UNIVERSITY OF ECONOMICS AND
BUSINESS, GREECE

1 INTRODUCTION

After carrying out research for a number of years and writing technical papers on various issues related to the position of women in the labour market in Greece, I decided to do some more practical work about some of the problems that I had encountered.[2] In my research I found that among the most serious problems for women in Greece were those faced by non-working educated women who wanted to re-enter the labour market after some years of absence from it because of family obligations. Under present circumstances this is extremely difficult because of extensive unemployment among university graduates, the drastic changes during recent years in the types of knowledge and skills required by the business world, and the prejudices that exist in the labour market against women and particularly against those who have not worked for some time.

The purpose of this paper is to describe an experimental training programme which I initiated in Greece with the aim of helping women university graduates in economics or business administration, who wanted to re-enter the labour market after an absence from it. This programme had some specific features which made it particularly successful, and for this reason the experience gained from it may be useful in other countries where women face similar problems.

Older non-working women university graduates have maturity and

227

other personal characteristics which make them particularly suitable for various administrative and middle- and high-level managerial positions. However, in order to obtain such positions they need encouragement, the opportunity to project themselves and, most important, some additional knowledge and skills which were not provided at universities at the time they obtained their degrees. It is of the utmost importance that these women, besides the additional knowledge and skills, are given a boost to their morale and a chance to come into contact with prospective employers and convince them of their capabilities.

In view of the above, I organised a project at the Economic Research Centre of the Athens University of Economics and Business with the following goals:

1. To collect information concerning the aspirations, capabilities, needs and general characteristics of women with degrees in economics or business administration, who were unemployed or outside the labour market and wanted to work;
2. To identify the openings in the labour market that could be filled by these women after some retraining and to investigate the views of prospective employers about the knowledge and skills as well as the other qualifications that the candidates for these openings should have;
3. To organise an experimental training programme for providing a selected sample of women from the target group with the knowledge and skills necessary to enable them to fill the existing openings; and
4. To establish a channel of communication with a relatively large number of big firms with the purpose of
   a. informing them about the programme,
   b. investigating the possibility of placing in these firms, even on a trial basis, one or more of the women who would be trained,
   c. selecting high and middle-level managerial staff to be used as trainers in the programme, and
   d. arranging for educational visits to the offices and plants of these firms by the trainees during the programme.

It is worth mentioning that for the preparation and implementation of the project, to the extent that it was possible, I involved only women who had an interest in matters related to the position of women. This proved to be a very good decision because they worked with unprecedented enthusiasm and zeal. Just the idea that they were doing something to help other women proved a great motivating force.

2 SURVEY OF THE CHARACTERISTICS OF WOMEN IN THE TARGET GROUP

To obtain information about women who were outside the labour force I conducted a survey by sending a questionnaire to a randomly selected sample of 1803 women who had graduated from the Athens School of Economics and Business Science during the period 1970–84. The questions referred to their personal and family characteristics, their employment status and history, their capabilities, aspirations and attitudes and their views about various issues concerning women and work. There were special sections in the questionnaire for the employed, the unemployed and those who were outside the labour force. An effort was made to collect as much information as possible about the need for retraining and the prospects for finding and holding a job for those who were not employed and wanted to work.

Out of the questionnaires that were sent, 433 (24 per cent) were filled in and returned within a relatively short time. The relatively low response rate may not have biassed the results because it was due mainly to changes of address; a large number of the questionnaires did not reach the addressees and were sent back by the post office. However, it seems that of those who were contacted, even those who were employed and could not participate in the planned training programme, answered the questionnaire with great enthusiasm. There were 337 answers from employed women and 96 from women who were not employed and wanted to work. All of them were very eager to participate in the planned training programme and most of them seemed to be very good candidates. Tables 13.1, 13.2 and 13.3 present data on the age, number of children and family status of the 96 unemployed women seeking training. About 85 per cent of them were over 30, 47 per cent had children under 10 and 25 per cent were heads of a family.

The answers to the questionnaires gave extremely valuable information but it is not within the scope of this paper to go into the details.[3] I will simply summarise the main conclusions, which are as follows:

Table 13.1 Age distribution of unemployed women seeking training

Age	Number of women	Percentage of total
Under 25	–	–
25–29	15	16
30–34	31	32
35–39	15	16
40–44	29	30
45–49	4	4
50 and over	1	1
No answer	1	1
Total	96	100

Table 13.2 Children of unemployed women seeking training

Number of children	Number of women	Percentage of total	Number of women with children under 10	Percentage of total
0	26	27	51	53
1	26	27	24	25
2	39	41	19	20
3	5	5	2	2
4 or more	–	–	–	–
Total	96	100	96	100

Table 13.3 Family status of unemployed women seeking training

	Number	Percentage of total
Heads of households	26	27
Members of male-headed households	70	73
Total	96	100

1. Most of the unemployed women who wanted to work were without a job for a relatively long time (see Tables 13.4, 13.5 and 13.6). Most of them, after working for a few years had withdrawn from the labour market because of family obligations, while others, for various reasons, had never entered it. Because of the long duration of their unemployment, additional training for both categories seemed essential. The women themselves expressed emphatically their need for such training. It is worth noting that of those who did not work, 85 per cent were without a job for more than a year and 95 per cent believed that if they had additional training it would be easier for them to find employment.

Table 13.4 Period not working since leaving college of unemployed women seeking training

Months	Number of women	Percentage of total
Less than 6	10	10
6–11	2	2
12–17	7	7
18–23	3	3
24–29	4	4
30–35	2	2
36 and over	68	71
Total	96	100

Table 13.5 Period not working since last job of women unemployed women seeking training

Months	Number of women	Percentage of total
Less than 6	11	11
6–11	3	3
12–17	9	9
18–23	3	3
24–29	2	2
30–35	7	7
36 or more	61	64
Total	96	100

Education and Family Policy

Table 13.6 Time since last effort to find work of unemployed women seeking training

Months	Number of women	Percentage of total
3 or less	26	27
4–6	7	7
7–12	8	8
13–24	8	8
25 or more	35	37
No answer	12	13
Total	96	100

Table 13.7 Additional training after graduation of unemployed women seeking training

	Number of women	Percentage of total
Women with additional training	19	20
Women without additional training	60	62
No answer	17	18
Total	96	100

2. A relatively small proportion of those not working had had training after they obtained their university degrees (Table 13.7) and this despite the fact that almost all of them were very eager to have such training. It seems that because of their special characteristics (for example older age, outdated knowledge, feeling of discouragement, etc.) these women were not successful in being selected for participation in such programmes. This indicates that there is a real need to organise special programmes for these women since it seems that those responsible for making the selection for such programmes do not take into account the particular circumstances of this category of candidates.
3. The main subjects in which the non-working women felt that

Table 13.8 Views of unemployed women seeking training on discrimination in the labour market

	Number of women	Percentage of total
Believed that discrimination against women exists	69	72
Believed that discrimination does not exist	2	2
Could not express opinion with certainty	20	21
No answer	5	5
Total	96	100

additional training would increase their possibilities to find jobs were the following, in order of the size of the frequency of the answers: (a) use of electronic computers, (b) marketing, (c) business management, and (d) personnel management and industrial relations.

4. The positions in which the non-working women had the greatest interest and felt that they had a comparative advantage were those of assistants to middle- and high-level managerial staff and those of specialists in the departments of public relations, marketing and personnel.

5. The women who were not employed were willing to work anywhere in the private or public sector and they did not put any unreasonable restrictions on the place or type of work. However, because of a feeling of discouragement, their efforts to search for jobs were not intensive or continuous.

6. Most of the non-working women believed that women face more obstacles in finding a job compared to men with similar qualifications (Table 13.8). Since so many of them had this belief one could infer that there were some reasons for it. However, even if this belief was unjustified, the mere fact that these women thought that such discrimination existed, put them at a disadvantage. It should be noted that a large number of non-working women who had previously worked, indicated that they had experienced specific acts of adverse discrimination, coming mainly from their superiors. It is also interesting to note that similar views were also

held by the women who were employed: about 80 per cent of them indicated that they believed that women face more obstacles in finding jobs compared to men.

3 SURVEY OF THE NEEDS OF FIRMS

Questionnaires were sent to 418 big firms, and answers were received from 145. More than two-thirds of the firms replying indicated that they had a need for specially trained assistants to presidents, managing directors and high-level executives. They expressed the opinion that the planned training programme should focus on subjects such as modern management techniques, public relations and the use of electronic computers. About 60 per cent of the firms indicated their interest in employing one or more of the trainees after the completion of the programme. This was surprising because of the apparent reluctance of firms to hire older women who were without work for a long period. It seems that the prospect of providing these women with some modern knowledge and skills through training made them more attractive to prospective employers. About twenty managing directors or high-level executives offered to assist in the programme by making presentations themselves or holding discussions with the trainees about various issues related to the operation of their firms. Given the serious pressures on their time faced by high-level executives, this response was very encouraging.

4 DETERMINATION OF THE DIRECTION, CONTENT AND NATURE OF THE TRAINING PROGRAMME

From the answers of the firms on the one hand and of the interested women on the other it became clear that the programme should be designed to train women to take positions initially as assistants to high- and middle-level managers with the ultimate goal of being able later on to get independent managerial positions. To enhance the employment prospects for the trainees it was decided that one-third of the time of the programme should be devoted to the use of various computer packages and about one-fifth of the time to marketing and public relations. Table 13.9 summarises the subjects that were included in the programme and the total number of hours devoted to each.

Table 13.9 Content of the training programme for women graduates in economics or business administration

Subject	Number of hours
Computer packages:	
DOS	12
PC-Write	16
Lotus 1-2-3	20
DBase	18
Accounting package	14
Economic analysis for decision-making	8
Macroeconomics for management	4
Organisation of industrial firms	10
Contemporary developments in management	12
Personnel management and training	12
Organising retail trade outlets	4
Industrial relations	4
Communication within a firm	12
Office organisation techniques	6
Self-promotion techniques and professional guidance	8
Marketing and market research	16
Advertising	4
Public relations	12
Collection and utilisation of economic information	4
Financial management	8
Banking procedures	4
Tax accounting and financial analysis	12
Visits to firms	20
Total	240

To enable the trainees to come into contact with real-life problems and to give them the opportunity of meeting some prospective employers, it was decided that the instructors should come mainly from industry and the business world. After some consultation, about 25 executives were invited to make presentations and have discussions with the trainees. Specialists from personnel management firms were also invited to give professional guidance and encouragement to the participants. Furthermore, arrangements were made for visits by the trainees to selected big firms so that they could see how they operated and discuss various matters related to management as they actually occurred.

The programme lasted two months and included six hours of instruction per day, of which two hours were devoted to training in the use of electronic computers. Twenty-two women took part in the programme, selected from a sample of about 96 candidates.[4] All participants showed an extremely keen interest in the training and the instructors were particularly impressed by the women's maturity, interest, problem-solving ability and other favourable characteristics.

It is worth noting that at the beginning of the programme some participants showed signs of lack of self-confidence and doubts about whether they could actually be successful in finding employment. However, after the completion of the programme almost all of them appeared ready to overcome whatever obstacles cropped up on their way towards a new way of life.

5 STEPS TO PLACE THE RE-TRAINED WOMEN AFTER THE COMPLETION OF THE PROGRAMME

From the first stages of the preparation and organisation of the project, one of the main objectives was to establish the foundations for the fast placement of the women in jobs, after completion of the training programme. Indeed, this was the main reason for our efforts to seek and establish communications with firms and ask for instructors from their staff.

After the completion of the programme we embarked upon a vigorous campaign to find jobs for the women who participated in it. We sent letters with the résumés of these women and a description of the programme to all firms which had indicated an interest in employing one or more of the women and to all those who had some involvement in the programme. The response was very good and six months after the completion of the programme 90 per cent of the participants had interesting jobs.

The programme is being repeated for two years but, because of financial limitations, again for a very small number of women.[5] Unfortunately its limited scale restricts its scope and effectiveness in solving the problems that exist in this area. Its most important achievement is that it shows the possibilities that exist to utilise the great potential of a significant number of women who because of special circumstances are without work.

6 SUMMARY AND CONCLUSIONS

The problem of re-entry into the labour market of women graduates who have been out of it for some time is very serious in Greece and in many other countries of the world as well. Because of the rapid changes in the skills and knowledge required, the prejudices that exist and other inhibiting factors, these women need special assistance to be able to find employment and realise their potential. The general training programmes that are available to all university graduates cannot be of much help in this regard. Because of their age and other personal characteristics on the one hand, and the keen competition from recent graduates on the other, these women do not have a fair chance of being selected for participation in such programmes.

The experience of the project described in this paper is very encouraging. Women, who otherwise would be unemployed and would be wasting valuable human capital, found an opportunity to do productive work and realise their potential. The results of this experiment suggest that the programme should be expanded to include more non-working women and in this way make a real contribution towards the solution of the problem. This programme could be repeated in other countries as well, where women university graduates face similar problems and difficulties in re-entering the labour market successfully after a long absence. The experience of this project shows that the involvement of private firms in the design and implementation of the training programmes and a survey to identify the specific needs and capabilities of the women in the target group are two factors of decisive importance for the effectiveness of such programmes.

Notes

1. The author would like to thank the Economic Research Centre and the European Social Fund for financial support for this project. She would also like to thank Dr Rita Maurice, Ms Bina Agarwal and Ms S. Gordon for useful comments, Dr N. Papalexandri for her assistance during the implementation of the training programme, Dr J. Halikias for his help in the design of the questionnaires and the processing of the information and G. Gorgas and J. Zorios for carrying out the computer work. Special thanks are due to two students – N. Varzelioti and A. Grammatikou – for undertaking with enthusiasm all the work related to sending out the questionnaires.

2. For analysis of the problems that women face in the labour market in Greece, see Kanellopoulos (1982), Kottis (1984, 1987, 1988a, b and c, and 1990), Kottis and Demelis (1990), Meghir *et al.* (1989), Psacharopoulos (1982 and 1983) and Tzannatos (1987).
3. A detailed analysis of the answers is included in a 90-page report in Greek (Kottis, 1989). For an econometric analysis of the data collected from this survey, see Kottis and Dimelis (1990).
4. The seminar was advertised in the press and some applicants had not participated in the survey. On the other hand, some who had participated were not invited for interviews because it became apparent from their applications that their prospects of benefiting from the training programme were much inferior compared to those of the other candidates.
5. The training programme was repeated for 24 additional women during the autumn of 1989 and 22 during the autumn of 1990 and was equally successful. In the case of the autumn 1990 programme, the two-month training programme was combined with two months of on-the-job training in private firms.

References

Kanellopoulos, C. (1982) 'Male–Female Pay Differentials in Greece', *Greek Economic Review*, vol. 4, no. 2, pp. 222–41.

Kottis A. Petraki (1984) 'Female–Male Earnings Differentials in the Countries of the European Economic Community: An Econometric Investigation', *De Economist*, vol. 132, no. 2.

Kottis, A. Petraki (1987) 'Earnings Differentials in Manufacturing in Greece: A Statistical Exploration', *International Journal of Manpower*, vol. 8, no. 4, pp. 26–32.

Kottis, A. Petraki (1988a) 'Sources of Growth of Female Employment in Greece 1971–1981: A Shift Share Analysis', *International Journal of Manpower*, vol. 9, no. 1, pp. 18–20.

Kottis, A. Petraki (1988b) 'The Impact of Economic Development on Women's Labour Force Participation Rates in Greece: An Analysis by Age Groups', *Equal Opportunities International*, vol. 7, no. 2, pp. 9–15.

Kottis, A. Petraki (1988c) 'The Position of Women in the Labour Market in Greece: Need for Measures of Positive Action' (in Greek). Presented at the Symposium of the Office of the European Community in Greece and the Greek Association for Women's Rights, 11–12 May.

Kottis, A. Petraki (1989) *A Pilot Project for Re-training Chronically Unemployed Women Graduates of Economics and Business Administration*, Economic Research Centre, Athens. (A 90-page report in Greek).

Kottis, A. Petraki (1990) 'Shifts Over Time and Regional Variation in Women's Labor Force Participation Rates in a Developing Economy: The Case of Greece', *Journal of Development Economics*, 33, 117–32.

Kottis, A. Petraki and Dimelis, S. (1990) 'Labour Force Participation of Women Graduates in Economics and Business Administration in Greece: A Cross Sectional Analysis', Proceedings of the thirty first Conference of the Applied Econometrics Association on Modelling the Labour Market, Strasbourg, December 1990.

Meghir, C. Ioannides, Y. and Pissarides, C. (1989) 'Female Participation and Male Unemployment Duration in Greece', *European Economic Review*, vol. 33, pp. 395–406.

Psacharopoulos, G. (1982) 'Earnings and Education in Greece, 1960–1977', *European Economic Review*, vol. 17, pp. 333–47.

Psacharopoulos, G. (1983) 'Sex Discrimination in the Greek Labour Market', *Modern Greek Studies*, vol. 1, no. 2, pp. 339–58.

Tzannatos, Z. (1987) 'The Greek Labour Market: Current Perspectives and Future Prospects', *Greek Economic Review*, vol. 9, pp. 224–348.

14 Women in Higher Education: Recent Changes in the United States

Mariam K. Chamberlain
NATIONAL COUNCIL FOR RESEARCH ON
WOMEN, NEW YORK

1 INTRODUCTION

During the last 15 years significant, and in some cases dramatic, changes have taken place in the status of women in higher education in the United States. Under the pressure of the women's movement the issue of equal opportunity was brought under growing scrutiny by academic women and civil rights groups during the 1970s. Widespread practices of sex discrimination, both overt and subtle, moved on to the research agenda of scholars and became subjects for legal redress.

Two landmark volumes, published in 1973, documented the situation of women in higher education as it then existed. One was a volume of essays entitled *Academic Women on the Move*, edited by Alice Rossi and Ann Calderwood and published by the Russell Sage Foundation. The other was a report of the Carnegie Commission entitled *Opportunities for Women in Higher Education*. Both dealt with problems and issues relating to women as students, as faculty members, and as administrators. The reports presented research findings on topics ranging from sex differences in student enrolment patterns, degree attainment and financial support to the under-representation of women in senior faculty and administrative positions. They also identified and chronicled the forces for change that were then newly emerging – the mobilisation of academic women's groups to press for reforms, the use of affirmative action as a remedy for employment discrimination in higher education, and the development of women's studies as a means of dealing with sex bias in curriculum content.

The decade following the publication of these studies was a period of continued efforts by women's rights groups, government agencies and foundations to improve educational opportunities for women. In 1982 a Task Force on Women in Higher Education was established at the Russell Sage Foundation, with joint support from the Ford Foundation and the Carnegie Corporation, to examine the progress women made during this period. Following a four-year study, the report of the Task Force was published by the Russell Sage Foundation under the title *Women in Academe: Progress and Prospects* (Chamberlain, 1988). The purpose of this paper is to present the main findings of that study.

2 HISTORICAL BACKGROUND

By way of background, it was noted that the entire history of higher education for women is much shorter than that for men. In the United States women first gained entry to institutions of higher education in 1837. That was more than 200 years after Harvard College was founded for the education of young men. In colonial America, as elsewhere in the world, there was no precedent for higher education for women. European universities, some of which were established as early as the eleventh and twelfth centuries, were open only to men.

Although it is now 150 years since college education became a reality for women, opportunities at first were limited. Women did not enter higher education in substantial numbers until the latter part of the nineteenth century. By 1900 women constituted 30 per cent of the student body in higher education. The foremost reason for the growth in enrolment of women during this period was the need for school teachers. The public school system was expanding rapidly throughout the country and women were hired as teachers because they worked for salaries that were half or less than that required for men. Moreover, teaching was considered an appropriate occupation for women since it was seen as a natural extension of the mothering role. By 1918, 84 per cent of teachers in the United States were women, and teaching has remained a traditional and stereotypical occupation for women ever since. In 1986 the proportion of public school teachers in the United States who were women was 69 per cent (National Center for Education Statistics, 1988, p. 54).

During the early decades of the twentieth century women entered higher education in ever increasing numbers in response to employment opportunities in other fields such as social work, librarianship, and nursing. These too were perceived as 'helping' professions. Employers were willing to accept women workers in these occupations and, due to women's exclusion from other professional jobs, could get them cheaply. Thus employers set low salaries for these jobs, and these were salaries for which few if any men were willing to work.

From 1900 to 1930 the proportion of women receiving a bachelor's or first professional degree increased from 19 per cent to 40 per cent (US Bureau of the Census, 1975, p. 386). The proportion remained steady during the 1930s while the actual number of degrees awarded to both men and women increased. The increase in college attendance during the Depression may seem surprising, but widespread unemployment apparently made college a better option for young men and women, even though most families had less income to spend on college education. In addition, the Depression demonstrated the advantage of having a degree as college graduates in white-collar occupations fared better than other kinds of workers (Jencks and Riesman, 1977, p. 108).

During World War II, with many college-age men in the services and some college-age women engaged in war work, the number of male students declined sharply and the number of women students remained at about pre-war levels. After 1945, returning veterans, with federal support under the GI Bill, fuelled a dramatic rise in male enrolments. At the same time, the pattern of early marriage and childbearing that characterised the 1950s kept many qualified women out of college. As a result, men dominated the campus from the late 1940s and throughout the 1950s. Although the enrolment of women and the number of degrees earned by them increased somewhat during this period, women lost ground relative to men. In 1950 women represented only 24 per cent of those receiving the bachelor's and first professional degrees compared with 41 per cent in 1940. By 1960 the proportion had increased to 35 per cent but the pre-war rate was not regained until 1970. By that time the aftermath of World War II had played itself out and the women's movement had created a climate of rising aspirations for women. As the influx of veterans into higher education began to taper off, colleges and universities with their expanded facilities became receptive to other constituencies of students. These conditions brought women into higher education in unprecedented numbers and with them a drive for equal educational opportunity.

3 THE DRIVE FOR EQUITY

When the decade of the 1970s began, there were no laws prohibiting sex discrimination in higher education. The Fourteenth Amendment to the Constitution, which assures all persons equal protection of the laws, was applied to race but not sex discrimination. Title VII of the Civil Rights Act of 1964 prohibited discrimination in employment, but did not apply to educational institutions. Executive Order 11246 prohibited discrimination by all federal contractors in employment, including colleges and universities, on the basis of race, colour, religion, and national origin, but not sex. In the early 1970s a battery of federal laws and regulations was passed mandating equal educational opportunities for women. Title VII, as amended in 1972, prohibits sex discrimination in employment in educational institutions. Title IX of the Education Amendments of 1972 prohibits sex discrimination in all educational programmes receiving financial support from the federal government, including discrimination against students as well as discrimination in employment. These provided the legal remedies for the campaign against sex discrimination in higher education.

How have women fared since that time? With the elimination of discriminatory policies in admissions and financial aid, women made spectacular gains in enrolment and degree attainment. Enrolment data are shown in Table 14.1. As indicated, in 1979 the number of women students in higher education institutions surpassed that of men and by 1988 women accounted for 54 per cent of total enrolment. In terms of degree attainment, women now earn the majority of all bachelor's and master's degrees and they have increased their share of doctorates from 13 per cent in 1970 to 35 per cent in 1988, as indicated in Table 14.2. At the same time there has been a large-scale movement of women into the traditionally male-dominated fields and a narrowing of the disparity in fields of concentration between men and women. Particularly striking is the massive entry of women into the professional fields of business administration, law, medicine and theology. The proportion of master's degrees in business administration earned by women increased from less than 4 per cent in 1970 to 33 per cent in 1988, and there was a similar increase for first professional degrees such as in law, medicine and theology. The figures are shown in Tables 14.3 and 14.4. Women also made significant advances in the social sciences, where in some fields – psychology, sociology, and anthropology – women now exceed men in the num-

Table 14.1 Enrolment in institutions of higher education, by sex, 1970–88

	Men	Women	Total	Women as percentage of total
		Number (thousands)		
1970	5 044	3 537	8 581	41.2
1971	5 207	3 742	8 949	41.8
1972	5 239	3 976	9 215	43.1
1973	5 371	4 231	9 602	44.1
1974	5 622	4 601	10 224	45.0
1975	6 149	5 036	11 185	45.0
1976	5 811	5 201	11 012	47.2
1977	5 789	5 497	11 286	48.7
1978	5 641	5 619	11 260	49.9
1979	5 683	5 887	11 570	50.9
1980	5 874	6 223	12 097	51.4
1981	5 975	6 397	12 372	51.7
1982	6 031	6 394	12 426	51.5
1983	6 024	6 441	12 465	51.7
1984	5 864	6 378	12 242	52.1
1985	5 818	6 429	12 247	52.5
1986	5 885	6 620	12 505	52.9
1987	5 932	6 836	12 768	53.5
1988	5 998	7 045	13 043	54.0

Source: National Center for Education Statistics, US Department of Education, *National Higher Education Statistics: Fall 1989*, Survey Report, December 1989, p. 9.

ber of doctorates earned. Economics ranked the lowest among the social sciences: in 1988 women earned only 19 per cent of the doctorates in that field (National Research Council, 1989, p. 57). Nevertheless, that represents a substantial increase over previous levels, which were:

1950–59	4.2 per cent
1960–69	4.6 per cent
1970–79	8.8 per cent
1980–87	15.8 per cent

The proportion of doctorates earned by women in economics currently is roughly similar to that in the physical sciences.

Although women have increased their representation in the traditionally male-dominated fields, they have continued to enter the

Table 14.2 Doctor's degrees conferred by institutions of higher education, by sex, 1970–88

Academic year	Men	Women	Total	Women as percentage of total
		Number		
1969–70	25 890	3 976	29 866	13.3
1970–71	27 530	4 577	32 107	14.3
1971–72	28 090	5 273	33 363	15.8
1972–73	28 571	6 206	34 777	17.8
1973–74	27 365	6 451	33 816	19.1
1974–75	26 817	7 266	34 083	21.3
1975–76	26 267	7 797	34 064	22.9
1976–77	25 142	8 090	33 232	24.3
1977–78	23 658	8 473	32 131	26.4
1978–79	23 541	9 189	32 730	28.1
1979–80	22 943	9 672	32 615	29.7
1980–81	22 711	10 247	32 958	31.1
1981–82	22 224	10 483	32 707	32.1
1982–83	21 902	10 873	32 775	33.2
1983–84	22 064	11 145	33 209	33.6
1984–85	21 700	11 243	32 943	34.1
1985–86	21 819	11 834	33 653	35.2
1986–87	22 061	11 980	34 041	35.2
1987–88	22 592	12 247	34 839	35.2

Source: National Center for Education Statistics, US Department of Education, *National Higher Education Statistics: Fall 1989*, Survey Report, December 1989, p. 13.

traditional 'women's fields' in large numbers and have increased their concentration in the humanities and in the professional fields of teaching, social work, library science, and nursing. Notwithstanding the predominance in the number of women in these professions, there is no field other than nursing that is female-dominated in terms of control of the profession. In the humanities, education, social work, and library science, as well as the scientific fields and more prestigious professions, men hold the preponderance of senior faculty and administrative positions on campus. They also hold the leading positions in the professional associations. To some extent, the discrepancy between doctoral degree attainment and control of the discipline or profession may be reduced over time as larger cohorts of women make their presence felt. But the discrepancy is also a result of the fact that within individual fields men have had greater success than women in entering the more prestigious and

Table 14.3   Master's degrees in business and management conferred by institutions of higher education, by sex, 1970–88

Academic year	Men	Women	Total	Women as percentage of total
		Number		
1969–70	20 792	769	21 561	3.6
1970–71	25 443	1 038	26 481	3.9
1971–72	29 166	1 201	30 367	4.0
1972–73	29 481	1 526	31 007	4.9
1973–74	30 491	2 153	32 644	6.6
1974–75	33 185	3 062	36 247	8.4
1975–76	37 559	4 953	42 512	11.7
1976–77	39 766	6 654	46 420	14.3
1977–78	40 150	8 176	48 326	16.9
1978–79	40 701	9 671	50 372	19.2
1979–80	42 722	12 284	55 006	22.3
1980–81	43 394	14 504	57 898	25.1
1981–82	44 243	17 056	61 299	27.8
1982–83	46 457	18 862	65 319	28.9
1983–84	46 565	20 088	66 653	30.1
1984–85	46 624	20 903	67 527	31.0
1985–86	46 288	20 849	67 137	31.1
1986–87	45 145	22 216	67 361	33.0
1987–88	46 184	23 246	69 430	33.5

Sources: National Center for Education Statistics, US Department of Education, *Digest of Education Statistics, 1988* p. 230; and unpublished data, National Center for Education Statistics.

upwardly mobile specialties. Future studies should take a closer look at the reasons for this and at relative changes in the subspecialties.

While there has been much progress for women in higher education at the student level, the gains have been slower or halting at the faculty and policy-making level. The percentage of women as full-time faculty members increased from 22 per cent in the early 1970s to 27 per cent in the early 1980s, but most of the gain was in untenured positions and in two-year institutions rather than in four-year colleges and universities. Over the same period the increase in the percentage of full professors was small, as shown in Table 14.5. In administrative positions, the progress of women is somewhat better, having increased from 23 per cent in the mid 1970s to 30 per cent in the 1980s. On the negative side, however, salary differentials between men and women faculty members and administrators have widened rather than narrowed during this period. There is relatively

Table 14.4 First-professional degrees* conferred by institutions of higher education, by sex, 1970–88

Academic year	Men	Women	Total	Women as percentage of total
		Number		
1969–70	32 794	1 784	34 578	5.2
1970–71	35 544	2 402	37 946	6.3
1971–72	40 723	2 688	43 411	6.2
1972–73	46 489	3 529	50 018	7.1
1973–74	48 530	5 286	53 816	9.8
1974–75	48 956	6 960	55 916	12.4
1975–76	52 892	9 757	62 649	15.6
1976–77	52 374	11 985	64 359	18.6
1977–78	52 270	14 311	66 581	21.5
1978–79	52 652	16 196	68 848	23.5
1979–80	52 716	17 415	70 131	24.8
1980–81	52 792	19 164	71 956	26.6
1981–82	52 223	19 809	72 032	27.5
1982–83	51 310	21 826	73 136	29.8
1983–84	51 334	23 073	74 407	31.0
1984–85	50 455	24 608	75 063	32.8
1985–86	49 261	24 649	73 910	33.4
1986–87	46 523	25 094	71 617	35.0
1987–88	45 288	25 127	70 415	35.7

Source: National Center for Education Statistics, US Department of Education, *National Higher Education Statistics: Fall 1989*, Survey Report, December 1989, p. 14.

Note: * Comprises law, medicine, dentistry, theology and related fields.

little historical data on the representation of women on boards of trustees of higher education institutions, but recent studies indicate an increase from 15 per cent in 1977 to 20 per cent in 1985.

At least as important as the other advances that women have made in higher education since 1970 is the introduction and growth of women's studies as a formal area of teaching and research. Virtually unknown prior to 1970, women's studies began as a marginal enterprise on a few campuses, more often than not conducted on a voluntary basis by committed feminist scholars. Women's studies courses are now given on most campuses, whether as courses within existing disciplines or as an interdisciplinary field of concentration. There is now also a network of approximately 60 campus-based and other centres or institutes for research on women. These provide supplementary research opportunities to academic women. Further

Table 14.5　Women as a percentage of total full-time instructional faculty in institutions of higher education, 1972–73 and 1984–85 (per cent)

Academic rank	1972–73	1984–85
Professors	9.8	11.4
Associate professors	16.3	23.5
Assistant professors	23.8	37.3
Instructors	39.9	42.7
Lecturers	34.9	47.3
No academic rank	32.8	37.7
All ranks	22.3	27.5

Source:　Vetter, Betty M. and Babco, Eleanor L. (1987) *Professional Women and Minorities* (Washington DC: Commission on Professionals in Science and Technology), p. 132.

evidence of the growth of women's studies is the establishment during the 1980s of endowed chairs in women's studies on at least a dozen major campuses.

4　THE ROLE OF ACADEMIC WOMEN'S ORGANISATIONS

The gains that women have made in higher education since 1970 did not come about without a struggle. To an extent that is not generally appreciated, women's groups in professional associations have played a strategic role. They have functioned as pressure groups on behalf of academic women, with two primary goals – to improve the status of women in the profession and to encourage scholarly research on women. Most of these groups were formed between 1968 and 1971 as caucuses, committees or commissions on the status of women in their respective professional associations. The American Economic Association's Committee on the Status of Women in the Economics Profession, for example, came into being in 1971. Some disciplines also have independent associations of women as, for example, Sociologists for Women in Society, the Association for Women in Psychology, and the Association for Women in Science. There are today well over 100 such groups in the USA, ranging across the academic disciplines and professional fields.

Nearly all academic disciplines have standing committees on the status of women. Usually the first task of these committees was to conduct surveys of departments in their fields to determine the number of women in faculty and administrative ranks. In addition, they have lobbied for better representation of women among the officers of the associations, greater participation in the programmes of annual meetings and a more significant role in the editorial policies of the association journals; and they have been largely successful in these efforts. Their influence in departmental hiring is more problematical, although some have developed guidelines to assist departments in improving the representation of women.

The next 10 years are expected to be a critical period for women from the viewpoint of faculty hiring and tenuring. Demographic trends indicate a high rate of faculty retirement and an upturn in the college-going age group of the population, a combination of factors that should make for an increase in the number of faculty openings unless offset by adverse economic or other external circumstances. It is the task of caucuses and commissions of professional associations as well as other academic and women's rights groups to monitor hiring practices and outcomes closely. The pool of qualified women candidates is large and growing, but without vigorous efforts, this may not be translated into proportional representation on college and university faculties.

References

Carnegie Commission on Higher Education (1973) *Opportunities for Women in Higher Education* (New York: McGraw-Hill).

Chamberlain, M. K. (ed.) (1988) *Women in Academe: Progress and Prospects* (New York: Russell Sage Foundation).

Jencks, C. and Riesman, D. (1977) *The Academic Revolution*, rev. ed. (Chicago, Illinois: University of Chicago Press).

National Center for Education Statistics (1988) *Digest of Education Statistics, 1988* (Washington DC: US Government Printing Office).

National Research Council (1989) *Summary Report 1988: Doctorate Recipients from United States Universities* (Washington DC: National Academic Press).

Rossi, A. and Calderwood, A. (ed.) (1973) *Academic Women on the Move* (New York: Russell Sage Foundation).

US Bureau of the Census (1975) *Historical Statistics of the United States: Colonial Times to 1970*, Bicentennial Edition, part 2 (Washington DC: US Government Printing Office).

15 The Impact of Population Policies on Women in Eastern Europe: The German Democratic Republic

Lynn Duggan[1]
UNIVERSITY OF MASSACHUSETTS, AMHERST

1 INTRODUCTION

Most of the literature on family policy in Eastern Europe has focused on the impact of population policies on birth rates and fertility rates.[2] However important this question may be, it narrows unnecessarily the analysis of the impact of family policy. Feminist theory suggests that this restrictive approach reflects a patriarchal bias which sees women only as instruments in achieving optimal growth rates. In this paper I develop a broader economic approach which includes the impact of family policy on women's economic position in society, and, in addition, considers the impact of factors not usually considered part of family policy, including housing policy and male/female wage differentials. This analysis is within the context of Eastern European family policies in general but focuses chiefly on the German Democratic Republic.

2 THE BACKGROUND OF POPULATION POLICY IN EASTERN EUROPE

In the period following World War II labour force participation rates of women in most Eastern European countries rose rapidly, except in those countries where they were already high. This upward trend was well established by the late nineteenth century in most of Europe, but the switch in the late 1940s from market economies to central plan-

Table 15.1   Females as a percentage of the labour force

	1960	1970	1980
Western Europe			
Belgium	30.7	32.7	37.2
Denmark	31.8	39.4	47.3[a]
France	37.8[b]	35.2	38.5
German Federal Republic	37.8	36.6	38.0
Greece	32.8[c]	26.4[d]	30.1
Italy	30.1	28.3	33.3
Spain	20.1	23.9	28.5
Sweden	36.1[e]	39.4	45.2
United Kingdom	34.4	36.3	39.1
Eastern Europe			
Bulgaria	42.0[f]	44.0[g]	46.8[h]
Czechoslovakia	41.0[c]	44.6	46.7
German Democratic Republic	44.2[i]	46.3[d]	49.9
Hungary	35.1	41.2	43.4
Poland	43.3	46.0	45.4[j]
Romania	45.2[f]	45.2[k]	45.6[l]

Sources: For Western European countries OECD *Labour Force Statistics* 1959–70 and 1969–80. For Eastern European countries ILO *World Labour Report*, vol. 1, 1984.

Notes: a 1979
　　　 b Calculated from UN Demographic Yearbook Statistics

c 1961	f 1956	i 1964	l 1977
d 1971	g 1965	j 1978	
e 1962	h 1975	k 1966	

ning, along with the post-war low wage levels and the shortage of men, led to higher female labour force participation in the East than in the West of Europe. By 1980 the female contribution to the labour force ranged from 43 per cent in Hungary to 50 per cent in the GDR, while it remained around 30 to 40 per cent in most of Western Europe (see Table 15.1)

This rapid transition, coupled with the liberal abortion policy after the mid 1950s in Bulgaria, Czechoslovakia, Hungary, Poland and Romania (following the Soviet example of reliberalisation in 1955) led to correspondingly swift declines in birth rates. Although birth rates in socialist Eastern Europe started out at a much higher level than in Western Europe in general at that time (an average of 23.8 per thousand in the East and 18.5 per thousand in the West in 1950)

Table 15.2 Percentage of the female population in the labour force

	1950	1960	1970	1980
Western Europe				
Belgium	n.a.	23.2	25.6	30.7
France	37.5[a]	28.8[b]	28.8[c]	32.5
German Federal Republic	31.4	33.6	30.6	31.5
Italy	21.7[c]	24.6	19.3	26.4
Spain	11.8	15.3	17.7	20.0
Sweden	23.2	25.7	38.4	46.5
United Kingdom	27.4[d]	31.1	32.2	35.9
Eastern Europe				
Bulgaria	n.a.	45.7[e]	45.7[f]	47.6[g]
Czechoslovakia	32.9[h]	37.8[i]	42.3	46.7
German Democratic Republic	33.1	39.8[j]	39.8[k]	46.2
Hungary	25.2[l]	33.4	38.6	39.9
Poland	42.4	40.0	46.4	45.4[m]
Romania	n.a.	52.7[e]	48.1[n]	45.1[o]

Sources: For Western Europe UN Demographic Yearbook and otherwise OECD *Labour Force Statistics* 1959–70 and 1969–80. For Eastern Europe ILO *World Labour Report*, vol. 1, 1984.

Notes: a 1946 d 1952 h 1947 l 1949
       b 1958 e 1956 i 1961 m 1978
       c 1951 f 1965 j 1964 n 1966
             g 1975 k 1971 o 1977

n.a. = not available.

they fell much more swiftly in Eastern Europe to a lower level than in the West (see Table 15.3). The average birth rate of all Eastern European countries (excluding Yugoslavia and Albania) fell from 1950 to 1955 by 7 per cent; then, with the legalisation of abortion, dropped an additional 20 per cent by 1960. Within these figures, the GDR's birth rate rose 4 per cent over the years 1955–60, probably because the GDR did not liberalise abortion with the rest of Eastern Europe. In contrast, the average birth rate for Western Europe fell by only about 3 per cent from 1950 to 1960, as shown in Table 15.3.

By the late 1950s, population growth rates had fallen to near replacement in several countries and below replacement in Hungary. Fearing future labour shortages, East European planners began as early as 1962 explicitly to pursue a policy of population growth, offering economic incentives which favoured larger families, and, at

Table 15.3 Birth rates
(births per 1000 population)

	1950	1955	1960	1965	1970	1975
Western Europe						
Belgium	16.5	16.7	16.9	16.4	14.7	12.2
England and Wales	15.8	15.0	17.1	18.1	16.1	12.2
France	20.5	18.5	17.9	17.8	16.7	14.1
German Federal Republic	16.2	15.7	17.4	17.7	13.4	9.7
Greece	20.0	19.4	18.0	17.7	16.5	15.7
Italy	19.6	17.7	18.1	18.8	16.8	14.8
Netherlands	22.7	21.3	20.8	19.9	18.3	13.3
Spain	20.1	20.4	21.3	20.9	19.5	18.9
Sweden	16.5	14.8	13.4	15.9	13.7	12.6
Average	18.5	17.7	18.0	18.1	16.1	13.7
Eastern Europe						
Bulgaria	25.2	20.1	17.8	15.3	16.3	16.6
Czechoslovakia	23.3	20.3	15.9	16.4	15.9	19.5
German Democratic Republic	16.5	16.3	17.0	16.5	13.9	10.8
Hungary	20.9	21.4	14.7	13.1	14.7	18.4
Poland	30.7	29.1	22.6	17.4	16.8	18.9
Romania	26.2	25.6	19.1	14.6	21.1	19.7
Average	23.8	22.1	17.8	15.5	16.4	17.3

Source: Mitchell (1980) *European Historical Statistics* 1750–1975, pp. 131–34.

the same time, restricting abortion rights, thus effectively forcing women to have more children. Czechoslovakia was the first to restrict abortions, and the other countries gradually followed suit, Romania most harshly. Maternal mortality rates rose sharply as women resorted to illegal abortions.

Subsequently, all of these countries liberalised abortion laws to varying degrees. Romania's policy remained the most restrictive, with abortion legal only for women aged over 40 and women with four or more children. There was also a ban on the import of birth control pills and intrauterine devices. In the other five countries abortion legislation was never used as instrumentally to raise birth rates as it was in Romania. From 1972 abortion was legal and free in the GDR.[3] From 1959 it was a woman's right in Poland, although doctors have had the right to refuse to perform abortions there. In

Hungary, Czechoslovakia, and Bulgaria abortion was not generally available to married women under 40 with less than two children, but an appeals committee could consider psychological and social factors, for which the approval rate is said to have been high in all three countries.

3 THE ASSUMPTION OF THE WOMAN AS PRIMARY PARENT IN FAMILY POLICY

As evidenced by the curtailment of abortion rights, governments in Eastern Europe have used women, to varying degrees, as instruments to achieve optimal population growth rates. The economic incentives offered to 'reconcile motherhood with female employment', and thus increase births were, however, in some ways an important economic and political gain for women who were mothers. These 'positive incentives' included longer maternity and child care leaves, subsidised nursery care or child care allowances, family allowances, birth grants, access to low interest loans, and preferential housing, among other benefits.

Yet although state support for motherhood recognises and compensates women's household and child care work to some degree, it has the disadvantage of reinforcing the traditional belief that the woman is and should remain the primary parent. This approach has adverse implications for the position of women in the labour market.

Aside from government exhortations to husbands to help women with domestic work, no action has been taken to persuade men that they need to reconcile their working lives with their domestic lives. Thus, the 'vicious cycle' of women's responsibility for the domestic sphere perpetuates itself: women periodically take time off from their jobs to have and care for children; they do not work overtime; and they resort to part-time work in a much greater proportion than men. In the GDR, for example, in 1988 about 27 per cent of women worked part-time and 90 per cent of all part-time work was done by women (SZS, 1989b). In the other five countries women typically leave the labour force for two to three years after each birth. Accordingly, women tend not to be promoted and to earn less than their husbands. Their lower incomes reinforce and reproduce the tendency for the mother, rather than the father of a child, to take paid and unpaid child care leave, and to see herself as the primary parent.

While post-maternity child care leave is now offered to fathers as an alternative to mothers and grandmothers in the GDR, Hungary, Bulgaria, and Poland, it has not been offered in Romania and requires special permission in most of the other countries; regardless of legislation, only a small fraction of men take advantage of these leaves where they are offered. The availability of child care varies widely in Eastern Europe. In Poland, 33 per cent of all children below school age are in nurseries and child care centres, in the GDR this figure is 89 per cent, and the other countries range somewhere in between (excluding Romania, for which these figures are not published) (SZS, 1989c). Hungary, Poland, and Czechoslovakia have encouraged child care in the home until the age of three, while the GDR has been committed to providing state child care for infants and small children.

4   BIRTH INCENTIVES IN THE GDR: A CASE STUDY

Economic incentives favouring larger families were introduced in the GDR in 1972 and have mainly increased in value since then. At the time of writing (1989), family policy in the GDR included nearly fully paid maternity/family leave for six weeks before delivery and 20 weeks after delivery. Additional leave extended to the child's first birthday at 65–90 per cent of pay, depending upon how many children the woman had had. The 'baby year', as this is called, was introduced in 1976, but was only available with the second birth, not the first, until 1986, when it was extended to all birth orders. In that year, paid maternity leave was increased to 18 months for the third and additional children. Families received a 'birth grant' of 1000 Marks for each child and a family allowance of 50 Marks for the first child, 100 for the second, and 150 Marks for each additional child. (The median monthly wage in the GDR was about 800–900 Marks.)

Families with three or more children received special health care, highly subsidised meals in pre-school and school facilities, and preferential allocation of housing, of nursery and kindergarten places, and of children's camps and holiday trips.

As a policy to promote marriage, newly-weds since 1972 receive an interest-free loan to furnish a home and/or to buy into a housing cooperative or build a house. This is available only until age 30 and is progressively cancelled upon successive births, with a maximum of 70 per cent cancellation when the third child is born. The borrowing limit was increased from 5000 Marks to 7000 Marks in 1986, and the age limit was raised from age 26 to 30.

It is only as of 1986 that married fathers have had the legal option of paid post-maternity leave in place of their wives, and the number of men who have taken advantage of this new legislation is correspondingly negligible.[4] In 1989 two laws were still on the books in the GDR which were obvious examples of the government's bias towards women as the primary parent: all married women who work full-time and single parents were allowed one day off per month to catch up on housework, *plus* married women with two children and single parents were allowed a shorter working week at full pay – 40 hours rather than 43¾ hours. Neither of these ambiguous privileges is open to married fathers in place of mothers, except by special permission (Ministerium der Justiz, 1988).

5 WOMEN'S ECONOMIC POSITION IN THE GDR

The GDR has come a long way towards proving the feasibility of its stated goal of 'reconciling motherhood with women's employment'. In 1988 its labour force was about 49 per cent female, even though approximately 92 per cent of women aged 35–39 were mothers. Since biological infertility can be expected to keep 5–10 per cent of any population of women from bearing children, this is a very high proportion, especially in a country with almost universal employment for women.[5] Women in the GDR have their children on average about four years earlier than women in the Federal Republic of Germany: in the GDR about 70 per cent of all births are to women aged 25 or below, while in the FRG this figure is only one quarter. 91 per cent of all births take place by age 30 in the GDR, 92 per cent of all FRG births by age 35 (Speigner, 1989; UN, 1988)

Despite the high percentage of mothers in the GDR, fertility is low; since 1971 it has been below replacement level, which would be about 2.1 births per woman. In 1988 an average of 1.6 children were born per woman of childbearing age. The population policy, encouraging births, along with the state's commitment to providing nurseries, has raised fertility by a small amount – the incidence of second and third births has risen slightly – but basically the incentives can be said to have only moderated the trend of decreasing fertility (Dinkel, 1984).

Table 15.4   Births out of wedlock as a percentage of all births
in the GDR

1955	12.8	1972	16.2
1956	13.1	1973	15.6
1957	13.1	1974	16.3
1958	12.2	1975	16.1
1959	11.8	1976	16.2
1960	11.4	1977	15.8
1961	10.9	1978	17.3
1962	9.9	1979	19.6
1963	9.1	1980	22.8
1964	9.4	1981	25.6
1965	9.8	1982	29.3
1966	10.0	1983	32.0
1967	10.7	1984	33.6
1968	11.5	1985	33.8
1969	12.4	1986	34.4
1970	13.3	1987	32.8
1971	15.1	1988	33.4

Sources: SZS (1989a, 1989c).

In association with the birth incentives there has been an increase
in the percentage of out-of-wedlock births in the GDR. After falling
in the late 1950s and early 1960s it has risen in two large swings from
the mid 1960s to 1972 and from 1977 to 1986, as shown in Table 15.4.
By 1984 about a third of all children were born to single mothers. The
corresponding percentage of out-of-wedlock births in the FRG, was
9.4 per cent in 1986 (UN, 1988), though such a comparison is of
limited usefulness.

In 1967 and 1977, laws were passed which improved the living
conditions of single, as well as married, mothers. In 1967 the new
development consisted mainly of paid leave for single mothers to care
for sick children. A yet more compelling package was introduced in
1977: (a) paid maternity leave was increased from 18 weeks to 26
weeks, and, beginning with the second birth, up to the child's first
birthday; (b) single mothers were given the baby year from the
first birth on; (c) single mothers received an increase in paid leave to
care for sick children; and (d) financial support was instituted for
single mothers to care for their children at home if a nursery place
could not be found in their vicinity. This brings us to an additional

Table 15.5 Births out of wedlock as a percentage of total births
out of wedlock in the GDR, by age group

Age group of mother	< 20	20–24	25–29	30–34	35–39	40 and over
1977	47.5	35.6	10.8	3.6	2.1	0.4
1982	33.0	47.5	13.5	4.4	1.1	0.3
1985	25.8	52.0	15.1	5.4	1.3	0.2

Sources: SZS (1989c); UN (1988).

important factor facilitating the rise in single motherhood: the rapid
expansion of child care facilities. In 1960 only about 15 per cent of
children aged 1–3 were cared for in state nurseries, and 65 per cent of
children aged 4–5 in state child care centres. By 1986, these figures
had reached 88 per cent and 89 per cent respectively (Speigner and
Winkler, 1988).[6]

Since 1977, the main age group of single mothers has moved
upwards in age. Whereas 15–19 year olds accounted for nearly a half
of all single parent births in 1977, in 1985 they accounted for only
about one quarter (see Table 15.5). Although the absolute number of
single parent births rose for this age group, women in all other age
groups were giving birth to much greater numbers of illegitimate
children, exceeding the increase in the younger age group; while
20–24 year olds accounted for about one third of all illegitimate births
in 1977, in 1985 they accounted for about one half. The number of
single 20–24 year olds giving birth increased by 320 per cent over this
period, the number of 25–29 year olds by 250 per cent, and the
number of 30–34 year olds by 210 per cent. Single mothers were
nevertheless still mainly young women, 78 per cent of all illegitimate
births in 1985 being to women aged 24 or under (UN, 1988).

This information alone shows that women in the GDR are post-
poning or neglecting marriage. But it is not clear how many women
remain single because they prefer not to share parenthood with a
male partner or because they haven't (or want to be sure they have)
found 'Mr Right', as distinct from how many remain single despite
living with a male partner, as a strategy to maximise income.[7]
Sociological studies have shown that about one quarter of single
women between 18 and 35 live with a male partner, and that most
who do so within this age group are younger, were never married,
and have young children (Gysi, 1988).

Table 15.6   Births out of wedlock as a percentage of all births in the
GDR, by age group

Age group of mother	< 20	20–24	25–29	30–34	35–39	40 and over
1977	40.3	11.4	7.4	9.1	11.5	12.5
1982	68.2	28.5	14.9	15.8	19.0	21.1
1985	75.9	36.0	18.4	19.5	21.1	26.7

Sources: SZS (1989c); UN (1988).

By not marrying until later, women can maximise their income
security and time off from work through the turbulent early child-
hood years. Single mothers are offered longer paid leaves to care for
sick children, and until 1986, only single mothers were offered the
'baby year' from the first child on. As of 1986, the loan newly-weds
were eligible for was available until the couple reached the age of
30, and payments could be cancelled retroactively based on the number
of existing children. Thus there was no penalty and only economic
advantage to postponement of marriage until the age of 30.[8]

The increasing postponement or neglect of marriage may be a
possible factor influencing the GDR's low fertility rates, but surveys
show that low fertility is due to a small 'ideal family size', and this is
low to begin with. According to Speigner (1988), 20 per cent of all
GDR women aged 18–40 desired only one child, and an additional 60
per cent desired no more than two. Less than 3 per cent desired four
or more children.

However, increased support of single mothers made it possible for
women to spend an increasing number of years outside of marriage or
partnership. To the extent that they did so, the high incidence of
out-of-wedlock births may be associated with lower fertility, since
two parents usually undertake to care for more children than a single
parent does. Thus, insofar as the increased support of single mothers
brought on an increased number of years spent outside of marriage or
partnership in the GDR, such incentives have led to lower birth
rates. GDR sociologists cite the increased economic independence of
women as the fundamental condition which made a rising divorce
rate possible there (see Table 15.7).

One problem with the rising incidence of single motherhood was
that, regardless of whether child rearing is actually shared with a
non-marital partner, it was only the mother who was allowed to take

Table 15.7   Marriage and divorce rates in the GDR
(numbers per 1000 population)

Year	Marriages[a]	Divorces
1950	11.7	2.7
1955	8.7	1.4
1960	9.7	1.4
1965	7.6	1.6
1970	7.7	1.6
1975	8.4	2.5
1980	8.0	2.7
1985	7.9	3.1
1988	8.2	3.0

Source: SZS (1989c).
Note: a Including second marriages.

paid post-maternity leave under 1989 legislation. On the other hand, the higher the proportion of single mothers who do not have such child rearing partners, the higher the proportion of men in the GDR who are free of any child care responsibilities and the greater the burden of parenthood for women. This in turn feeds the vicious cycle: more leaves of absence and part-time work; consequent lack of job advancement, career attachment, and promotions; and women's continued identification with the role of primary parent, which is then passed on to the next generation of women.

6   MALE/FEMALE INCOME DIFFERENTIALS IN THE GDR

In focusing on these explicit components of population policy, the birth incentives, we run the risk of leaving out other, possibly more important, factors and relationships that are not normally considered part of family policy. Male/female income differentials and housing policy are two such additional variables, each of which explains a bit more of the picture of women's situation in the GDR economy.

Feminist theory postulates, and empirical research shows, that when male/female wage differentials decrease, the incidence of non-marriage tends to rise, because women have less income to gain by marrying (McCrate, 1985). Although the male/female wage ratio has not decreased in recent years in the GDR, at about 100:75 it is lower than in some Western countries. In addition, the standard deviations of average wages for men and for women are probably lower in the GDR than in the FRG and other Western European countries. This may be seen to have a similar effect of lessening the potential gain in income that an individual woman can achieve through marriage.

Perhaps a more important factor than wage differentials in influencing non-marriage in the GDR was state enforcement of child support payments. Since 1965, single parents as well as divorced parents have been entitled to child support from the other parent. This legislation was actively enforced and was insured by the state when the other parent was not in a position to make such payments. It was thus possible for single mothers to benefit from a male wage without the marriage contract, lowering the cost of non-marriage to women never married, as well as to divorced mothers and fathers.

7 HOUSING POLICY IN THE GDR

Another economic relationship worth mentioning here is the link between early age at marriage or single motherhood and housing rationing in the GDR. Although the government devoted a large part of its budget to housing construction, there was usually a wait of many years for a non-inherited apartment outside of Berlin.[9] This wait could be shortened if one had connections or if one could move to a higher priority on the waiting list by marrying or having a child. Pregnant students were also given rooms of their own in student dormitories. As the household grew, it received a higher priority rating from the housing authorities. In fact, according to sociological studies, the three main reasons for marriage listed by young men and women were love, tradition, and 'to receive one's own apartment' (Gysi, 1988).

Preferential access to housing was an explicit birth incentive, but usually this incentive was not associated with the rate of marriage or single motherhood. When the housing shortage is considered from a young, single adult's perspective, this factor acquires a new significance. The average age of first marriage is 22.9 for women, half of these marriages occurring by age 21, and three-quarters by age 23, with a two-year lag for men (SZS, 1989c). It is common knowledge in the GDR that apartment rationing was one reason for the young age at marriage.[10] It is not improbable, however, that the desire to escape from the parents' apartment also played a role in some young women's decisions whether to abort or continue a pregnancy.

8   CONCLUSION

This initial case study of the GDR has shown, schematically, that a family policy which uses raised fertility rates as the chief criterion of its success seeks to solve perceived population problems at women's expense. This population policy goal not only uses women as an instrument but also does not raise birth rates substantially except by way of a diminished quality of women's labour force participation.

An examination of the effects of family policy on the position of women shows that more is at stake than fertility rates. The real question is not 'will the population be reproduced', but 'how should the population be reproduced'. To quote Enders (1984, p. 48): 'As long as policy claims to reconcile motherhood, but not fatherhood, with employment, the employment of women will remain a disposable factor, and with it, equality of men and women will remain a formal claim.'

Notes

1. This paper reports on work in progress which is funded by a fellowship granted by the Berlin Program for Advanced German and European Studies of the Social Sciences Research Council and the Free University of Berlin. I would also like to thank the Demographic and Family Research Groups of the Institute for Sociology and Social Policy of the Academy of Sciences of the GDR for their helpful comments on this work. However, the conclusions, opinions, and other statements in this paper are the author's and not necessarily those of the sponsoring institutions. In general the paper describes the situation in 1988–9.
2. The 'fertility rate' is not a biological term but a demographic term for the ratio of the total number of children born to each woman in a certain population to the size of that population. It corresponds to the biological term fecundity.
3. Abortion was legalised due to high maternal mortality rates resulting from the widespread incidence of illegal abortion.
4. In the GDR parental leave for married fathers was only available on a case by case basis, subject to employers' approval. The overwhelming majority of men who have taken the 'baby year' (or some fraction thereof) are students or intelligentsia, according to Dr Jutta Gysi, Director of the Family Research Group of the Institute for Sociology and Social Policy, Academy of Sciences of the GDR.
5. In the Federal Republic of Germany only 75 per cent of young women are expected to become mothers, according to Speigner and Winkler (1988) but this is a different measure – of expected (future) rather than actual (past) fertility.

6. According to many GDR women I have spoken with as well as Helwig (1987, p. 97), despite improvements in the quality of nursery care, the state's endeavour to integrate women into the full-time labour force has taken place without due regard to the well-being of their children.

7. According to Speigner (1989) 99 per cent of GDR women and 96 per cent of men regard living together with a partner as an important aspect of life. The gender of the partner was not specified in this survey. There is a small but growing gay rights movement in the GDR, but the family research group at the Academy of Sciences of the DDR does not think this group is large enough to have any impact on the above numbers.

8. In an interview with Dr Jutta Gysi, Director of the Family Research Group of the Institute for Sociology and Social Policy, Academy of Sciences of the GDR, I was told that only 7–10 per cent of GDR young people do not want to marry, thus the benefits of single mothers and the loans to newly-weds mainly affect the timing of the marriage decision.

9. If the workplace was in the same town as the parents' residence, and a room would have been made empty in their house by moving out, one was not allowed to apply for an apartment of one's own until age 26.

10. According to many GDR acquaintances, the rationing of apartments is one factor influencing the divorce rate. In order to leave their parents' households yet remain in the same town, many young people had no legal alternative other than marriage, whether or not they were ready for such a commitment.

References

Dinkel, R. (1984) 'Haben die Geburtenförderungsmaßnahmen in der DDR Erfolg?' (Have the Pronatalist Policy Measures in the GDR Been Successful?) *Ifo-Studien*, vol. 11, pp. 139–62.

Enders, U. (1984) '". . . damit sie ihre Pflichten als Berufstätige, Ehefrau und Mutter immer besser vereinbaren kann." Zu einigen Aspekten der Lebensbedingungen von Frauen in der DDR' ('". . . In Order that She Can Better Reconcile her Duties as Worker, Wife, and Mother." On some Aspects of the Living Conditions of Women in the GDR') in Spittman-Ruhle, I. and Helwig, G. (eds), *Lebensbedingungen in der DDR* (Cologne: Verlag Wissenschaft und Politik), pp. 37–48.

Gysi, J. (1988) 'Familienformen in der DDR' (Forms of the Family in the GDR), *Jahrbuch für Soziologie und Sozialpolitik 1988*, (Yearbook of Sociology and Social Policy), pp. 508–24.

Helwig, G. (1987) *Frau und Familie: Bundesrepublik Deutschland – DDR* (Woman and Family: German Federal Republic–German Democratic Republic) (Cologne: Verlag Wissenschaft und Politik).

International Labour Organisation (1984) *World Labour Report*, vol. 1 (Geneva: ILO).

McCrate, E. (1985) 'The Growth of Nonmarriage Among U.S. Women 1954–1983', unpublished PhD thesis, University of Massachusetts, Amherst, USA.

Ministerium der Justiz (1988) *Ehe und Familie* (Marriage and the Family) (E. Berlin: Staatsverlag der DDR).

Mitchell, B. R. (1980) *European Historical Statistics 1750–1975* (London: Macmillan).

Organisation for Economic Cooperation and Development (1973) *Labour Force Statistics 1959–1970*, OECD, Paris, France.

Organisation for Economic Cooperation and Development (1983) *Labour Force Statistics 1969–1980*, OECD, Paris, France.

Speigner, W. (1989) 'Die Geburtenentwicklungen in der DDR' (The Birth Developments in the GDR), *Wirtschaftswissenschaft* (Economics), vol. 37, no 1, pp. 19–35.

Speigner, W. and Winkler, G. (1988) *Wie wächst unser Lebensbaum?* (How Grows our Tree of Life?) (E. Berlin: Dietz Verlag).

Statistisches Zentralverwaltung für Statistik (SZS) (1989a) *Die Frau in der Deutschen Demokratischen Republik: Statistische Kennziffernsammlung* (Women in the GDR: a Collection of Reference Statistics), Ministerrat der Deutschen Demokratischen Republik, Berlin, GDR.

Statistisches Zentralverwaltung für Statistik (SZS) (1989b) *Jahresbericht Arbeitskräfte- und Lohnstatistik* (Yearly Report on Labourpower and Incomes), Ministerrat der Deutschen Demokratischen Republik, Berlin, GDR.

Statistisches Zentralverwaltung für Statistik (SZS) (1989c) *Statistisches Jahrbuch der DDR* (Statistical Yearbook of the GDR), Ministerrat der Deutschen Demokratischen Republik, (Berlin, GDR: Staatsverlag der DDR).

United Nations (1988) *Demographic Yearbook*, Department of International and Social Affairs, New York, USA.